ALL ACCESS
THE MAKING OF THIRTY
EXTRAORDINARY
GRAPHIC DESIGNERS

WRITTEN AND DESIGNED BY
STEFAN G. BUCHER

GLOUCESTER MASSACHUSETTS

ROCKPORT
PUBLISHERS

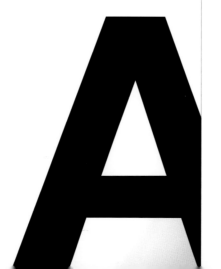

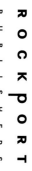

FEATUR

THE

Australia
Austria
Brazil
Germany
Great Britain
Holland
Iceland
Japan
Norway
Switzerland
United States
Yugoslavia

ING
STORIES OF

BUT FIRST:

IMPORTANT INFORMATION

FOR THE DETAIL ORIENTED READER This stuff could save your life someday.

First published in the United States of America by
Rockport Publishers, Inc.
33 Commercial Street
Gloucester, Massachusetts 01930-5089
Telephone 978 282-9590
Fax 978 283-2742
www.rockpub.com

Library of Congress Cataloging-in-Publication Data
Bucher, Stefan G.
    All access : behind the scenes : the making of thirty
  extraordinary graphic designers / Stefan Bucher.
        p.   cm.
    ISBN 1-59253-079-6 (hardcover)
    1. Commercial artists—United States—Biography. 2. Commercial art—United States—History—20th century. 3. Graphic arts—United States—History—20th century. I. Title.
NC999.2.B83 2004
741.6'092'2-dc22

2004009990
CIP

ISBN 1-59253-079-6

10 9 8 7 6 5 4 3 2 1

Design: Stefan G. Bucher
       for 344 Design, LLC
       Pasadena, CA
       www.344design.com
       344 LOVES YOU

       Printed in China

Allow me to give you a few helpful hints about the design.
I'm sure you'll figure this out on your own,
but hey, I want to be helpful:

Each of the chapters in Part 1 has a timeline
that shows all the work included in that chapter,
along with the year each piece was made.
The pieces on the page you're looking at are raised,
and—nifty detail—the little numeral
below the year is the age of the designer at that time.
I think it's interesting. Don't you?

2003   2004
        31

You got all that? Excellent! Then, please...
by all means, commence reading.

NOW THEN:

WHO A
PEOPLE,

Early on my friend Jed suggested this title for the book:
"How the People You've Never Fucking Heard of Got So Famous:
How Graphic Designers Become Design Heroes." Jed's a writer.

Edmund Burke said: "The only thing necessary for the triumph of evil
is for good men to do nothing." Substitute "mediocrity" for "evil" and you've got
good words to live by for any Designer Who Cares." Don't forget to vote, either!

Fifteen of the people I talked with are "famous designers," well established,
widely known practitioners with years of brilliant work under their belts.
The other fifteen are designers who are also doing beautiful, engaging work,
but who haven't received the wide exposure of the first group yet.
I'm betting that it's just around the corner for them, though.

I also asked the "famous fifteen" to show me work from along the way,
including the early pieces they removed from their portfolios long ago.
Usually, I see the bulk of their work at shows, in books, or on
high-profile assignments—an automatic Greatest Hits collection,
which adds to their allure, but doesn't necessarily inspire me
as I struggle to grow. Constant success is a lousy road map to follow.

Good news: They weren't born brilliant. They didn't radiate genius
the minute they picked up a pencil. Take a look at their *Frühwerk*
and you will see that they had to work at it as much as anybody else.
Before their switches got flipped, they slaved away at normal careers,
chipping away, getting gigs, doing OK. *Then* their lights came on
and they made their big contributions. There is hope.

I want to say thank you to all the people I interviewed and you should, too.
They all spent a lot of time responding to these and many other questions.
None of the people included gave pat answers. Everybody has been open
and honest and was willing to share their experiences with you and me.

I recognize something from my life in each one of these thirty stories,
some moment that mirrors my own experience. I'm sure it will be
the same for you. Despite huge differences in location, upbringing,
and style, our similarities far outnumber our differences.
We are all part of the same family.

"Blessed is he whose fame does not outshine his truth," said the poet.
Rabindranath Tagore. I heard this lovely quote a few days ago,
during George Harrison's induction into the Rock'n'Roll Hall of Fame.
It explains perfectly how I selected the thirty people I interviewed
for this book. No self-fellating hype-meisters here. Only designers
who care deeply, speak openly, and work hard. They are people
whose work I respect and whose dedication to the craft I admire.
Their truth shines bright.

Thank you for picking up this book. Have fun.

Thank you for reading the fine print, too. You are a person after my own heart. You and I—we'll get along just fine.

RE THESE ANYWAY?

FAMOUS GRAPHIC DESIGNER is a bit of a contradiction in terms. Paul Rand never appeared on the Ed Sullivan Show, Sagmeister isn't Prince, and *Graphis* isn't *Tiger Beat*. That's just as well, but as a Designer Who Cares® I still come down with a case of hero worship every now and again. I love graphic design and I can't help but look up to the people who are doing smart, beautiful work. They aren't rock stars, but they are further along the road I'm traveling and I want to know what's around the bend. So I asked thirty of them.

Did they always know that they wanted to design? Did they stumble into it by accident? Did they have a hard time making it? How do they deal with setbacks? Do they have Eureka moments? How do they go from inspiration to making something? How do they get their work produced? Do they still face The Fear? How do they balance their work with their private life? (Do they draw that distinction?) Does their work make them happy?

This is not a scholarly book. This is a book about community. It's about seeking out the village elders. It's about inviting the people in your trade guild to have a beverage with you, so you can ask them what it was like for them, to ask them for their advice and encouragement. It's about learning and growing and becoming part of the line. That's what it felt like for me and I hope that's what it will feel like for you.

Stefan G. Bucher

LET'S MEET OUR LOVELY CONTESTANTS →

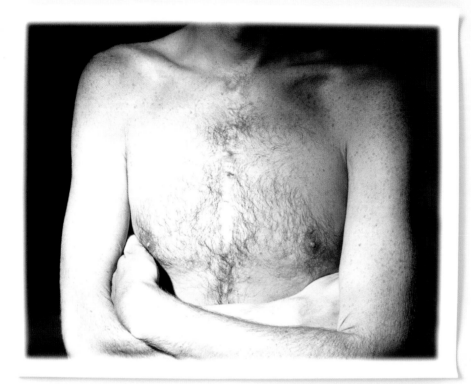

01

**Untitled selections from
"Faggot Series," photography**
"I placed these sticks in strong,
defiant positions in various landscapes—
heroic, almost. I had just come out,
so a whole range of emotion was open
for examination—from celebration
to close introspection—as in looking
at the kind of scarring one could
only hope to see as easily as a scar
left on the body."

ALLEN HOR

After a youth spent preparing for a future in medicine,
Allen Hori discovered art and went on a journey of learning
that would lead him from Hawaii to Michigan to Holland
to New York and from design to photography and back again.

" I grew up as a third-generation Japanese American *sansei* in Hawaii on the island of Kauai: very rural, country, small-town. Hard work, education, and achievement were central beliefs in my family." Hori's father worked as a surgical technician, his mother as a nurse at a dispensary. "Dinner conversations often involved descriptions of surgery, trauma, laboratory procedures, and disease." Accordingly, Hori was primed for a future in medicine or science. "I was a science geek in high school. As a sophomore, I did a National Science Foundation research project on testing toxicity of a local soft coral toxin on lymphoma cells. As a junior, I did research with the Hawaii Heart Association, sequencing a particular protein from bovine heart mitochondria—stuff that gave me a preview of what might be ahead for me."

After graduating from high school, he enrolled at the University of Hawaii. "I got as far as sophomore pre-med when I took an art history course—Art 101—as a humanities requirement, and here is where things radically changed. Art presented vistas I had never been exposed to. It was a totally alien activity. This was part of its allure and excitement. More classes followed, and I found myself gravitating toward graphic design, where a certain amount of precision and certainty was a necessary part of the process. Also, there was the prospect of commercial and practical application that minimally placated my parents' concern of self-support and future livelihood."

But the initial excitement didn't last. "I made it through to the last year of the design program and found myself with a kind of buyer's remorse. The excitement and expressive potential I had initially latched on to were slowly being reduced the further I progressed in the primarily Swiss-based program." Instead of finishing the final year of the design program, he switched his major to photography and finished his degree in 1987.

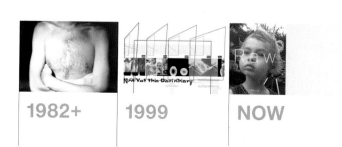

1982+   1999   NOW

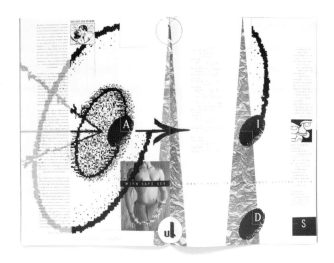

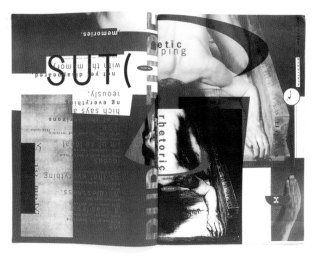

AIDS Matrices, spread from *Émigré* 10 While at Cranbrook, Hori had the chance to design for *Émigré* magazine—"Lots of bitmap, very little assimilation or integration of type, typography, and image."

Sutural Rupture, spread from *Émigré* 12 "This issue was about stripping— mechanical lithography in the offset printing process. I took it to mean, among other things, the stripping or unlearning of convention and tradition in design, the becoming new and naked at Cranbrook."

Fiber Content, exhibition catalog "This piece is still one of my favorites. I played with the word progression *content> contain>containment*. The catalog assumes to be a cardboard box while the graphic elements describe the change in form through forces of constraining containment."

THE MAINLAND "It took seven years to earn my BFA and realize that getting to the mainland—out of Hawaii—was essential and that continuing school was probably the only way I was going to find a larger landscape." He continued with independent studies in photography at the University of Hawaii until 1987 and got a job to make ends meet. "I worked as a 'camera lout'—operating a stat camera at a typography house called The Other Type. I moved up to paste-up artist and finally to designer. After three years of this, I applied to graduate school in graphic design, returning to the commercial and more-bankable-than-photography route." To his delight, he was accepted into the program at the Cranbrook Academy of Art and moved to Bloomfield Hills, Michigan.

CRANBROOK Hori was immediately fascinated with the school. "This was graphic design like I had never seen nor imagined. It involved theory, thinking, commitment, analysis, experimentation, and, for me, continuing with making photographs as well. I realized graphic design could be read in much the same way that photography could be read—this was the first most liberating moment—where typography had the power to communicate more than the actual words it represented, where additional meaning was formed on the intentions of the designer."

The second year was dedicated entirely to producing designs. The experience had a lasting impact on Hori's aesthetic. "Making work, experimenting with thresholds of

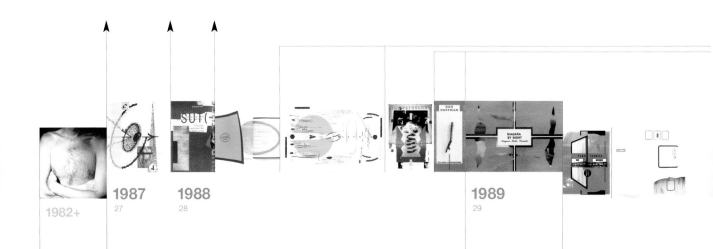

1982+

1987
27

1988
28

1989
29

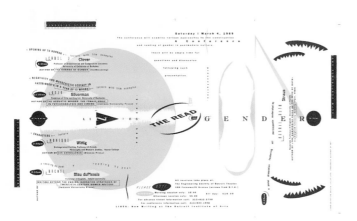

The Reading of Gender, event flyer "This project actually produced a piece of mail from an incensed museum patron addressed to Roy Slade, then the President of Cranbrook Academy of Art, criticizing the academy, the design department, and me for producing this so-called example of graphic design. Roy gave me the letter to keep and said to keep up the good work!"

readability and visibility, and inserting liberal amounts of literary and semiotic theory—there were long, long nights fueled with beer and cigarettes, going back and forth between the design studio and the darkrooms in the photo department. It really was the best period of growth and discovery for me. I loved it so much, I asked for permission to stay, and after some lobbying and pleading, I was granted a third year. Even today, I still try to re-create the energy and attitude within myself that began at Cranbrook."

HOLLAND Hori received his masters degree in 1990, and he decided to continue on the journey he had begun at Cranbrook. He received a Fulbright scholarship to The Netherlands and landed internships at Studio Dumbar in The Hague and at *Hard Werken* in Rotterdam. "It felt like a continuation of experimenting, relearning, making adjustments, and growing. All that in which I had previously been invested—literary and semiotic theory— quickly came to a full stop in Holland because the language of the projects— Dutch—was now basically inaccessible to me. This limitation forced a different development, one of focusing on form language, on the 'graphic' of graphic design. And what better place to do that than in Holland? This was second heaven. Studio Dumbar was an amazing place then, with Gert Dumbar providing a lively and spirited lead. I spent two internship periods at Studio Dumbar and then moved to Rotterdam to intern at *Hard Werken*."

Cranbrook Academy of Art, museum exhibition, announcements "You don't have to do much when you start with great material," Hori says of his announcement for Dan Hoffman's *Bio-Logic Constructions* show. *Saarinen in Finland* is a different story. "I'm so busted on this one. Stretching type is so, so wrong. It's the one rule I impose in my typography class."

"THIS WAS GRAPHIC DESIGN
LIKE I HAD NEVER SEEN NOR IMAGINED.
IT INVOLVED THEORY, THINKING, COMMITMENT, ANALYSIS, EXPERIMENTATION,
AND, FOR ME, CONTINUING WITH MAKING PHOTOGRAPHS AS WELL."

Niagara by Night, manipulated postcard, personal project "I loved stenciling over postcards with silver Krylon!"

1990   1991   1992   1999   2000   2001   2003   NOW

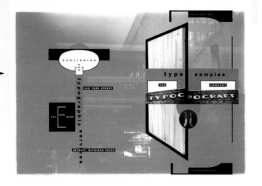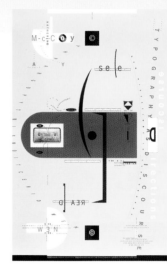

Typocraft Type Samples, book covers (left and middle) "Typocraft was the Detroit printer that allowed me to experiment and learn an enormous amount by working with them. This was an homage to their down-and-dirty, roll-up-your-sleeves-and-get-it-done beneficence."

Typography as Discourse, poster (right) "I designed this poster for the seminal lecture by Kathy McCoy on new directions in typography and her paradigm of see–read–image–text, in which all are equally viable in communication."

"NON–DESIGN STUDIO EMPLOYERS HAVE CONVINCED ME THAT I CAN'T WORK AS AN EMPLOYEE.

OPENING MY OWN STUDIO WAS THE ONLY THING I COULD DO."

Monotonous Beauty, spread from *Émigré* 13
"A moment of reductivist hyperbole—look at all that white space."

"This was a totally different studio—very male, very industrial and industrious, located near the international shipping ports of Rotterdam. Very blue-collar. Working with Willem Kars, Gerard Hadders, and Rick Vermeulen was pragmatism-in-training: Be direct, be practical, be creative—very *Hard Werken*. I liked the atmosphere and the work, and they seemed to like me. I stayed on as a senior designer when the internship ended."

NEW YORK After spending three years in Holland, Hori decided to return to the United States. He moved to New York and dipped his toe into a culture that was more corporate than he had been used to. He became an art director for Atlantic Records. "It was great fun—big budgets, location shoots, lots of expensing, lots of long days and nights. I fell in love with the creative director, Richard Bates, also a Cranbrook grad. But mixing love and work in this arrangement grew too complicated, so I left the job and kept the relationship." He worked for the cosmetics brand Prescriptives for six months but hated the experience. "Non–design studio employers have convinced me that I can't work as an employee. Opening my own studio was the only thing I could do. I don't do well with someone above me. I launched Bates Hori with Richard in 1993 and got a couple of cats—Book and Myth—to keep me company in our basement studio."

THE DOUBLE EDGE OF SUCCESS Since his time at Cranbrook, Hori had been a darling of the design scene, and it had an unexpected impact on his work. "There was a string of years from Cranbrook to Holland to Atlantic

1982+   1987   1988   1989

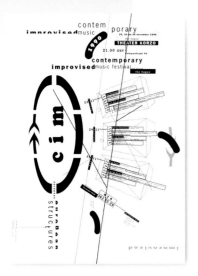

Subjective Reasoning, The Phases of Water; The Faces of Man, brochure (right, top) Hori worked with Gerard Hadders at Hard Werken to create this paper promo for Kromekote. "The funny thing was Champion Paper wanted a European viewpoint as part of this promo series, so they contacted Hard Werken to participate. I ended up getting the project, so it was an American in a Dutch studio presenting an American interpretation of a European situation." Of the spread shown here, he says, "It's way too complicated for its own good to explain. It involved the perfection of nature, imperfection of man, arrangement of the water molecule, movement of water, and images of then current political conditions and consequences in Eastern Europe. We also forced the printer to intentionally misregister film and print some of the images as mistakes."

CIM, Contemporary Improvised Music Festival, poster (left) "This poster was my first for Studio Dumbar. *Improvisation* was the operative word throughout the project. While at the press check, I saw the make-ready sheets from the lavender ink being put through the silk-screen press for the make-ready on the violet ink. This resulted in overlaps and overlays not present in the original design, but it made the piece so much better. I decided to keep that bit of improvisation and had them run the poster as they had on the make-readies. I thanked the press-men for collaborating on the design."

CIM, Contemporary Improvised Music Festival, catalog (left, bottom) "The show-through on the cover and outer pages is still pretty nice to see. This was a no-budget project for Studio Dumbar, so instead of going only slightly heavier than the text pages for a flimsy cover, I went in the opposite direction and spec'ed a very lightweight, thin text stock for the covers and made sure the page imposition on the cover and outer pages produced a visual sequence that capitalized on this transparency."

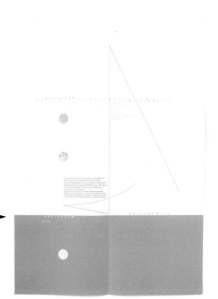

Records where I submitted everything I produced to design competitions such as the American Center for Design's (ACD) 100 Show and the *ID* magazine review, and almost everything got in and published. That was a great ego-boosting cycle but ultimately a destructive and disrupting cycle as well, because this recognition-getting became laced into my design process. It was as if the piece wasn't valid until it was validated from the outside and by other designers, you know? It became an insular, selfish practice. The recognition comes and goes very quickly for me. I needed a more secure, stable form of knowing for myself what was good, what was almost good, and what was enough. I actually stopped working for about six months to live with this dilemma and with myself in my head to figure this out. I can't say I've resolved all my insecurities and issues entirely, but I feel that I'm definitely far, far from looking for outside validation of anything I do."

Today, he has a balanced view of the benefits and dangers of recognition. "It has spoiled me, given me a big head, reaffirmed beliefs, produced new beliefs, humbled me,

Rotterdam Designprijs, call-for-entries poster
"Two American clichés: *the big cheese* and *a piece of the pie* were central motifs representing the first implementation of this design competition. The orange was used because the contest was Dutch." Hori designed this poster with Kai Zimmerman at *Hard Werken*.

1990
30

1991
31

1992
32

1999

2000

2001   2003   NOW

13

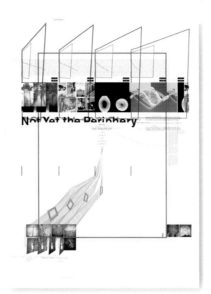

ETHER, The 8th Annual Edition, The Alternative Pick, poster "The separate halves of the infinity symbol were completed when the posters were street sniped next to each other in a long row. The two dark blue dots at the middle right are pictures of my two cats, Book and Myth."

Not Yet the Periphery, The 23rd Annual 100 Show, American Center for Design, poster "Dream project: chair the show, select the jurors, set the agenda. Too bad the ACD folded prior to publishing the catalog. It would have been quite charged because we made 52 selections instead of the usual 100." Hori created this poster in collaboration with his panel of judges, Gaye Chan, Siobhan Keaney, and Harmine Louwé [p.140]. The writing came courtesy of Max Bruinsma.

Things in the Making, Contemporary Architecture and the Pragmatist Imagination, Museum of Modern Art, symposium poster "An enlightened client requested a 'poetic read' to promote this symposium."

"POETIC INTERPRETATION OF WORDS, IDEAS, AND FORM OF LANGUAGE IS THE MOST ENJOYABLE PART OF MY PROCESS."

scared me, developed my self-confidence and self esteem, frustrated me, energized me, allowed me opportunities to lecture all over the place, put more money in the bank, lost me some jobs, made me happy, made me bitter, and made me jealous. Really, though, I don't think recognition is a good or bad thing. I just hope I do okay with what I have."

METHODS In his work, Hori refers back both to his education at Cranbrook and to the habits of his earlier pre-med days. "I still hold a semi-scientific method close to heart—research, thorough analysis, hypothesizing, experimenting, data analysis, conclusions. I try to let things stew in my head as long as possible, connecting ideas and formal scenarios in as many ways as possible, before actually starting the visual producing process. I think poetic interpretation of words, ideas, and form of language is the most enjoyable part of my process. Sometimes I go too far out on a tangent, but making it link back up to a core idea of the originating content is also pleasurable. Convincing people of these links and the coherency of it all is sometimes a challenge, though."

Considering this personal approach and his complex aesthetic, it's no surprise that Hori executes most of his work alone. "I'm not great at sharing or compromising. I love collaborating in the verbal, idea-based stages. When that stage is over I tend to isolate myself over the rest of the project."

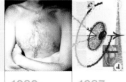

1982+

1987

1988

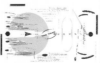

1989

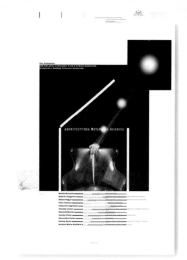

The Rescinded Muse, panel from the poster "What started as a designer's take on the music industry evolved into an elliptical musing on sound-making—rewriting the brief opened up the project and was a good lesson on realizing possibilities." Both Hori and Gaye Chan provided photography, Augustine Hope pitched in with words.

Lecture Series, spring 2001; Graduate School of Architecture, Princeton University, poster "Printing disaster. I experimented with very cheap marbled stock and warm gray metallic ink—sounded good, looked bad. I paid for the second color out-of-pocket. The client was surprised a little, too, with the pink. They never called again."

Architectures, Metaphors, Sciences; Graduate School of Architecture, Princeton University, poster "This piece is apparently straight-forward but actually a little concertino of metaphors."

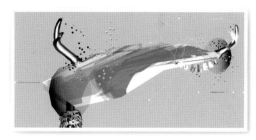

Bates Hori, The Alternative Pick, ad "I'm very proud of the ad copy: *SYNTHETIC.POETIC.POINTED.*"

SUCCESS Ten years after opening his own studio, Hori still happily works from home. Book and Myth still keep him company, as do two French bulldogs, Beluga and Ivan. In 2000, he joined the graduate faculty at the Yale University School of Art and teaches a class on typography. While telling his story, Hori notices a pattern. "There were a few concentrated periods of intense discovery linked by quieter periods of more organic evolution. I'm looking for another one of those concentrated periods. I've been lazy for too many years now." He recognizes the need to keep growing. "Teaching at Yale is definitely pushing me in ways that are productive—away from a passive comfort level—but I definitely think a more substantial shift is necessary."

Ultimately, Hori just wants to do his job. "I'm successful when I am able to really understand what the client wants in addition to hearing what the client is saying—when I produce something that exceeds their expectations using my voice, all the while maintaining and growing the relationship between the client and myself with humor and dignity. And when they come back and want more of the same—that's when I feel really good." ✀

Raw One, Rafael Fuchs Photography, promo book series "Rafael keeps pushing me to be more intrusive with the design. I keep pushing to just let his photographs be."

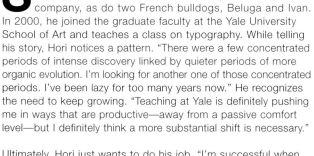

1990

1991 1992

1999
39

2000
40

2001
41

2003
43

NOW

02

Red Hot Chili Peppers, postcards Freelancing, Burdick designed this set of postcards for Capitol Records, promoting the 1987 Red Hot Chili Peppers album *The Uplift Mofo Party Plan*, proving that she wasn't afraid of bold, illustrative typography and bright red ink.

ANNE BURDICK

Born a design Brahmin, Anne Burdick worked hard to earn the place she holds among her peers. Her passion for critical writing led her to move beyond print into the bold new world of interactive typography. Her digital efforts ultimately allowed her to gain worldwide recognition for a decidedly old world book design.

Anne Burdick's roots are in the Los Angeles design community. Born in 1962, she was surrounded by design from birth. "My father, Bruce Burdick, is an industrial designer. From the time I was little, his passion for design was a defining presence." An alumnus of Art Center College of Design in neighboring Pasadena, Bruce Burdick worked for Charles and Ray Eames and various other designers in the area. He later started his own studio and headed the Environmental Design Department at Art Center in the 1970s. "My father's dedication to his career and his ability to achieve the goals he defined for himself have been the number one influence on me."

It was impossible for Burdick not to be caught up in her father's passion for design. "After I graduated from of high school, I took a year off and worked in my father's studio, The Burdick Group—my initiation into the culture of high design and design celebrity. For summer vacations we went to the International Design Conference in Aspen, Colorado, every year for about 12 years. I remember walking across a meadow with Saul Bass, who talked to me about design." This deep and constant immersion in the field at a young age formed Burdick's approach. "I took for granted that design was a philosophical pursuit as well as a formal one. I expected that designers should have something to say. For me this was an integral part of being a good designer."

Considering her father's position, Art Center seemed the inevitable academic destination for Burdick. "It was always assumed that I would go there. Before committing to the rigor and narrow focus of a small, private art school, I decided to attend a large university with a reputation as a party school, getting a broad liberal arts education, testing my limits, and refining my portfolio." She enrolled in the liberal arts program at San Diego State University in 1981 before transferring to Art Center two years later. Unaware of the value of a degree in design, she tailored her Art Center experience to suit her needs at the time. "I took only the courses I wanted to—I had no intention of graduating."

1987   1995   NOW

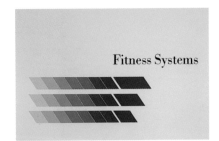

Fitness Systems, identity (left, top) After weekends out on the town, the nature of Burdick's second job at the decidedly conservative studio Cross Associates forced her to re-dye her hair to a natural shade every Monday. The same shift is apparent in this piece of corporate identity. More than anything, it displays Burdick's ability to suppress her own identity in the service of a corporate master.

Children's Hospital Los Angeles, logo (left, bottom) Aiming to lively up herself, Burdick switched employers, getting a job with designer John Coy. He had other plans, however, and wanted her for her experience with conservative clients. This competent but listless design for the Children's Hospital Los Angeles was one of the resulting pieces.

Stanford Conference, poster (right) Working for John Coy finally did give Burdick a chance to design for less conservative cultural clients, such as the 1988 Stanford Conference for Design. Her use of imagery and fonts shows the influence of *Émigré* and are of their time, but the simple, elegant layout stands the test of time.

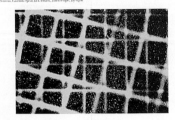

07 / 28 - 30 / 88

Frank Gehry event, invite (below) While still at Coy, Burdick designed this event invitation for architect Frank Gehry, mirroring his then signature angular shapes and muted color scheme. One can tell that Burdick was reasserting her personality in the context of the design studio world.

"I WAS INTO GLAM, PUNK ROCK, AND NEW WAVE.
I HAD TO RE-DYE MY HAIR AT THE END OF EVERY WEEKEND."

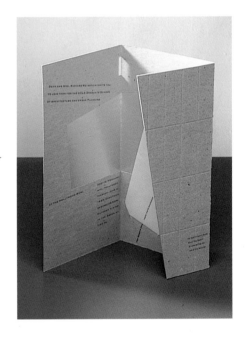

CULTURE SHOCK "After four terms, I took my polished portfolio and looked for a job. My first position was at a firm called Garber SooHoo, where I designed Rambo and Barbie and the Rockers doll packaging. Eight months later, I got a job in the design office of Jim Cross," a prominent L.A. designer who handled large corporate accounts. "Jim was a good friend of my father's, but his office was definitely too conservative for me. I learned valuable lessons about the practice of design, but I wasn't comfortable with the politics. In addition, it was the mid-'80s and I was into glam, punk rock, and New Wave. I had to re-dye my hair at the end of every weekend. It was around this time that I discovered the more artistic cultural work of John Coy and sought refuge in his New Age haven."

Ironically, John Coy hired Burdick for her corporate experience and placed her on conservative assignments before eventually giving her more interesting projects. "I also started to do work for friends who were in bands or working at record companies. Through the library at John's office, I discovered the work of Neville Brody, early *Émigré* magazines, Henk Elenga, *Hard Werken*, and the Dutch design scene. It was all exciting, fresh, hip. I wanted to be a part of it."

1986
24

1987
25

1988
26

1991
29

1992

1993

1994

1995

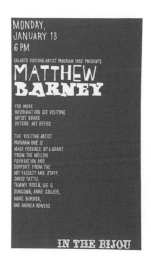

Julie Becker, poster (left) Julie Becker allowed Burdick to explore more avant-garde imagery and livelier typography for her gallery opening. The resulting piece looks modern but also carries itself with the elegance of a poster from the early twentieth century.

Matthew Barney, Visiting Lecture, poster (right) Silk-screening posters to advertise visiting speakers is a tradition for students at CalArts. With this poster for artist Matthew Barney, Burdick made a fairly straightforward layout her own through the use of consciously rough-hewn, hand-drawn typography.

Even in the day-to-day reality of a busy design office, Burdick's inquisitive nature would not be denied and it caused frustration. "I had too many questions about the cultural context of design, where stylistic languages came from, the politics of representation, and so on, and none of the designers I worked with were thinking this way." Luckily, several things happened to make Burdick's life more interesting. "First, John Coy recommended me for a job teaching at Otis Parsons School of Design (now Otis College of Art and Design), which was brilliant. I loved the dialogue, and the educational context seemed like the right place to pursue my burgeoning ideas about design." The second major event was far less pleasant. "I got in a car accident that led to a lawsuit that led to a settlement. What would I do with a tidy sum of money? Go back to school and get a graduate degree so I could get further into teaching! I applied to CalArts," the California Institute of the Arts in Valencia, north of Los Angeles, "where they let me get both my BFA and MFA in two years."

GRADUATE SCHOOL "Going to graduate school was the single most transformative experience of my career. I learned to go deep—dive straight into the content and ideas that are most interesting to me and learn how to

"I GOT IN A CAR ACCIDENT THAT LED TO A LAWSUIT THAT LED TO A SETTLEMENT. WHAT WOULD I DO WITH A TIDY SUM OF MONEY? GO BACK TO SCHOOL AND GET A GRADUATE DEGREE."

ADVENTURES in the SKIN TRADE

"PERHAPS I HAD SOMETHING TO SAY THAT WAS WORTH SAYING."

turn them into visual ideas. I also learned that I wasn't crazy. I found a community of like-minded designers who were asking the same sorts of questions and were interested in similar ideas." As part of the CalArts community, Burdick was introduced to visiting designers, among them *Émigré* founder Rudy Vanderlans. Vanderlans invited Burdick's teacher, Jeff Keedy, to edit an issue of his magazine using his students' work. The assignment was a combination of critical writing and design. "Rudy responded positively to my writing and asked to see my thesis when it was finished. Later, Lorraine [Wild, the department chair] quoted me in her talk at the Millennium conference. To have my point of view affirmed by two of the people in the design community who I respected most made me think that perhaps I had something to say that was worth saying."

HOLLAND After finishing her degree in 1992, Burdick went to Holland, following in the footsteps of two of her design heroes, Allen Hori and Robert Nakata. Based on a referral from Vanderlans, she connected with Vincent van Baar, who was working on the *Made in Holland* issue of *Émigré*. Van Baar had recently left Studio Dumbar to open his

Adventures in the Skin Trade, thesis (above, left) A spread from Burdick's thesis project displays a prototype of the restrained yet eclectic typography she would soon develop fully for her work with *Émigré* magazine. In fact, *Émigré* editor Rudy Vanderlans soon asked her to reprint her thesis in the magazine, touching off a long-running collaboration between the two.

Unisource, wine label (above, right) During her time in Holland, Burdick worked for Barlock, a firm run by Studio Dumbar alumni. This label for Saulheimer Ritterhundt—Knight's Hound—wine dates to that period and shows the intersection of Burdick's freshly minted graduate sensibilities with the necessities of a rarefied but ultimately commercial branding project.

Melissa Etheridge, billboard (opposite, top) If you're a designer in Los Angeles, you will eventually work for the music industry, and Burdick was no exception. She designed this billboard while working for Margo Chase and saw it go up on the side of the legendary Whiskey-A-Go-Go in 1993. To this day many music industry billboards on Sunset Boulevard aren't digital outputs but are individually airbrushed.

77s, CD packaging (opposite, middle) Working for Margo Chase, Burdick discovered that she loved designing CD packages. *Drowning with Land in Sight* was the 77s first album for the gospel label Myrrh and gave Burdick a chance to revisit the typographic style of her CalArts work in a commercial context.

Crowded House *Locked Out,* CD packaging (opposite, bottom) Year in and year out, record companies produce hundreds of CDs that are sent exclusively to radio stations and the press to promote upcoming singles and album releases. As such, they are often subject to a less painful approval process than CDs intended for sale to the general public. Accordingly, Burdick was able to be more adventurous in her use of typography and color on these 1994 discs for Crowded House.

Mouthpiece 1 and 2, magazines "Rudy Vanderlans allowed me to guest-edit an issue of *Émigré*, which was dedicated to the intersection of writing and design. I sent out a call for papers and projects and got a tremendous response—enough to fill two issues. This project paved the way for all the design-writing projects that followed." The right hand page of the open spread was designed by Louise Sandhaus.

own firm—Barlock—with two other Dumbar alumni. Even though they didn't yet have enough work to offer her an internship, they would soon play an important part in her life. "I got a call from Rudy saying that the *Made in Holland* issue was running behind schedule and that he wanted to publish my thesis, *Neomania*, in the upcoming issue of *Émigré*. He also wanted me to do an interview with David Carson, who was just starting work on *Ray Gun,* 'the bible of style and culture.' This was exciting, but I was sitting on a farm in Veldhoven in the south of Holland without the necessary tools to create work." After discussing her situation with van Baar, she was able to use his brand-new Macintosh on the condition that she teach him and his partners how to use it. Working at Barlock put Burdick in a uniquely privileged position. "Not only did I get the benefit of the feedback and support of the Barlockians, I also got to participate in the design, writing, and production of *Made in Holland*. It felt like I was at the center of the Dutch design universe; an endless parade of interesting young designers came through for coffee, to show work, and to drink beer." After she had completed her work for *Émigré*, she continued to handle jobs for Barlock and Studio Dumbar, remaining in Holland until money and work ran out a year later.

BACK TO THE U.S.A. Burdick returned to Los Angeles in the spring of 1993, and started freelancing for Margo Chase [p.110]. "I ended up working for Margo for about

"I WAS AT THE CENTER OF THE DUTCH DESIGN UNIVERSE.

AN ENDLESS PARADE OF INTERESTING YOUNG DESIGNERS CAME THROUGH FOR COFFEE, TO SHOW WORK, AND TO DRINK BEER."

1996 1997 1998 1999 2000 2001 2003 NOW

EAT

'ING BOOKS

m someone else, VOLER UN LIVRE, Voltaire, of course, said it in French, I am

ER UN LIVRE, Voltaire, of course, said it in French, I

***electronic book review* 2.0** "Eating Books" is part of ebr 2.0, which Burdick considers one of her breakthrough projects. "It gave me a natural stepping-stone into the digital realm. I was interested in the Web, but needed a real reason to investigate it. Working with e-lit was the perfect entrée." Burdick's ongoing engagement with *ebr* can be seen at www.electronicbookreview.com.

American Center for Design, poster In 1997, Burdick designed this beautiful call-for-entries poster for the 20th 100 Show hosted by the now sadly defunct American Center for Design in Chicago, showing her deft handling of large amounts of information and her touch for fusing type and imagery into one mesmerizing visual.

"I LEARNED HOW TO RUN A SUCCESSFUL BUSINESS AND HOW TO CREATE AN ATMOSPHERE THAT NURTURES CREATIVITY AND HARD WORK WITHOUT SACRIFICING THE FUN."

a year and a half, and it was excellent. I learned how to run a successful business and how to create an atmosphere that nurtures creativity and hard work without sacrificing the fun. For the first time, I felt the confidence to follow my own creative impulses, primarily in the context of record-industry work. I love CD packaging—the various components, the emphasis on formal innovation." But despite enjoying the work, she couldn't resist when North Carolina State University offered her a one-year appointment as a visiting professor. "I missed the hard-core questioning."

"Living in Raleigh, North Carolina, was boring, but it was perfect. It gave me both the freedom and support to pursue my own interests. While teaching there I produced *Mouthpiece*, two special issues of *Émigré* magazine. Thanks to the copious amounts of free time—there was little else to do—and the financial support of the university, I was able to undertake this elaborate project." *Mouthpiece* gave Burdick a chance to further investigate the intersection of writing and design, by now a central focus of her work.

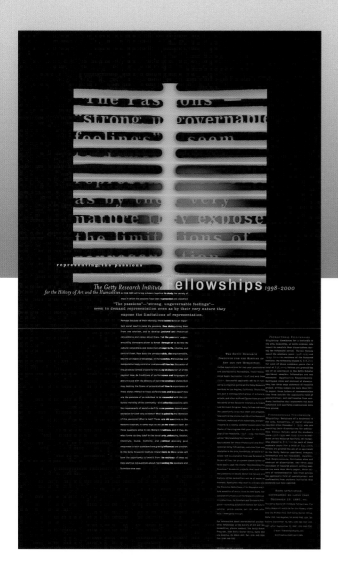

representing the passions

Getty, Passions poster (left) Burdick created this poster as a call-for-entries for the fellowship program offered by the Getty Research Institute for the History of Art and the Humanities. The type behind the glowing orange ribs reads: "The passions—strong, ungovernable feelings—seem to demand representation even as by their very nature they expose the limitations of representation." It's true, you know.

On Site Locations, website (below, top) Burdick developed the identity and website for this publisher of location guides, introducing a clean, high-end look to an arcane corner of the movie industry that shows her growing interest in the world of interactive design and online publishing.

phon:e:me, website (below, bottom) "Mark Amerika asked me to collaborate on this net.art project. As a result of this project and my work for *ebr*, my focus shifted from my own writing to collaborations with experimental fiction and critical writers, along with theorists, filmmakers, sound designers, programmers, and many others. It also inspired me to think about the performative aspects of the interface." You can see the site at phoneme.walkerart.org.

"This project was the second-most defining moment of my career. It brought together the opportunity to grow my own ideas, expand as a designer, and try new things with editing and collaboration." It also introduced her to like-minded individuals who would become future collaborators, friends, and contacts.

Among them was Joe Tabbi, a pioneer of Internet-based self-publishing. He invited Burdick to collaborate on his online literary journal *electronic book review,* in which she is still heavily involved today. She was also placed on the shortlist for a teaching position at CalArts, but ultimately didn't get the job due to her inexperience in new media. Instead she decided to go it alone and opened her own studio.

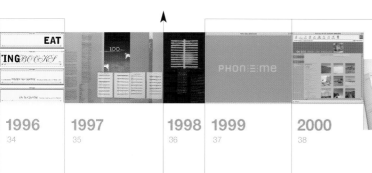

1996
34

1997
35

1998
36

1999
37

2000
38

2001

2003

NOW

23

"ONE OF MY KEY INTERESTS BECAME SPATIAL WRITING, OR DIAGRAMMATIC WRITING—

WRITING WITH A SEMANTIC OUTCOME THAT IS EQUAL PARTS WORDS AND FORM."

SPRECHEN SIE DEUTSCH? In the early days of 1997, the Viennese chemist-cum-book designer Walter Pamminger invited Burdick to give a lecture in Vienna. The promotional material for the event described her work as the "bridge between literature and design." This description drew the attention of the snappily titled Austrian Academy of Sciences' Commission for Non-Literary Text Types. "They asked me to meet with them about a project, which turned out to be the *Fackel Wörterbuch.*" They needed a designer who understood their vision for an experimental dictionary dedicated to *Die Fackel,* Karl Kraus's turn-of-the-century journal of media. "The only hitch: the project was entirely in German."

But it was too late. Burdick was in love with the project. She spent the next year in an intensive e-mail dialogue with the editors. "It was entirely about the structure and editorial strategies of the dictionary." She drafted Pamminger as her liaison in Vienna and also relied on him to help her think through the structure of the book. "When I finally felt that I had a thorough understanding of the dictionary, I tackled the structure, which was strongly influenced by my work in the electronic realm. One of my key interests became spatial writing, or diagrammatic writing—writing with a semantic outcome that is equal parts words and form." While consulting with type designer and design historian Jens Gelhaar on the book's typography, Burdick recalls spending countless hours "sitting on the floor of the Getty Research Library pouring over the entire set of original issues of *Die Fackel.* Our typographic choices were driven by our concerns for interpreting and re-presenting history in an informed way."

Negating the Enlightenment, announcement Created for the UCLA Center for Germanic Studies, this conference announcement was printed in fluorescent ink and shows that even highly academic topics are made better by the merciless use of high-octane colors.

Fackel Wörterbuch: Redensarten, dictionary "This unconventional dictionary grew out of a year-long collaboration with literary scientists at the Austrian Academy of Sciences. Initially, it was meant to be an Internet-based project, but it ended up being a printed book." Burdick's magnum opus later received the coveted Leipzig Award, also known as "The Most Beautiful Book in the World" award.

Writing Machines, mediawork *Writing Machines* is a collaboration between Burdick and literary critic N. Katherine Hayles. The book introduces a vocabulary for addressing materiality in the critique of literature. "Users can customize their own copy of the Writing Machines book with printable components that are only available online. The resulting Web and print components demonstrate what one critic called 'a new, composite reading mode.'"

electronic book review **4.0, website** "*ebr* 4.0 is built upon a database and re-conceives the site as an ongoing hypertext archive. Whereas 2.0 focused on individual projects, 4.0 is about the site as a whole, providing readers with an interface that is both reading and writing tool. There is no fixed, final meta view of the site; it changes constantly in response to activity at the site and the interests of the individual reader."

"~~THIS IS THE PINNACLE.~~
~~I FEEL LIKE I CAN RETIRE NOW.~~
I'M AT THE TOP OF MY GAME
AND READY TO MAKE
A REAL IMPACT."

The *Fackel Wörterbuch* is Burdick's magnum opus. It commits to paper the advances she made while exploring interactive design and stands as a monument not only to her skills as a designer but also to her stamina. Both were justly rewarded when the book received the Leipzig Award, the highest honor in book design, also known as "The Most Beautiful Book in the World" award. "It came as a complete surprise. The editors had entered the book in the contest, unbeknownst to me." The Los Angeles *Times* ran a piece on Burdick on the front page of the Sunday Style section. "The quote beneath the photo read, 'This is the pinnacle. I feel like I can retire now.' My father scolded me: That will never get you clients! You should have said 'I'm at the top of my game and ready to make a real impact.'"

EXPANSION In 2002, Burdick downsized her business and upsized her family. "I had my first son, bought a house, and converted the garage into a studio. I took a full-time job teaching in the graduate Media Design Program at Art Center. Now I take on only large-scale, long-term collaborative projects that allow me to push my work in new directions or to pursue a line of questioning that I've been following already." Burdick gave birth to her second son in January 2004. When I asked her about her plans for the future she answered "I'm at the top of my game and ready to make a real impact." ✄

EAT

'ING *BOOKS*

PHON:E:me

WRITING
MACHINES

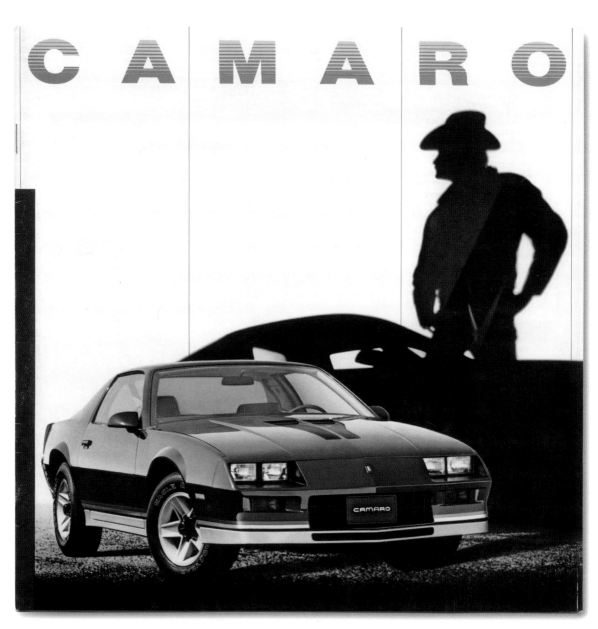

Camaro, car catalog cover Fella designed this catalog cover a year after his 1979 *You As Well As Me* poster. At this point in his career, his personal aesthetic had moved far away from his commercial work.

ED
FELLA

After thirty years of working for the Detroit advertising machine as an illustrator and layout man, Ed Fella went back to school and got his MFA. When he started teaching, he suddenly realized that he had become the hot new thing on the design scene—at the tender age of forty-nine. Teaching at the California Institute of the Arts allowed him to become, in his own words, an exit-level designer.

ED Fella was born in 1938. His parents had come to the United States from Europe and settled in the Detroit area. Like most immigrants, they adapted to their new surroundings well enough but never fully assimilated. His mother came from a family of artists and was always working on various craft projects. His father was employed as an autoworker, but used his free time to sculpt. Fella inherited their artistic temperament. He remembers drawing since early childhood. For this, his mother called him the easiest of her five kids. "All we had to do was give you a pencil, and you'd be gone all day," she later told him.

DETROIT BAUHAUS Striving to give their son the best possible education, his father enrolled him in a local college preparatory school. The steady diet of math, Latin, and theology classes didn't sit well with Fella, and his grades reflected it. Art and drawing were more to his liking, so in 1955, his father placed him at Cass Technical High School, a trade school. "I had to be dragged kicking and screaming, but once I was there I immediately felt at home." He still flunked English.

At Cass, Fella received "a Bauhaus model of high school design education"—a thorough trade education complemented by extended trips into twentieth-century art history. He trained extensively in the techniques of the day, leaving him with lettering, illustration, and production skills that would form the basis of both his commercial career and his later personal work.

1965   1987   NOW

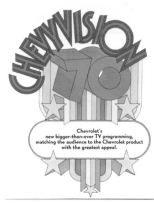

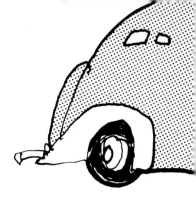

"IT WAS ALL GOOD, HARDCORE MODERNISM, AND I LOVED IT. BUT AS FOR THE PREVAILING MODERNISM IN DESIGN,

I WANTED SOMETHING DIFFERENT AND BEGAN LOOKING TO HISTORICISM AND THE VERNACULAR."

1915 Chevrolet, illustration
(above, left) This rendering of an early Chevrolet turned into a series of more than fifty cars used to illustrate the book *The Chevy Story.*

ChevyVision 70, promotional display (above, middle) This display shows the tongue-in-cheek Art Deco–inspired typography Fella often used during this phase of his career.

Charlie Rasch, *Ragtime Down the Line,* record sleeve (detail) (far left) This piece of 1967 lettering clearly foreshadows Fella's later interest in irregular vernacular letterforms.

Celebrating the Moon Landing, poster (near left) This announcement of the Apollo 11 moon landing was a breakthrough for Fella. It was the first time he realized that he could self-publish his work by getting it printed affordably.

Car, illustration (above right) Fella drew this cartoon car for an article in *Motortrend* magazine in 1972.

1965 27

1967 29

1969 31

1970 32

1972 34

1973 35

1975 37

1978

1979

1980

He graduated at the age of eighteen and, in 1957, got his first job in the Detroit design and advertising business that would be his home for the next thirty years. Not going on to college after high school, he started taking night classes at Wayne University, developing a particular taste for avant-garde literature and poetry. "It was all good, hardcore Modernism, and I loved it. But as for the prevailing modernism in design, I wanted something different and began looking to historicism and the vernacular." He was also becoming a bit of a hep-cat. "Remember, this was still the '50s. Art types aspired to the high culture, classical music, cool jazz, folk. We wouldn't be caught dead listening to Elvis."

COMMERCIAL DESIGN Fella's life at a string of advertising-oriented design studios in the Detroit area revolved around cars and health care. His day-to-day work consisted of drawing headlines and layouts where he further refined his technical skills. His illustrations clearly reflect the trends and flavors of their moment, whereas his typography often made ironic reference to commercial Art Deco lettering, a style then years away from its renaissance. But it worked, and Fella's often-whimsical illustration style ultimately earned him the nickname "The King of Zing."

Throughout the '60s and '70s, Fella was doing well. He had a string of well-respected, well-paying jobs that allowed him to take care of his two daughters. Occasionally, he would pop up in design annuals. But his commercial work was not enough to satisfy his artistic desires. He became active in Detroit's cultural scene, offering his services to alternative art organizations with the motto "Free work in due time." Among other things, he became the designer for the Detroit Focus Gallery, creating dozens of event posters and art-directing the *Detroit Focus Quarterly*.

These pro bono assignments gave Fella a welcome excuse to print the kind of experimental designs he was already doing privately. This was work that would never have been possible in the context of his day job. He did, however, use his employers' facilities to produce the pieces. These were the predigital days when type had to be ordered from a typesetter. Fella would piggyback pro bono type onto whatever job he was working on at the time. Predating the now-grating term *vernacular*, he'd use a direct-positive Photostat machine to create collage with found images and whatever type he could lay his hands on. "My work for nonprofits was based entirely on the fact that I had these big studios at my fingertips. I had the board to do the mechanicals, type, wax, pencils—all of that. I would always give credit to the company I worked for. They didn't mind."

Advertising illustrations In his commercial illustration work, Fella followed the style of the times, such as in these mid-'70s ads for GMC, Osmond's Clothing Store, and Hudson's Department Store.

Fact, Not Opinion, poster Though aesthetically still far removed from his later poster designs, this was one of the first personal pieces Fella designed using the Photostat machine to create collages from found images and leftover type.

Henry Ford Hospital brochures When the need arose, Fella easily channeled corporate design, such as this series of pamphlets for the Henry Ford Hospital.

You As Well As Me, poster *You As Well As Me* is an early breakthrough piece from Fella's personal oeuvre and illustrates the transition from a modernist aesthetic in the background to the frenetic collage in the fore that suggests his later compositions.

1965   1967   1969   1970   1972   1973   **1975**   **1978**   **1979**   **1980**

37   40   41   42

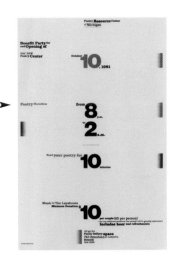

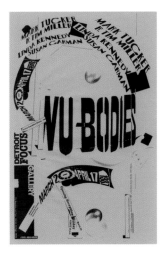

"I ALWAYS HAD AN ALTERNATIVE PRACTICE, A COUNTER CAREER,

BECAUSE OF MY EARLY SCHOOLING AT CASS TECH AND THEIR IDEOLOGY OF FINE ART AND COMMERCIAL ART BEING CONSIDERED ONE AND THE SAME."

Beyond the need to play, Fella gives another motivation for his experiments: "The biggest reason I did this was to avoid doing the work I really had to do. Experimental work is easy and fun for me, so coming into the studio, it was much simpler to start with some playing around before getting into the much more difficult job of really making something that solves a problem, has specific meaning, or fills a demand."

NO MORE CLIENTS Starting in the 1980s, Fella would occasionally present his growing body of experimental work to the design students in Katherine and Michael McCoy's class at the Cranbrook Academy of the Arts in nearby Bloomfield Hills. The McCoys were at that point creating Cranbrook's graduate design program, and when he retired from advertising in 1985, Fella decided to enroll.

Studying at Cranbrook afforded Fella the freedom to concentrate entirely on his artistic explorations, and his work from that period reflects the fertile creative environment he occupied. "I don't think I ever had a moment of change, as such, because I always had an alternative practice, a counter career so to speak, because of my early schooling at Cass Tech and their ideology of fine art and commercial art being considered one and the same. Since day one, I have always pursued my experimental work. My kids used to call them 'fun sheets' when they saw me working on stuff that wasn't 'the job.' Those fun sheets later became my sketchbooks. For years they were just loose sheets. I started doing the books in 1976. It's a much more disciplined way to work. They become a sort of a designer artist's book."

"When I stopped doing client work, I just continued my other work. It was a progression of the fussing around that I had always done anyway. Now I just did it full-time and made a new career out of it—without payment." As a student, Fella used the freedom that came with retirement to give his creativity free reign but then applied his thirty years of skill to whatever emerged. As spontaneous as his typography may look, it is always painstakingly rendered, spaced, and balanced.

CALIFORNIA His work evolved into highly elaborate pseudo-anarchic compositions. They were different than any graphic design of the time but struck a chord with a new generation of designers who were staking their claim during the aesthetic land-grab following the wide availability of the computer as a design tool. During his two years at the school, Fella had become an undeniable presence for his fellow students and teachers alike, and they carried forth the word

1981
43

1986
48

1987
49

2000

2002

2003

NOW

CalArts
*Dance*Ensemble
10th

Anniversary

Cristyne Lawson Artistic Director/Choreographer
Larry A. Attaway Producer
Dancers:
Rebecca Bobele
Laurence Blake
Clare Duncan
Kurt Weinheimer
Tina Yuan
Lance Fuller Erin White

Costume Design: Martha Ferrara
Mod Scenographer:
COMPOSERS:
LARRY A. ATTAWAY
JOHN CAGE   Robert Benedetti
ORNETTE COLEMAN   Toshiro Ogawa: Light Design
FEATURING DAVID ROITSTEIN
AND THE CALARTS JAZZ ENSEMBLE
AND THE BRAZILIAN PERCUSSION ENSEMBLE
CONCERTS NOVEMBER 30, DECEMBER 1,2, 8, 9 (1989)
AT 8:00PM CALARTS MODULAR THEATRE AND MAIN GALLERY
TICKETS ARE $6 GENERAL ADMISSION AND $3 FOR STUDENTS AND SENIOR CITIZENS
CALL (818)362-2315 OR (805)253-7800 FOR RESERVATIONS

CalArts Dance Ensemble Tenth Anniversary, poster As a freshly minted faculty member at the California Institute of Arts, Fella designed this poster for the school's dance ensemble. Aesthetically he focused on the art of uneven letter, line, and word spacing.

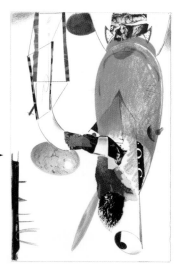

Sketchbook page Fella has filled sketchbooks for years. This abstract page is part of his thesis project at the Cranbrook Academy of Art.

T-shirt design Fella designed this type composition to be used on a T-shirt for CalArts. As with all his work, the lettering and design are drawn entirely by hand and then modified using a black-and-white photocopier.

***Letters On America,* book cover** In 2000, Fella published *Letters On America*, a Polaroid survey of vernacular typography throughout the United States.

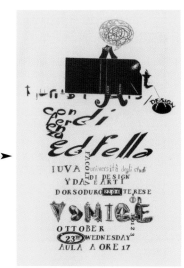

After-the-fact flyers Over the years, Fella has printed an ongoing series of posters advertising both visiting speakers at CalArts and his own appearances around the world. The twist is that he designs them either to be handed out at the event or to be sent to participants days, weeks, or months after the fact, thus negating their use as advertising tools.

1965   1967   1969   1970   1972   1973   1978   1979   1980

Hamtramck, illustration
Used for the cover of a Polish design magazine, this is a good example of the intricate lettering that fills Fella's sketchbooks. A better example of the lettering that fills Fella's sketchbooks can be seen below, on a page from one of Fella's sketchbooks.

about his designs. Before long, Fella had a fan base. At the age of fifty, he was suddenly a controversial new designer. He was championed by *Émigré* magazine, adopted as a graphic godfather by young designers, and Steven Heller famously dissed his design as "ugliness" in a 1993 *eye* magazine article.

It was only natural that Lorraine Wild hired Fella as a teacher when she took over the graduate design department at the California Institute of the Arts in 1987. Since then, CalArts has become Fella's home base. He maintains a small office on campus from which have come some of his most famous designs.

AFTER THE FACT Besides continuing to fill one sketchbook after another with his surrealistic type compositions, Fella's main creative outlet is his ongoing series of after-the-fact posters, cheaply reproduced black-and-white compositions advertising past events. "I make all these announcements for things that are already over. I pay for them myself. There are no editions; there is just the archive edition. In advertising, you send out 200 posters and hope that twenty people come to the event. When you do it after the fact, you make just the twenty and give them to people who actually came to the event." This gives Fella the freedom to ignore any considerations of marketing or sheer mailworthiness. Most important, it allows him to grow his body of work. He has designed announcements for visiting lecturers and for his own past appearances. He even made one piece advertising a dinner engagement with a friend. He just loves the work.

Sketchbook spread Stefan Sagmeister claims that flipping through Ed Fella's sketchbooks was one of the experiences that convinced him to embark on his famous Year Without Clients, so he could get back to free experimentation. Having spent an afternoon on a guided tour of the sketchbooks while talking with Fella, I can see Sagmeister's point. It is worth noting that Fella draws exclusively with a four-color ballpoint pen and two small pencils in yellow and light blue.

Fella now calls himself an exit-level designer. Since 1957, he has built a totally unique and undeniable body of work, but he now says that his statement is made—he has reached an endpoint, his particular one. "I'm still involved in design, but I've become my own client, which is kind of like being an artist. My work constantly evolves. Now it can evolve totally in the direction that I'm interested in. The thing about being an exit-level designer is that you don't have to worry about being in the mix. You're basically done. The truth is, my work entered history, so to speak, fifteen years ago. It had its blip through the culture, and now I'm history and totally free of it. I'm all finished with the necessity of proving anything anymore. I'm my own history! Now I can do what I want." ✌

FELLA CALLS HIMSELF AN EXIT-LEVEL DESIGNER:
"I'M MY OWN HISTORY! NOW I CAN DO WHAT I WANT."

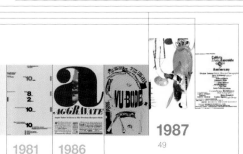

1987
49

2000
62

2002
64

2003
65

NOW

1981   1986

04

Image As Symbol, graduate thesis poster, Join The NRA! "The National Rifle Association used to offer $100,000 of free accidental death and dismemberment insurance as a recruitment inducement. You'd think that would scare people away, right? A gun goddess pleasures herself while a group of impotent men watch. I still hold the record for most phallic symbols in a graduate thesis," says Sahre.

PAUL SAHRE

Escaping from a series of uninspiring jobs, Paul Sahre used a small silk-screen setup in his basement to gain his artistic freedom. Soon art directors and editors took note and brought his work into the light.

"I don't know if I would call it a mission exactly, but I do feel that the work I do as a graphic designer is important. It is what I have chosen to do with most of my time, but it is also the primary way I express myself. It is a job. It is a hobby. It is probably the closest thing I have to religion. It is something that defines me. It is a lifelong pursuit. I feel very lucky that, most of the time, I can work very hard and not feel like I am working at all."

Born in upstate New York in 1964, Paul Sahre was the third of four children. "I was obsessed with sports as a kid. I played them, watched them, and talked about them. Baseball was my favorite. I got as far a Division III baseball in college before I realized that I wasn't good enough to go any further with it." Luckily, Sahre had a parallel passion for art. "From as far back as I remember, I liked to draw. By high school I had progressed to pencil drawings of cars, athletes, and band logos. I also drew a cartoon strip."

This early interest eventually led Sahre to study graphic design. He chose his alma mater for its political history. "I went to Kent State University in Ohio, because I thought it would be a radical place to go to college. It wasn't." Still, Sahre enjoyed immersing himself in graphic design. As part of his undergraduate studies, he participated in a summer design workshop in Switzerland. "Through the programs developed by j. Charles Walker at Kent State, I was able to study with Rudy Ruegg and Fritz Gottschalk and was exposed to so much in a short period of time. The experience is still with me."

UNDERGROUND ENERGY Sahre also vividly recalls discovering the work of Seattle designer Art Chantry. "It totally changed the direction I was going in with my work while I was an undergrad. For the next few years at school I saw as much of his work as I could and ripped him off a lot, trying to figure out what he was doing and why I responded to it so strongly. I eventually bugged those responsible at Kent State to bring Art in for a workshop and was able to study with him for a few weeks as a graduate student." The bold underground energy of Chantry's work inspired in Sahre a love for the medium of poster art and showed him the potential for artistic expression in graphic design. Both seeds would flower years later in his personal and professional work.

1987

1996

NOW

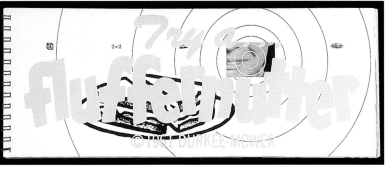

"I also developed a strong work ethic in school. By my junior year I was becoming successful in school, mainly because I worked harder than almost everyone. But it didn't feel like work. I am the same today—I can work very long hours and not notice time passing. I like when that happens." Sahre received a bachelors of fine arts degree in graphic design and was offered a teaching assistantship near the end of his senior year. He stayed on to get his masters degree, and perhaps, as a reaction to the unexpected political apathy that he found on campus, he designed a series of activist posters as part of his graduate thesis. "College was a transformative experience for me. I had a focus when I left. I knew what I wanted, and I felt that I had found something that I loved to do."

Sahre was ready to change the world with new designs, but it didn't happen that way. "I graduated in 1990, got married, moved to Baltimore, Maryland, and got a job at a marketing communications company called Barton-Gillet.

MORE THAN 25 PERCENT "Barton-Gillet specialized in work for colleges and universities. We also did quite a bit of corporate work—annual reports, identities, stuff like that. The creative director, Bill Shinn, was trying to do quality work, but it was a constant struggle. The company was top heavy, with a handful of designers in the art department supporting dozens of writers and account executive-vice-presidents and support staff. We were on the lowest rung of the corporate hierarchy. I was frustrated with everything about the place and remember constantly getting into arguments with the account executives about the work."

"From the beginning, I started to look at the work I was doing as a percentage. Starting out, I was perhaps doing work that was interesting and that I was proud of 25 percent of the time. My modest goal on the job was to get that percentage up somehow."

Working in an environment that was at best indifferent to good design further stoked the fires of artistic rebellion in Sahre that had been ignited during his college years. "My favorite part of that job was the people I worked with in the art department. There was a strong camaraderie between us. We felt we were the underdogs, trying to care about the work we were doing, even if no one else in the company did."

Fluffernutter, composition (left) "This was my first printed piece. It was part of a promotion called *Edible Encounters*, put out by TSI—Typesetting Service, Inc. At the time, they were Cleveland's largest typesetter. They put out a call for entries all over northeast Ohio for designers and clients to send in their most memorable food experience. I loved eating Fluffernutter sandwiches as a kid."

Concept Architecture, catalog cover (right) "As part of my graduate studies, I designed a number of catalogs for the School of Art Gallery at Kent State. This catalog was for an exhibition called 'Concept Architecture for a Post-Conceptual Age.' I incorporated my own photography as well as a few original typeface designs (executed with the help of a new type design program called fontographer)."

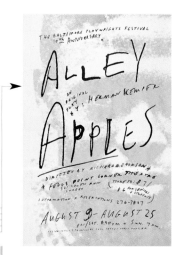

1987
23

1988
24

1989
25

1991
27

1994
30

1996
32

1997+

2000

Image As Symbol, graduate thesis poster, American Warts "I liked this quote from Hunter S. Thompson: 'In America we decorate the warts, sell them, cultivate them.' My graduate studies culminated with a series of personal advocacy posters in which I focused on symbolism as it pertains to visual communication. Looking at these posters now, I see the ideas I was working with still hold a lot of influence over my work. Art Chantry's influence is visible, but I also feel I was taking my college experience full circle, justifying my original decision to attend Kent State."

Summer Exhibitions, poster (above) "This poster announced a series of summer exhibitions at the School of Art Gallery at Kent State University. I convinced my father to allow me to reproduce some of our old summer vacation slides on the poster. My mother and my aunt appear in their bathing suits, and my sister appears twirling a baton."

Fells Point Corner Theatre, poster series "I printed each of these posters with my own two hands."
Alley Apples (opposite, below) "A historical play based on race relations in the late 1960s in Baltimore."
Baby with the Bathwater (below, far left) "A poster for the comedy *Baby with the Bathwater* by Christopher Durang. The typography on this poster was manipulated with a stat camera." Sahre designed this poster with David Plunkert.
A Lie of the Mind (below, left) "A dark play by Sam Shepard in which two families deal with the after-effects of an instance of severe spousal abuse." Once again, David Plunkert helped.
Abstract Purple (below, right) Sahre pushed minimal design and the aesthetics of silk-screening for this play by Steve Harper. "This is one of my favorite posters in this series and my client's least favorite."
Ghosts Play One (below, far right) "Three homeless people meet around a campfire and spontaneously act out a typical middle-class breakfast scene." Sahre used irregular spacing and an open composition to make the traditional typestyle and illustration contemporary.

"In retrospect, I did learn quite a bit—mainly about production, printing, and working in a business environment. But at the time, fresh out of grad school and full of optimism, it was hell." Sahre quit after two years and took a job at Rutka Weadock, a smaller, more creative design firm.

"Partially due to my creative frustrations at work I began to do pro bono poster design for the Fells Point Corner Theatre, a local company. I set up a crude silk-screen studio in my basement and began designing and printing posters for all of the theater's productions. After everyone else left the office, I would design these posters, then go home to print until 3 a.m. Then I was up again at 8 a.m. for work. I designed posters for the theater for five years."

"THERE WAS A STRONG CAMARADERIE BETWEEN THE PEOPLE I WORKED WITH IN THE ART DEPARTMENT.

WE FELT WE WERE THE UNDERDOGS,

TRYING TO CARE ABOUT THE WORK WE WERE DOING, EVEN IF NO ONE ELSE IN THE COMPANY DID."

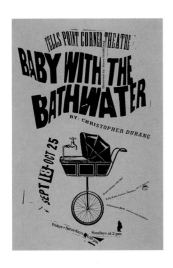

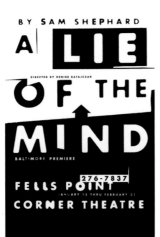

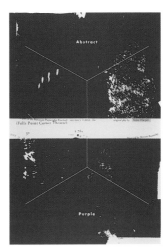

2001　　　2002　2003　　　　NOW

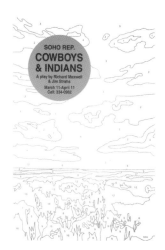

Soho Rep, identity To advertise productions for Soho Rep, an experimental black-box theater that operates on a very low budget, Sahre devised a sticker logo. For each production, a new sticker is designed in a consistent un-designed format and printed in a run of 2,000. "These stickers have many lives. Attached to business cards and stationery they become part of the theater's singular visual identity, whereas as an element in the design of flyers and posters they become part of an evolving graphic scheme." Shown here are the stickered posters for the plays *The Escapist* and *Cowboys & Indians.*

Jim White, *No Such Place,* CD package Sahre collaborated with Jim White and designer Cara Bower on this package. "Jim White's music has been described as hick-hop, somewhere between Johnny Cash and Beck. The CD package design includes photographs, diagrams, drawings, and odd collections from the artist, as well as heavy doses of UFO evidence. I designed this while at Doyle Partners."

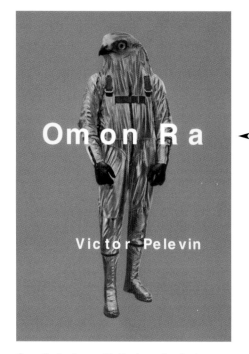

Omon Ra, book cover Working for creative director Michael Ian Kaye, Sahre designed and illustrated the cover for this book about a Russian cosmonaut in 1986. "This is my first book cover, and it is still one of my favorites."

Art directors took notice of his typographically challenging theater posters that were beginning to make the rounds on the design awards circuit, and he started getting calls from New York publishers. Michael Ian Kaye of Farrar Strauss and Giroux and John Gall of Grove Press were at the head of the line. "They were the first to hire me to design book covers."

OVERLOAD These assignments were a thrill for Sahre and would soon become one of his signature creative outlets. At that time, however, they added more work to an already packed schedule. "I kept myself very, very busy during this period. I was working full-time. I began teaching design at the University of Baltimore and doing posters for the Fells Point Corner Theatre, which I also printed. I had bought a row home in south Baltimore that I gutted and was renovating room by room by myself. I was married and had a dog. And I was also doing some personal work with all of my 'free time.' It was nuts."

"All of this eventually took a toll on my marriage, and we separated. My wife moved to New York to continue her career as a fashion designer. This set off the hardest period of my life to date, because I was stuck in a half-finished house, trying to save my marriage long distance."

1987   1988   1989   1991   1994   **1996**   **1997**   **2000**

32   33   36

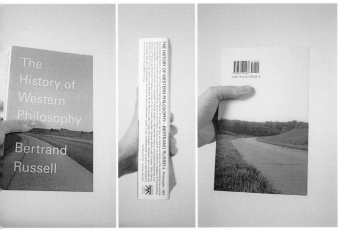

A History of Western Philosophy, book cover "Since its first publication in 1945, Lord Russell's *A History of Western Philosophy* has been universally acclaimed as the outstanding one-volume work on the subject. For the redesign of the cover, photography functions as metaphor."

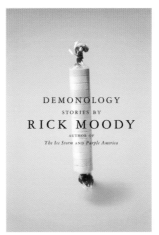
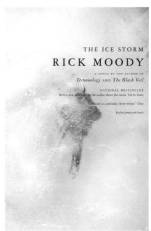

Rick Moody, book cover series Based on the success of his design for the hard-cover edition of Rick Moody's *Demonology,* Little, Brown asked Sahre to redesign the author's backlist as a series.

The changes in his private life brought about a professional change as well. "After one year at Rutka Weadock, I realized I needed to make more money, so I took a job at an advertising agency as a design director. This position led to more frustration, mainly because it was another poor fit. In retrospect, I should never have worked there, but I needed the money. I lasted two years before it mercifully ended with the agency totally disbanding the design group. It was only after I was fired that I began working for myself."

During this period, Sahre kept a list on the wall of his unfinished studio:

In 1996, he checked off the final task on his list by moving to New York City. He began working inTribeca from a small, windowless office, aptly named *Office of Paul Sahre*. Now on his own, Sahre delighted in taking on projects that allowed for growth. He underwent an aesthetic transition. He abandoned his roughed-up typographic work of the '90s for a bolder, more minimal aesthetic that fuses the typography of his book covers with more prominent conceptual photo illustrations. The latter would find even wider exposure when Sahre was invited to contribute to the *New York Times'* op-ed page.

TO DO:
GET DIVORCED
FINISH RENOVATING HOUSE
GET RID OF STUFF
SELL HOUSE
SELL CAR
MOVE TO NEW YORK

2001 2002 2003 NOW

FIND THE NUCLEAR SECRETS HIDDEN IN THIS PICTURE

Paul Sahre and Brian Rea

New York Times **op-ed, illustration** "Two computer hard drives full of weapons secrets disappeared from the Los Alamos Nuclear Labs. The energy department said there was no proof that the drives had fallen into the wrong hands and that they had merely been 'misplaced.'"

him time to begin to change from the person who detonated that bomb?

Soul-searching is not an overnight process, and we cannot have it both

June 11, 2001 7:10 a.m.

June 11, 2001 7:14 a.m.

Paul Sahre

ways. We can either speedily execute, or we can force violent offenders to spend decades staring at walls, locked up with their minds.

New York Times **letters, illustration** (above, left) This illustration ran on the *New York Times'* letters page the day after Timothy McVeigh's execution. "This piece was a response to a number of letters to the editor that asked: what has changed?"

Tolerance, poster (above, right) Sahre collaborated with Tarek Atrissi on this project. "As part of the World Studio Poster Project, we were asked to design a poster that dealt with the idea of tolerance. Our poster introduces a new hand gesture to express this idea. We see it as a cousin to such positive hand gestures as the peace symbol, the thumbs-up sign, and the I Love You sign, even though it more closely resembles a well-known negative hand gesture. Literally, we are suggesting a way to turn a negative into a positive."

"I TRY TO ALLOW FOR EQUAL PARTS LOGIC AND INTUITION IN MY WORK, AS WELL AS EQUAL PARTS ALTRUISM AND SELFISHNESS.

MOST OF THE WORK I DO IS FOR SOMEONE OR SOMETHING OTHER THAN MYSELF, BUT, AT THE SAME TIME, IT IS ALWAYS FOR ME AS WELL."

A NEW START After years of working in restrictive situations, Sahre now values his independence. "Other than a brief experiment as an associate partner at Doyle Partners in 2000, I have been operating a small design studio—now featuring windows—and have generally worked on the projects that interest me, while trying to keep overhead low and make ends meet. I'll admit to not having that much interest in the operation of a business. It might be better for the bottom line if I did, but I don't." The studio is clearly not designed to be a moneymaking operation but rather it's a creative home for Sahre. The layout of the office itself illustrates the intersecting spheres of his work. "The front room is a design office, and the back room is a silk-screen studio, where I continue to print some of my work, mostly for pro bono clients and personal projects. I have also recently begun concentrating on the authoring side of publishing. I try to allow for equal parts logic and intuition in my work, as well as equal parts altruism and selfishness. Most of the work I do is for someone or something other than myself, but, at the same time, it is always for me as well." ✌

Notable American Women, book cover The book deals with a group of women who attempt to attain complete stillness and silence by various cultish means. From the book: "The Reading Wizard, a machine that scans and summarizes books to determine their themes and content, determined that this book was 'a documentary account of the role of the mouth in the art of deception and failure, with a specific focus on children who have been buried alive.'"

1987 1988 1989 1991 1994 1996 1997+

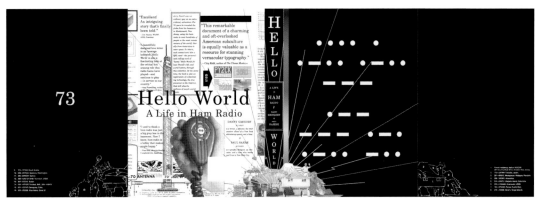

***Hello World: A Life in Ham Radio,* book** "This book, co-authored with Danny Gregory, was initiated by a flea market find. Danny bought an album full of QSL cards (postcards ham radio operators exchange after they make contact on the air for the first time). The collection belonged to a man named Jerry Powell, who communicated with people all over the world for seventy-five years from his basement in Hackensack, New Jersey. The book documents Powell's hobby through the cards. Through this information we learned about the people and the places he communicated with."

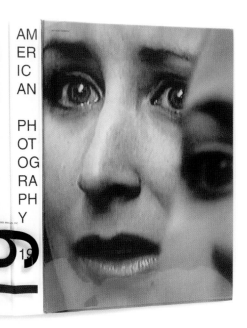

***American Photography 19,* book design**
"*American Photography* is an annual juried show of the year's best commercial photography. The visual pacing of the book is dictated by the photography. The images run uninterrupted like a giant jigsaw puzzle from the cover until they are done. Then the typography takes over, eventually spilling over onto the back cover. The sparse and strict system was a response to the prevailing mood of 2002." Tamara Shopsin helped with the design.

SAGM

05

STEFAN SAGMEISTER

There are bands you listen to and then there are bands that make you want to start a band. Stefan Sagmeister is a designer that makes you want to be a designer. Over the past ten years, he has created a body of highly visible work that is driven not by style—which in Sagmeister's world still equals fart—but by intelligent thoughts, funny ideas, and a good heart. At a time when ironic detachment is still the safe choice, Sagmeister is making it acceptable for designers to be sincere.

Stefan Sagmeister was born in 1962, in Bregenz, a small town by Lake Constance, where the very western tip of Austria meets Switzerland and Germany. Early memories of school involve teachers that would not have seemed out of place in a German language version of Pink Floyd's *The Wall*. They quickly awakened Sagmeister's rebellious nature but left him otherwise uninspired.

Declining to follow in the footsteps of his two older brothers who had received business degrees and become fashion retailers, he went to engineering school. In a student body of respectable young men on their way to becoming engineers, Sagmeister's long hair and counter-culture attitude won him few friends among his fellow students or the faculty. He stuck it out for three years and managed to join a band in the meantime, an experience that taught him one valuable lesson. "We spent most of our time looking through amp and guitar magazines, dreaming of grand equipment out of conviction that we'd be just as great as our heroes if only we could get our hands on that great loudspeaker/amp/microphone. I did not make that silly mistake again as a designer. My tools make me only marginally better."

After engineering school, he transferred to the college of the neighboring town of Dornbirn. He joined the editorial team of the left-wing quarterly *Alphorn* and took over its design. "I found out I liked doing layouts more than writing."

THE MASTER CLASS SYSTEM Sagmeister graduated from Dornbirn at age ninteen and soon moved to Vienna to finish his academic career with a masters degree from the prestigious University of Applied Arts, known in Austria as Die Angewandte. "Die Angewandte has a master-class system: You are with the same professor for the entire four years. This system works well if your professor is great, and less so if not. Our professor was old and had not kept up with developments in design, so what we could learn from him were the basics: composition, typography, and grid systems."

1982

1997

NOW

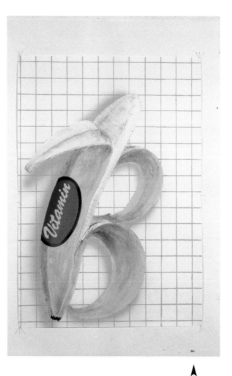

Zoo Schönbrunn, poster (far left) A poster from Sagmeister's time at art school in Vienna appropriates Lichtenstein to convey the fierceness of Austrian lions.

Vitamin B, poster (left) An early rendering from Sagmeister's time at the University for Applied Arts in Vienna shows his visual sense of humor already in effect. *Vitamin B* is a German slang term for getting your way by being well-connected.

Schauspielhaus, theater posters (below) The poster designs for the Schauspielhaus in Vienna gave Sagmeister a chance to have his work seen on billboards all over the city. *Bruder Eichmann* deals with the life of Nazi war criminal Adolf Eichmann. The play *Abendrot* ("Sunset") dealt with protests about the construction of a power station in the region. Several copies of the poster were silk-screened onto Austrian flags and hung in cafés around town.

"THERE IS AN ENORMOUS DIFFERENCE
IN SEEING SOMETHING CRAPPY
YOU DESIGNED PRINTED
TO SEEING SOMETHING YOU ARE
VERY HAPPY WITH ALL OVER THE CITY. →

More challenging educational opportunities presented themselves elsewhere. His sister's boyfriend introduced Sagmeister to Hans Gratzer, the director of the Schauspielhaus, Vienna's modern theater. Gratzer invited Sagmeister and three of his classmates to submit poster designs for upcoming productions. The students dubbed themselves "Gruppe Gut"—the Good Group—and took over as the de facto agency of record for the Schauspielhaus. All four students would submit poster designs for each play, and Gratzer would select one. More often than not, Sagmeister's idea ended up being the one posted all over the city.

Then as now, he takes pleasure in seeing his work out in the world. "There is, of course, an enormous difference in seeing something crappy you designed printed to seeing something you are very happy with all over the city. The latter came about when my first Schauspielhaus posters were appearing in Vienna. I think a poster for the play *Bruder Eichmann* was the first one I was happy with. That was a big thrill for me as a student. When a piece comes back from the printer now (if it came out the way we hoped), I still get a huge, huge kick out of it."

1982
20

1983
21

1985
23

1986
24

1997

Ronacher, posters (left) Schauspielhaus director Hans Gratzer started a campaign to save the well-loved Ronacher music hall when it was threatened with demolition in 1984. For posters he turned to Sagmeister. The theater is still going strong today.

Interactive postcards (below) For his thesis project at the Angewandte, Sagmeister designed a series of twenty postcards using a number of paper construction tricks and optical illusions. Shown here are a sundial and a hand-operated (fully functional) record player that would be resurrected years later when the band Aerosmith commissioned Sagmeister to design a Christmas card for them.

WHEN A PIECE COMES BACK
FROM THE PRINTER NOW—
IF IT CAME OUT THE WAY WE HOPED—
I STILL GET A HUGE, HUGE KICK OUT OF IT."

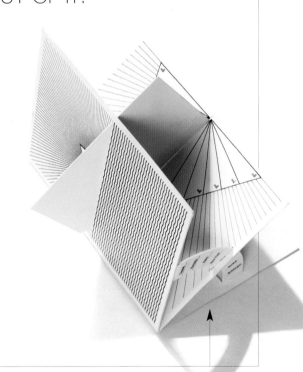

BRIGHT LIGHTS, REALLY BIG CITY While in his last year at the Angewandte, Sagmeister applied for a Fulbright scholarship to study at Pratt Institute in New York. He had fallen in love with the city when he joined his brother-in-law on a week-long trip at age eighteen. Now he was eager to return. Based primarily on his Schauspielhaus posters, he got the scholarship and was on his way to the United States. "Having grown up in a tiny town in the Austrian Alps, I always dreamed of living in a big city, so winning a full scholarship to Pratt was truly exciting. Besides being in New York, I just loved art school and probably would still be enrolled now if I could have figured out how." Sagmeister thrived in his new environment. He spent three years at Pratt, indulging in the design styles of the day and in the delights of New York City life.

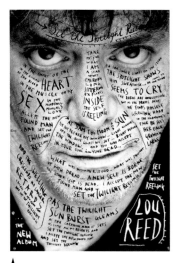

Lou Reed, poster (left) "We designed a poster announcing the new album by Lou Reed. The lyrics are extremely personal, and we tried to show this by writing those lyrics directly over his face."

AIGA New Orleans Conference, Jambalaya, poster (right) "It became clear that the event was planned with seventy-five speakers speaking at six different venues. Headless chickens running about came to mind. AIGA sent over massive amounts of copy. For the backsides we tried to do the information-graphics thing with different weight rules, color coding, and so on. After a day or so we threw out all that and wrote it any which way. Subsequent corrections were easy because they could just be written on top of the existing artwork."

> "THERE IS A LOT OF STUFF TO BE LEARNED FROM BAD JOBS:
> THAT IS, HOW TO AVOID DOING THEM IN THE FUTURE."

CIVIC DUTY (INTERLUDE) Unfortunately, Austrian law demands that all Austrian men report for eight months of military or community service before turning thirty. After three years of living in New York, Sagmeister had to return home in 1989 to work at a refugee center outside Vienna. Luckily, the demands of the job were reasonably light and allowed for freelance work on the side. After completing his service, he continued practicing design in the capital for another year, until another vacation brought about the next step in his career.

HONG KONG While traveling in Hong Kong with a friend, he decided to look at the local design scene by pretending to apply for work. Eight less-than-serious interviews into his survey, he suddenly had before him a job offer from the ad agency Leo Burnett. Not really interested in the position, Sagmeister named a high salary to end the discussion and was surprised to find his figure accepted without so much as a flinch. He was now the creative director of the Leo Burnett Hong Kong Design Group.

He stayed for two years, frequently working eighteen-hour days, creating a nonstop stream of identity systems, annual reports, brochures, and announcements and managing a sizeable staff. "Out of any two years of my design-y life, I learned the most in Hong Kong, simply as a result of having worked the most. I found out there is also a lot of stuff to be learned from bad jobs (that is, how to avoid doing them in the future). I can still switch back into that mode, but I do not enjoy it." He left the agency in 1993.

BACK IN NEW YORK Following a three-month stint of running an office out of a beach hut in Sri Lanka—Stefan's Propaganda Shack—Sagmeister returned to New York to work for Tibor Kalman's M&Co, allowing Kalman to focus on his work with *Colors* magazine. Working for one of his heroes proved rewarding, a little bit tricky, and mostly short-lived. Only six months into Sagmeister's stay at the studio, Kalman decided to close up shop and move to Italy to dedicate himself fully to *Colors*. The time had come for Sagmeister to open his own firm and pursue the kind of work he had wanted to do all along: music packaging.

1982   1983   1985   1986

1997

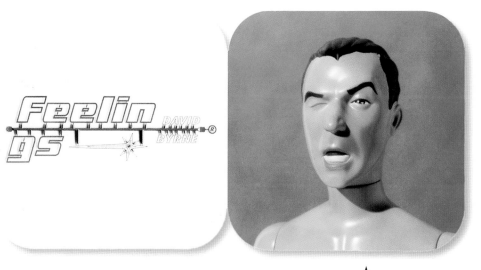

David Byrne, *Feelings*, CD
"This round-cornered *Feelings* CD packaging features happy, angry, sad, and content David Byrne dolls. The packaging includes a sophisticated, color-coded 'David Byrne Mood Computer' (printed on and under the disc) that lets you determine your current feelings. The type was actually made as a model and then photographed."

While in Hong Kong, he had saved as much as possible of his generous advertising salary and now used the money to go solo in style. He bought a two-story penthouse space in Manhattan, claimed the upstairs as his apartment and converted the lower level into a studio. By January of 1994 Sagmeister, Inc. was in business.

PACKAGING MUSIC Much of the new firm's early effort went toward putting the word out to record companies while working on nonmusic assignments to keep the lights on. Later that same year, Sagmeister's friend Hans Platzgummer invited him to design a package for his band's new album. H. P. Zinker's *Mountains of Madness* featured a close-up of an old man, looking calmly through a ruby-red jewel case. When you took out the CD booklet, however, the man was transformed into a crazy-eyed screaming demon. The effect was so startling, the idea so appropriate, that Sagmeister, Inc.'s first CD design was nominated for a Grammy in the Packaging category. The red filter was, in a way, the studio's first hit single and was appropriately revived for *Made You Look,* Sagmeister's first greatest hits album. "The H. P. Zinker CD was a neat trick that worked well and, because of it earning a Grammy nomination, really opened the doors of the music world-wide for us."

The years that followed brought a number of high-profile assignments that let Sagmeister experiment and exercise his sense of humor on an ever-greater canvas. A string of CD packages for the likes of Lou Reed, David Byrne, and the Rolling Stones, as well as an infamous troika of AIGA posters, kept clients hungry for more and seldom failed to whip the design scene into a frenzy.

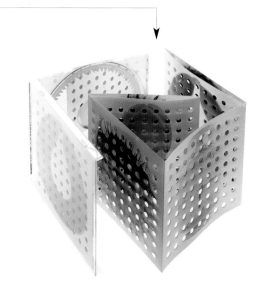

Skeleton Key, *Fantastic Spikes Through Balloon*, CD "True to the album title, *Fantastic Spikes Through Balloon*, we photographed all the balloonlike objects we could think of (sausages, fart cushions, blowfish, and so on) and punched a lot of holes through them— simple. Because the band did not want their audience to read the lyrics while listening to the music ('This is not a poetry affair'), the words to the songs are printed flipped so they are readable only when seen reflected in the mirror of the CD."

2001   2002   2003   NOW

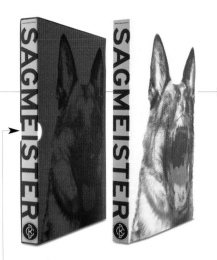

OK GO, CD "OK GO is a young band from Chicago that plays sophisticated pop. If their music were a car, it'd be a 1980's square Volvo. We asked."

Sagmeister, *Made You Look,* book "All the work we ever designed. Paperback in a red transparent slipcase—makes that dog go wild. When you bend the book in one direction, the title *Made You Look* becomes visible on the fore-edge; bend it in the other direction and the dog gets something to eat," because three bones appear.

Zumtobel annual report Zumtobel is a leading European manufacturer of lighting systems. The cover of this annual report features a heat-molded relief sculpture of five flowers in a vase, symbolizing the five subbrands under the Zumtobel name. All images on the inside of the report are photographs of this exact cover, shot under different lighting conditions, which illustrates the incredible power of changing light."

G **REED CONTROL** At a moment when he could have easily expanded into a big design operation, Sagmeister stuck to his plan and kept the studio small. At any given time, he works with only one designer and one or two interns, giving him the freedom to turn away clients if he feels that he couldn't do good work for them. "Opening my own place was definitely the best design decision, and not growing in size the second best. The designers who worked here—Veronica Oh during the first years, then Hjalti Karlsson for four years, and now Matthias Ernstberger—obviously had an enormous impact on the studio and myself. I think I would have turned into an even older fart if it had not been for all three of them constantly bringing in new ideas, techniques, and challenges."

When did Sagmeister first feel that he had made it? "There was a second of that feeling when I was picked up to fly to Los Angeles to meet the Stones for the *Bridges to Babylon* album packaging. But these feelings are sadly fleeting, and I felt like a complete jerk a couple of days later."

A **YEAR WITHOUT CLIENTS** In 1999, five years after starting his studio, Sagmeister decided to give himself a year without clients, dedicating himself to artistic experiments and leaving his then designer Hjalti Karlsson free to form his own firm with former Sagmeister intern Jan Wilker [p.160]. "At the time (1999), I was bored with the work in the studio. Also, I became influenced by a workshop I did with students at Cranbrook. They were mature and experimented on a high level, and I got jealous. And then Ed Fella visited the studio and showed me his beautiful sketchbooks [p.26]. That did it. The Year Without Clients was well worth my while: I found my love for design again."

Since returning to work, Sagmeister has stepped up his efforts to create real change in the world. In recent years, he has lent his skills to the political action group True Majority. "True Majority, a group composed of American business leaders led by Ben Cohen (Ben & Jerry's cofounder), is trying to get the U.S. government to adopt a number of long-term policies designed to make the planet a safer place. These policies include wide ideas such as eliminating world hunger and reducing our dependency on oil, as well as more specific points such as paying U.N. dues ungrudgingly. This is *not* a bunch of well-meaning hippies with a great cause and no way to get results. They have a chance."

Sagmeister is now spending a semester teaching design in Berlin and continues on his mission to touch someone's heart with design. ✑

1982   1983   1985   1986   1997

Anni Kuan, brochure (far left and middle) The Fall/Winter 2003 brochure for Anni Kuan, an Asian fashion designer working in New York, features some very low-tech production effects. "We bought ten irons and used them like printing presses. An iron burns through the sixteen pages of one brochure in five minutes."

Sagmeister on a binge, Japan, poster (near left) A poster advertising design exhibitions in Osaka and Tokyo with a classic before and after situation. The top picture shows Sagmeister at 178 pounds, the bottom picture shows him one week later and twenty-five pounds heavier, having consumed all the pictured food items. "Not an enjoyable binge."

"THE YEAR WITHOUT CLIENTS WAS WELL WORTH MY WHILE: I FOUND MY LOVE FOR DESIGN AGAIN."

"Having Guts Always Works Out for Me," magazine spreads for the Austrian magazine *.copy* "These are dividing spaces, each opening a new chapter in the magazine. Each month the magazine commissions another studio or artist for the design."

2001
39

2002
40

2003
41

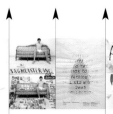

NOW

06

RANCHO MARÍA

A novel by the author of SWEET JUSTICE

Jerry Oster

DAVID CHACKO
WHITE GAMMA

a novel by the author of The Black Chamber

HAWKSMOOR

a novel by
PETER ACKROYD

E.F. Schumacher

SMALL IS BEAUTIFUL

Econ-mics as if People Mattered

YEHUDA AMICHAI

SELECTED POEMS

Newly translated by
Stephen Mitchell and Chana Bloch

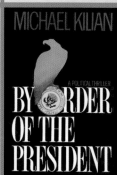

MICHAEL KILIAN

A POLITICAL THRILLER

BY ORDER OF THE PRESIDENT

Rancho María, **book cover** Victore got his first jobs with a portfolio of mocked-up book cover designs. This cover for Jerry Oster's novel *Rancho María* was his first real one.

1987 book covers All created in 1987, following the release of *Rancho María*, Victore's book cover designs closely follow the patented bestseller style of his mentor, Paul Bacon: Big names and titles and a small, simple illustration.

JAMES VICTORE

Describing himself as "just a working stiff who gives a damn,"
James Victore seeks truth and strives for the artistic liberation
that comes with it. His work is politically charged, not because
of any partisan agenda but because it has a clear point of view—
Victore's truth, shown his way. Sometimes brash, sometimes
seductive, but always immediate, his work makes it impossible
for you to close your mind.

Victore's search began early. "I grew up on a military base during the final years of the
Vietnam War. My father flew missions in an air-refueling KC-135"—a military tanker based
on the same design as the Boeing 707. "He was away most of my childhood. My mom
worked. I was a latchkey kid. This period is the basis of everything for me. The solitude forced me
to create a world to live in. I still do that. I have always had a very active imagination. I also gained
a healthy dose of 'Question Authority' from this period. This motto was printed on buttons back
then—I think the large questions that I ask of my country in my posters come from being reared
in this time and in the military. I had *Question Authority* drawn on my jeans. I drew heavily all
the time—monsters, dinosaurs, cars, planes, superheroes, nekkid ladies, usual kid's stuff."

TOMASZEWSKI "My mom worked at the university in the reference department of the
library. There I learned to love books and the value and skills of research." In the library he
also found old design annuals. "I was influenced by the work of American and European
designers. Remember, I was eight. I saw my influences very early on. When I saw some of the
work of the Eastern Europeans, I realized they couldn't really draw very well, either," Victore jokes.
He was immediately drawn to their spirit and command of the craft. "I loved them. Henryk
Tomaszewski especially appealed to me. His work was so completely free from any self-criticism.
Or so it seemed." Tomaszewski's work would prove a lasting obsession, and his influence
is clearly visible in all stages of Victore's work. "His stuff just didn't seem to follow any rules.
I grew up with rules—How to stand. How to follow the norm. How to get a college degree, even
if you don't want one. What I love about Tomaszewski's work and some of his students' work
is that it does the same job as regular design—gets people to buy, attend, and so on—but it has
a humanity to it. It looks like one person made it. When was the last time that happened here?
Fuck—we see work these days, bad work, with a list of seven creators, writers, AD, CD, PH,
but there is no opinion. Why is design always looking to the street for its message? Because
the street is the truth. The truth is always the best answer."

1987

1989

NOW

1988 book covers These covers from 1988 show Victore beginning to deviate from the formula, introducing less formal design elements and a sense of humor.

"I WANTED TO GO TO THE SCHOOL OF VISUAL ARTS IN NEW YORK.

MY PARENTS HAD NO DOUGH, SO I GOT LOANS AND A JOB AT A SKI SHOP IN NEW YORK CITY.

AT THIS TIME I WAS MAKING FIVE DOLLARS AN HOUR— THIS WAS GREAT MONEY! WHAT THE HELL ELSE WAS THERE IN LIFE?"

MOST LIKELY TO BE When Victore graduated from high school he questioned what to do next. "I did not know what I wanted to do. Let's see: What are my skills? I was smart but different. And I could draw naked ladies pretty darned good. But I ignored these skills and attended the local state university right off." Parallel to his first semester at Plattsburgh State College, Victore waited tables, worked with the ski patrol, and slept in his car to make ends meet. He received a 0.04 grade point average and was asked not to return. He was relieved. "Now I only had to deal with waiting tables and skiing. I floundered for a bit until the idea of art school came to me."

"The thought of drawing naked ladies from models appealed greatly to me. I applied to pretty much all the East Coast schools and was accepted to all of them. I wanted to go to the School of Visual Arts in New York. My parents had no dough, so I got loans and a job at a ski shop in New York City. At this time I was making five dollars an hour—this was great money! What the hell else was there in life?"

REDISCOVERY "Above the ski shop was a second-hand bookstore. I would spend my lunchtime breaks looking through the art and design books. I found a book called *Top Graphic Design* by F.H.K. Henrion. In it I found Tomaszewski again, as well as some other cool cats. The book cost sixty dollars. It took me two months to buy it. I went hungry for another two months, but it was better than just visiting the book."

"I found SVA really boring. My fellow students and the teachers just did not set me on fire. Plus, I was a shitty student. I knew I belonged there. I knew I wanted this thing—really badly. But at one point, I was taken aside by an instructor who explained to me that 'graphic design is very difficult, and there are a lot of people looking for the same job.' It was suggested that maybe I pursue another career. But, damn, I had no other skills. So I dropped out." Victore adds this as a coda to his academic career: "I am now an extremely popular teacher at SVA. The best revenge is success. I am the teacher I always wanted. I now set fires all over the place."

1989 book covers Only two years after his first published book cover design, Victore had evolved beyond Bacon's design template. His new work was more strongly influenced by the work of Henryk Tomaszewski. The handwriting he used on Don Byron's *Tuskegee Experiments* foreshadows a looser, more personal aesthetic he would use in years to come.

BESTSELLERS Frustrated with school, he sought alternative education. "I had an instructor I liked—book cover designer Paul Bacon. He was the Chip Kidd of the '60s, '70s, and '80s." Bacon had pioneered the bestseller cover: titles and author bylines set in huge type, arranged around a small, simple illustration. "He could draw type like nobody's business. He could draw, paint, photograph. In other words, he was exactly what I wanted to be: a master of his craft. He worked in a small studio on the top floor of Carnegie Hall. I went to see him and asked for an apprenticeship. He said 'Sure, nobody ever asked.'

"Just being near Paul was an education. He is my second father. He taught me how to throw shoes at news radio. He taught me about wine. He taught me about jazz—thank God! He is a fount of information and life and resource. Well, two months after dropping out of school, I had a small portfolio of book jackets—all fake." With this cache of work, mocked up in the style of his mentor, Victore went out and looked for work. "My first hit was Harper and Row, now HarperCollins. I got a freelance design job—a cover for *Rancho María*—and have been working steady ever since."

Victore's first covers still hewed closely to Paul Bacon's method, but his love for Tomaszewski soon came through. His work became more personal and expressive. Handwriting and lively conceptual illustration entered his designs. The new direction startled his clients and led to a drop-off in work. For a three-year stretch, his main work consisted of designing greeting cards on commission.

Celebrate Columbus, poster
When the media celebrated the 500th anniversary of Columbus' discovery of the Americas, Victore missed any mention of the disastrous impact European settlement had on Native Americans. "There was no mention of the pox-infected blankets. What is a celebration without mention of genocide?" To raise the issue, he invested his rent money to print and put up 3,000 posters around New York. This was Victore's first poster.

A **DISSENTING VOICE** Salvation eventually came courtesy of Elektra Records, who immediately inundated Victore with assignments to design almost 100 CD covers a year. This work sustained him financially but didn't offer the artistic satisfaction he sought. Victore is blunt in his assessment of the sleeves he designed. "It all sucks." Luckily, his time in the desert came to an end when he printed the first of his polemical pieces, a poster commenting on the 500th anniversary of Columbus's voyage to America. "I originally moved to New York because I wanted to make posters. Then, on arrival, I found there were no jobs making posters and no money in it. Still isn't. But, the 500th anniversary of Columbus Day was coming up, and I was paying attention to the hoopla.

"I noticed there was no mention of the pox-infected blankets. What is a celebration without mention of genocide? I realized it was my job to bring this part of the conversation to the public. I used my rent money to pay the printer (a bad habit) for 3,000 posters that were sniped professionally. This allowed me two moments that I hope all designers get in their lifetime: One, I got to watch real human beings, not designers, stop, look at, and read my poster. And two, I got to see the cops take my poster down. It was pasted very prominently at Columbus Circle in New York City, near Carnegie Hall, where the parade passes. They left Calvin Klein's naked kids posters alone."

"CONFIDENCE—THIS IS WHAT SEPARATES THE HUNTER FROM THE PREY. THIS IS WHAT GIVES WORK ITS FREEDOM, ITS CASUALNESS, ITS EASE, AND ITS COMFORT."

Racism, poster (near right) Following the race riots in Crown Heights, Brooklyn, and the ensuing media coverage, Victore reduced racism to its simplest, predatory form with this raw, violent typographic illustration.

Racism and the Death Penalty, promotion piece (opposite right) The NAACP (National Association for the Advancement of Colored People) asked Victore to design a promotion for their video *Double Justice*, which dealt with the inherent racism in the application of the death penalty in the United States. He used the children's game hangman as a metaphor. The poster was sent to teachers and to Legal Defense Fund lawyers with death row clients. It also found its way into the office of U.S. Supreme Court Justice Blackman, just before he reversed his opinion on the death penalty.

1987

1988

Totally Live, poster (above left) Victore went with proven strategies to boost attendance for a show of his work at the DDD Gallery in Japan: Girls and free beer.

Twelfth Night, poster (above right) To advertise the Shakespeare Project's production of *Twelfth Night,* a comedy involving love, longing, and cross-dressing, Victore voted for Bush in 1995.

Images of an Ideal Nation, poster (right) For an exhibit of political posters dealing with truth, justice, and the American Way, Victore replaced the American eagle with a plucked chicken.

Looking at Victore's oeuvre up to this point, one is surprised by the sudden shift in subject matter and style, away from a professional, polished, benign aesthetic toward something much more active and personal. "The moment of change. What you are talking about is the freedom in my work. To me, my work isn't even as free as I want it to be, but I am growing every day. The moment of change is about the confidence in my work. Confidence—this is what separates the hunter from the prey. This is what gives work its freedom, its casualness, its ease, and its comfort. My work, my process is thinking really hard—harder than anyone else and in a different vein than anyone else—to come up with a particular point of view: mine. Mine and, actually, a lot of other peoples'. James Joyce said that when he did a good job of describing the particular, he had actually described everywhere. In the particular lies the universal. So my job, the interesting part, is finding that tiny gem of an idea—the universal—then taking it to its easiest modes of translation—the doodle or the scribble or the bad drawing—to illuminate the point most powerfully. This shit is magic. And the funny thing is that it actually happens for me. This shit works! I love my job. And I love my girlfriend."

Less Is More, The New Simplicity in Graphic Design, **book design** Victore didn't use irony for the cover of Steven Heller and Anne Fink's book *Less Is More,* just a hell of a lot of black dots.

Come, postcard Victore contributed this invitation postcard to the identity for the AIGA V01CE conference in Washington, DC, designed by Los Angeles design firm AdamsMorioka. The event was intended to spur graphic designers into taking political action.

"MANY DESIGNERS MAKE GROOVY, BOUTIQUEY POSTERS, BUT DO THEY GET THEM UP ON THE FUCKING STREET?"

Victore strongly believes in the need for designers to engage the public with their work to raise the level of debate. "Many designers make groovy, boutiquey posters, but do they get them up on the fucking street? That is the ultimate high—paper crack. I believe in the public education aspect of our work. I have something to say—a lot of us do—not because I am an egomaniac (I'm not), but because I am smart. I take large, difficult ideas and create simple, memorable images to relay an aspect—pro or con—of this idea. I like to ask difficult questions. I love my country. This is my military upbringing talking, but what my country does, sometimes, is not universally right. We do some very fucked up things, and I like to be one of the folks who bring this notion to the fore."

Portfolio Center, various materials Victore has created materials for Portfolio Center, an advertising and design school in Atlanta, Georgia, for more than seven years. "They spoil me, and I spoil them. And together we have done great stuff. But, you see, they are not a client. I don't want clients; I want relationships. That is the only way to do great work."

Medea, play identity Victore matched a brash and terrifying new interpretation of this Greek tragedy about a vengeful woman with equally brutal aesthetics.

School of Visual Arts, billboard After a lackluster experience studying at New York's School of Visual Arts, Victore went on to become one of the design program's most popular teachers. He created this billboard for them in 2003, defacing a cookie-cutter portrait of a happy family with SVA graffiti.

THE KEY TO HAPPINESS Since the Columbus Day poster, Victore has designed numerous other polemics, both on his own dime and for larger organizations, such as the NAACP. It is the work he is now most recognized for, a fact that isn't without complication for him. "I am uneasy about my recognition. I have a solid reputation as a social/political poster designer. I don't want to sound spoiled, but I do a lot of other work." His passion extends to all his work, but he recognizes that in a homogenized world, passion sometimes scares people. "I know that it takes a certain type of brave client to work with me." And he finds them, allowing him to lead a principled and challenging life. "Life is choices. When you choose vanilla bean, you exclude all the other fifty-one flavors. You cannot have it all. But, nobody really wants it all. If we are really honest with ourselves we can find what we can live with. If you want huge success in this business, you have to accept sacrifice. Relationships, maybe. Kids possibly. Or any of the other trappings that success brings. But, you can figure out how to have what you need. The trick is how to be happy with that. That is the key."

Artistically, Victore refuses to coast. "I am beginning. Again. The work that I have done so far is a nice little portfolio. Now I am using that to take me to even more interesting places. I am very spoiled as a designer, and I thank my lucky stars for that. I love my job, and I want to realize my full potential. I am like a musician or actor who wants to play to a larger audience." I asked him if he experiences classic eureka moments. Victore's answer is his mission: "Every day, mutha'fucka!" ✌

"I AM BEGINNING. AGAIN.
THE WORK I HAVE DONE SO FAR IS A NICE LITTLE PORTFOLIO. NOW I AM USING THAT TO TAKE ME TO EVEN MORE INTERESTING PLACES."

1993   1995   1998   **1999** 37   **2001** 39   **2002** 40   **NOW**

radio rhythm **box** saga

oo.1

distributed by soul trader illustration by richard delingpole. designed by paul allen and tom hingston. the little men.

Box Saga, *Radio Rhythm,* **record sleeve** Hingston and Paul Allen, his design partner at the time, wrapped this 12" (30.5 cm) single by Box Saga in a silver Mylar sleeve and added an illustration by Richard Delingpole. They billed themselves as "the little men." "This was actually the first record cover I designed. The initial run was 1,000, and we individually packed each sleeve ourselves to keep the cost down."

TOM HINGSTON

Tom Hingston has revealed himself to be at the forefront of a music-packaging renaissance that flies in the face of shrinking sales and the migration to online music distribution. Like relics from a future past, his designs shine with special effects of feature-film quality and move with a debonair grace that belies his age.

" I still think out of all the disciplines, graphic design is the broadest. That's why I was drawn to it. I liked the idea that you could end up designing a typeface, making a film, or even designing clothes. Potentially, there can be a large crossover into lots of different media—and that's a really healthy thing."

Born in 1973, Tom Hingston grew up in Lewisham, in the southeast part of London. Creativity runs in his family. "My dad's a silversmith; my mum a florist. From quite an early age I became aware that I had some sort of raw artistic talent, and both my parents actively encouraged me to go off and explore this. They were never concerned that I should concentrate on anything academic, even though neither of them had ever made a great deal of money doing what they did. It was about being happy in what you do that's more important. Experiencing the love they had of their individual crafts was a big influence on me."

Being a boy with an interest in the arts, Hingston found himself in a favorable spot. "Up to the age of about eleven, my mum would often take me to art exhibitions and events. Living in London is a fantastic resource for that. In my early teenage years I'd take myself—getting the train after school to go and see shows like Hockney at the Tate and later Neville Brody's exhibition at the Victoria and Albert Museum. That had a really profound effect on me. It made me realize what a broad area this facet of design was and how much of our culture it affected."

Hingston left school at the age of sixteen to study at the London College of Printing and later went on to get his undergraduate degree at Central St. Martins. "Toward the end of St. Martins, I felt my time in education had reached a point where I could no longer gain anything from being in an environment like that. For me, the challenge of working and applying my approach to projects in the commercial environment was far more stimulating."

1994

1998

NOW

Faze Action, *Plans & Designs*, record sleeve One of Hingston's early successes, this 1995 sleeve for the British dance act Faze Action shows him moving from the necessary simplicity of his flyer work toward more complex compositions.

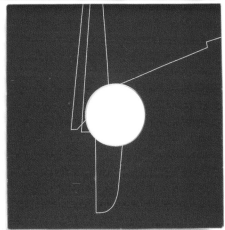

"NEVILLE TAUGHT ME A GREAT DEAL. IN MANY WAYS HIS STUDIO IS HOW COLLEGE SHOULD HAVE BEEN.

HE ENCOURAGED ME TO LOOK AT ALL PROJECTS AS PART OF AN ONGOING LEARNING PROCESS."

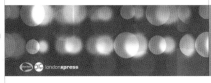

1994

1995
22

1996
23

1998

NEVILLE BRODY As it happened, one of Hingston's teachers was able to open an important door for him. Jon Wozencroft had been the author of the two-volume monograph *The Graphic Language of Neville Brody.* "He was also my personal tutor in my final year at college. Jon was a big influence on me at that time. I seriously thought about leaving college at one point and going off and doing something completely different. If it wasn't for him, I think I would have. We remained good friends after I'd graduated, and it was around that time that he introduced me to Neville. Later the same year there was a vacancy for a junior designer at Brody's studio. We'd got on well when we met, so it was all about good timing, really." Hingston remained with Brody for two and a half years. "In many ways his studio is how college should have been. Neville taught me a great deal. He encouraged me to look at all projects as part of an ongoing learning process. Sometimes it's not successful, but being given freedom like that can lead to some amazing work. I still feel very honored to have worked there."

WORKING THE CLUBS In his off hours, Hingston took on a number of freelance projects. "Record sleeves, club flyers, work for small fashion labels— I built up a handful of clients through friends who were making music, running club nights, or starting up independent labels." Over time, more and more assignments rolled in. "I was forced into making a decision between keeping a full-time job or setting up on my own. I decided to set up the studio. Initially, a friend of mine who runs a record label let me have a desk space in a ground floor storeroom in an office block in Brewer Street in Soho. We piled the boxes at one end and stuck a desk at the other. The rent was cheap and the location perfect.

"My work at that time was a mixture of club flyers and sleeve work. The flyer design was predominantly for the Blue Note Club in Hoxton Square. The club had become really successful, and my workload reflected that. It was an exciting two-year period in which I would produce ten to fifteen flyers a week. That was great, because there's a disposable quality to flyers, so you can afford to experiment with them, both in design and with print processes."

Various club flyers and posters (this page and opposite) Dance clubs were among Hingston's earliest clients. Chief among them was the Blue Note Club, a venue on London's Hoxton Square. As the club got more and more popular, Hingston's workload increased, giving him ample room to play. "There's a disposable quality to flyers, so you can afford to experiment with them, both in design and with print processes."

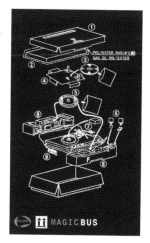

MAGIC**BUS**

"I WAS FORCED INTO MAKING A DECISION BETWEEN KEEPING A FULL-TIME JOB OR SETTING UP ON MY OWN
I DECIDED TO SET UP THE STUDIO."

2000   2001   2002   2003   NOW

61

Robbie Williams, *Millennium,* poster Advertising the single of the same design, Hingston and photographer Elaine Constantine cast Williams as a Bondesque secret agent being hurled through the air from the force of an explosion. "We wanted the sleeve to capture the same energy and dynamic he had when you see him perform on stage. We wanted it to feel exciting."

Massive Attack, *Singles 90/98,* box set Hingston and Robert Del Naja encased twelve individual single sleeves in a box covered in heat-sensitive ink. Entirely black in its neutral state, the box turns white wherever it is touched, revealing a hidden image by Del Naja.

MASSIVE ATTACK Hingston took a huge leap forward both artistically and professionally when he was commissioned to design the sleeve for Massive Attack's 1998 album *Mezzanine.* "In late 1997, I met Marc Picken, Massive Attack's manager. The band was finishing work on their third album and was consequently thinking about artwork. Previously, Massive Attack had collaborated with larger design studios, but they were now more interested in developing a creative relationship with an individual.

"I'll never forget seeing the first *Mezzanine* billboards go up, and looking at the sleeves racked in stores. There is this project that has existed in the confines of your studio for nearly four months and, all of a sudden it has a life of its own. It becomes a reality. I remember spending a whole weekend running all over London photographing it all. It was fantastic. I still get that same sense of excitement when I see work come to fruition now. It forms part of the passion for what we do, I guess.

"The Massive job also provided an opportunity for me to work with photographer Nick Knight, who I'd long admired." Working with Knight seems to have allowed Hingston to mature as a typographer. Having sumptuous images to work with, he restrained himself from using any ornamentation and relied entirely on strong, simple compositions. It's not surprising to hear that he counts Josef Müller-Brockmann and Wim Crouwel among his influences. "The project was undoubtedly an important milestone in my career. When I first set up, it was quite hard convincing big clients to commit when you're only a small studio. This project marked a change and eventually formed the impetus for expanding to three members."

When the time did come for Hingston to hire his first employee, he found the experience somewhat nerve-racking. "You're very aware that you've become responsible for somebody else's livelihood—it's not something to be taken lightly." The studio is now home to Hingston and three creative members—Danny Doyle, Simon Gofton, and Manuela Wyss.

1994

1995

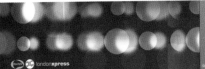

1996

1998

Massive Attack, *Mezzanine,* record sleeve Massive Attack's *Mezzanine* was Hingston's first chance to work with fashion photographer Nick Knight. Having Knight's beautiful imagery as a base, Hingston used the bare minimum of typography, creating a classic album sleeve in the process.

Robbie Williams, *Sing When You're Winning,* campaign For Williams' 2000 album *Sing When You're Winning,* Hingston teamed up with photographer Paul M. Smith to create a soccer match populated entirely by Williams. They covered every aspect of the game, from the team to the fans to the policemen and pedestrians outside the stadium. "This was an incredible amount of work to produce. We shot this over three days at Stanford Bridge with Robbie having to do a complete costume and make-up change for every character."

Planet Funk, *Inside All the People,* record sleeve Hingston collaborated with illustrator Kam Tang to create a series of collages that were surreal mixes of things from the Italian city of Naples (the band's hometown). The aesthetic was inspired by the graphic language of the '70s Archigram movement.

SING WHEN YOU'RE WINNING Robert Brownjohn is another of Hingston's design heroes. Brownjohn may be most famous for creating the iconic opening sequence for the James Bond movie *Goldfinger.* His influence would now come to the fore on another high-profile assignment, when Hingston was hired to create the sleeve for a new single by Robbie Williams that was based on a sample from John Barry's theme from *You Only Live Twice.*

The photo shoot appropriately cast the singer as a decidedly Connery-flavored James Bond. "I found the challenge of taking an image of a mainstream pop icon and doing something subversive really exciting. It was important that the sleeves embody the same humor and energy that I found in his personality. It formed the beginning of a long, successful working relationship that would allow me to collaborate with some much-admired imagemakers and photographers."

For Williams' next album, *Sing When You're Winning,* Hingston collaborated with photographer Paul M. Smith to create a soccer match that starred Williams in every role, from the players on the team to the fans in the stands to the policemen outside the stadium. The result was a Photoshop tour de force, but it was executed at a level that made it seem effortless. Once again, Hingston had the good sense to let the images speak for themselves and kept his typography to a graceful minimum. This combination of highly art-directed imagery adorned with minimal graphic design is becoming somewhat of a signature for Hingston, though projects like Planetfunk and the To Be Confirmed poster prove he has other arrows in his quiver and is not above choice ornamentation when the situation calls for it.

"WHEN I FIRST SET UP, IT WAS QUITE HARD CONVINCING BIG CLIENTS TO COMMIT WHEN YOU'RE ONLY A SMALL STUDIO."

2000
27

2001
28

2002

2003

NOW

63

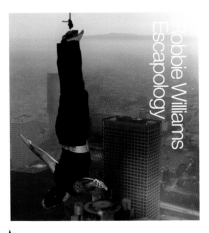

Zoot Woman
Grey Day

Robbie Williams, *Escapology,* record sleeve
Using high-concept images with minimal typography,
the creative partnership between Hingston and
Williams is a lighthearted echo of Storm Thurgerson's
collaboration with Pink Floyd.

Zoot Woman, record sleeves For '80s influenced
dance-pop act Zoot Woman, Hingston and studio
member Simon Gofton collaborated with photographers
Anuschka Bloomers and Niels Schumm to create
three-dimensional typographic compositions.

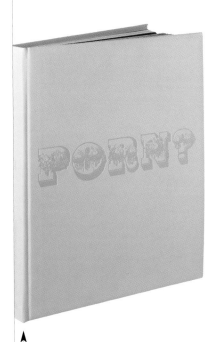

Porn?, book Edited and designed by Hingston
and studio member Simon Gofton in collaboration
with the makers of *Dazed & Confused* magazine,
the book *Porn?* invited a selection of photographers
and fine artists to explore the nature and impact of
pornography in today's media culture. Appropriately,
the book was bound in padded pink leather.

"I SPENT A LARGE CHUNK OF MY TWENTIES
WORKING INCREDIBLY LONG HOURS,
AND SOMETIMES THAT WOULD FEEL VERY
FRUSTRATING—ANOTHER WEEKEND AND
YOU'RE STILL IN THE STUDIO AT MIDNIGHT.
BUT YOU'RE ALSO AWARE DURING THAT TIME THAT IT'S PART OF THE PROCESS
OF BUILDING A STUDIO, PART OF THE PROCESS OF FORGING SOMETHING UNIQUE."

PATIENCE Hingston's success didn't come without effort, of course.
"I spent a large chunk of my twenties working incredibly long hours,
and sometimes that would feel very frustrating—another weekend and
you're still in the studio at midnight. But you're also aware during that time
that it's part of the process of building a studio, part of the process of forging
something unique. So I always felt it was a worthwhile sacrifice to make."
Even during the most successful periods, there were setbacks that didn't sit
well with Hingston, who admits to having been less than patient in the past.
"In the early days, we used to get asked to pitch a lot. Because I'd already
worked with some big acts I found it frustrating that I was being asked to
pitch anyway. I would then get even more disheartened when we didn't win
the work." Over time, his frustration has dissipated, however. "In hindsight,
maybe I just wasn't ready for those projects to happen at that time.
Years later I've ended up working with some of those bands or those clients
anyway. You've just got to be patient with things sometimes."

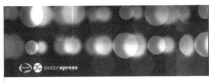

1994   1995   1996   1998

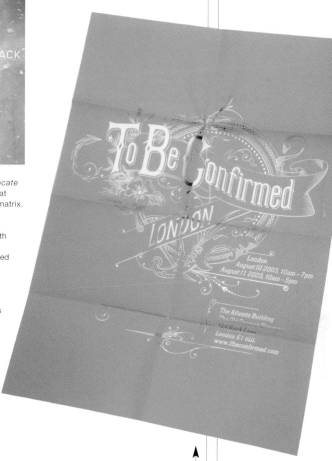

Dave Clarke, *Devil's Advocate*, record sleeve (above, left) For the 2003 album *Devil's Advocate* by influential British DJ and producer Dave Clarke, Hingston conceived a molded plastic box that slides out the CD tray toward the top. The gothic typography is the result of an embossed dot matrix. "We wanted to create and object that was a weird mix of something both gothic and digital."

Massive Attack, *100th Window*, record sleeve (above, right) Hingston once again teamed up with photographer Nick Knight for this album. Together with Massive Attack front man Robert Del Naja, they spent seven weeks supervising the fabrication of fifteen glass sculptures, which they then detonated in sections. Three days were then spent shooting stills of the sculptures exploding and two days shooting video and high-speed 35mm film. "It was about creating imagery that explored the theme of fragility and vulnerability and the idea of showing delicate objects in states of fracture."

To Be Confirmed, poster (right) "To Be Confirmed is a fashion trade show for independent labels that is held twice a year in London, New York, and Tokyo. It was set up as a reaction to the bigger, more corporate trade shows. As a way of the image reflecting this it was decided the identity should be completely redesigned each season." This poster, printed in gold leaf, advertises the 2003 event in London.

NEW GROWTH In 2003, the studio completed another complex sleeve for Massive Attack, building and detonating a series of custom-made glass sculptures. Hingston also expanded his client roster past the boundaries of the music industry, working on assignments for Christian Dior and the Italian luggage company Mandarina Duck. "I just had a desire to broaden the areas in which the studio was working. It's important to work in as many different areas as you possibly can. That was, after all, one of the reasons I first chose to study graphic design."

Although he gives a nod to the importance of time away from work, he never really considered dialing back his efforts. "I never thought I would get away with not working as hard as I am. Seeing something grow from nothing is very exciting. When you begin to realize that you can create your own tiny universe, that's a big motivation." ✌

"I NEVER THOUGHT I WOULD GET AWAY WITH NOT WORKING AS HARD AS I AM."

2000

2001

2002
29

2003
30

NOW

65

Untitled Paintings "These are all from 1991. Back then I had phases of dealing with some things intensely. It was the confrontation with everyday situations I always used the same fomat—19" x 27" (50 cm x 70 cm), heavy handmade paper, and Copic comping markers. And to make sure I wouldn't finish too quickly, I added outlines to everything with a silver marker at the end. That was a kind of meditation after the content was established."

KÖNIG

08

EIKE

Tired of being a champion athlete, Eike König turned to graphic design, made his name in the music industry, and opened a studio in Frankfurt that serves as a playground for himself and his collaborators. Together they turn out some of the most entertaining design Europe has to offer.

Eike König talks about his studio: "It started with the fact that I've always collaborated with different people, oftentimes with students. Sometimes I got the feeling that these were people who needed a particular space, a playground, to give their abilities the right expression."

Born in 1968 in Hanau outside of Frankfurt, König picked up a pencil early on. "My father was an architect. He would draw constantly. My grandfather was a painter and a writer. He challenged me to follow in this direction." A friend from König's school days remembers that he would draw hands unceasingly. His future was clear to her, even then. This insight puts her years ahead of König, who saw drawing as merely a hobby. His first love was artistic gymnastics—floor exercises, parallel and horizontal bars, rings, vault, and the pommel horse.

Having started the gymnastic program at the age of three, he spent the next thirteen years training for three hours every other day. His unwavering dedication led him to compete at the state level, netted him numerous awards, but ultimately left him straining to break out. He had trained with the same group of people from the very beginning and was eager for a change of scenery, for pursuits that wouldn't demand so much of his time. When his longtime trainer, a strong father figure, passed away, König left the sport. "I had never smoked or had a drink or done any of the other things you go through around that time in life. I just wanted to be a normal teenager. The urgency of youth finally broke the chains of discipline."

1991 **2000** **NOW**

Zoran, record sleeve "This was the first complete cover I designed, so it still holds a certain charm for me today. It was the first time I used the computer. Photoshop, scanning, layers, and then assembling it all in Quark at the end—it was an exciting experience."

Jacko, record sleeve "I created the logotype from scratch. It's reminiscent of Japan. At that time I loved manga comics. The rest is a cheap Photoshop filter, but it's very conspicuous," König admits with a smile.

Bamby, record sleeve "Bamby is Inga Humpe of Ideal, one of the great German bands I loved when I was a teenager. I created the artwork with the Japanese artist Akihiko Oshini."

ON-THE-JOB TRAINING He graduated from high school shortly thereafter and dedicated himself to his other passion, art. He joined an arts society in his hometown and started painting and contributing to group exhibitions. "Painting was more a means to an end for me to turn the inside out. It gave me a way to deal with things." Finally, he enrolled in the communication design program at the University of Darmstadt. As a requirement, students had to complete two internships while in school. Both would prove formative.

For his first internship König signed on for a six-month tour at the Frankfurt outpost of Swiss ad agency Wirz & Hafner. He now has only one word to describe the experience: deterring. He was fired when he decided to go AWOL. "I had fallen in love, and one night I decided to take my girlfriend to Paris for a few days. I let the agency know by dropping a note in their mailbox." When it came time to find a place for his second internship, he turned to his friend Fedi. König had designed a number of event flyers for Fedi over the years, and Fedi returned the favor by introducing him to Logic Records.

RECORDS König had been frustrated with school but loved working for a record company. He contemplated abandoning his studies in favor of his new job. Unfortunately, the company placed him under the supervision of a less-than-nurturing art director who kept him on a tight leash, exerted substantial pressure on his new assistant, and, of course, put his own name on everything König produced. But a lucky break presented itself in December 1992,

Yves Deruyter, record sleeve "We had a lot of fun developing this artwork for Yves Deruyter," using the German mosaic toy Ministeck (Miniplug). "After it turned out that it would take us a year to actually set all the little plugs, we had the base plate scanned and did the rest in the computer." Bernd Westphal shot the original objects and Ralf Hiemisch helped with the design.

1993
25

1994
26

1998
27

1991

Intrance, record sleeve "This is artwork I developed with Walter, the best 3-D operator in the world. Back in 1995, the flyer culture was awash with 3-D renderings. We just gave it the necessary quality. Back then nobody could afford Softimage or an SGI, except us."

Microbot, record sleeve "This is another collaboration with Walter of Silver Haze. This is a wonderful machine, a robot reminiscent of ordinary things that surround us every day. I never wanted to just make pretty pictures. The humor and the story were always much more important to me."

when his boss went on vacation over the holidays. "For the first time I was given the chance to design a complete record sleeve from beginning to end"—a sleeve for Zoran. "When I presented it to the client at the weekly meeting, they asked me why I didn't design more of their pieces." He had been on the verge of quitting, but when the head of the label took note of the situation, he extended the art director's vacation indefinitely and let König take over the department.

OPEN SPACES "Considering all my experiences up to that point, I decided to do things differently—completely differently." He made the art department into a space that allowed him to have fun, to experiment, and to grow, and that gave others the chance to do the same. It speaks volumes that several of his collaborators, assistants, and interns from this period went on to start successful design studios in London and Paris and remain his friends to this day. Without realizing it, König had created an early prototype of his ultimate creative home, the Hort.

> "CONSIDERING ALL MY EXPERIENCES UP TO THAT POINT, I DECIDED TO DO THINGS DIFFERENTLY— COMPLETELY DIFFERENTLY."

Dune, poster (far left) "I've accompanied Dune from the very beginning. I did their first cover in 1995 and their latest in 2003. If you've been with a project for that period of time, you can guide the design process. Dune was where I started working with old, used surfaces and developed a new aesthetic within my work."

Heaven 17, record sleeve (left) "The boys of H17 were enthusiastic, open, and really nice. They could laugh at themselves, and that's a quality I really like in people. 'Trust us, we're entertainers' was the theme. Ralf Hiemisch and Alek Mandrisch worked on the artwork with me. Gaby Gerster took the pictures."

1999   2000   2001   2002   2003   NOW

EXPN catalog "ESPN/EXPN was like a movie. We received an email from San Francisco. Howard Brown had seen our work in a book and wanted to know if we'd be interested in creating the images for a global launch campaign for the ESPN Web portal. At first, we thought it was a joke, but pretty soon we were working all night every night. First, we developed the posable dummies, their clothes, and the sets. Then we spent a month shooting the various scenes."

"THE DAILY EXCHANGE [WITH OTHER DESIGNERS] IS WORTH ITS WEIGHT IN GOLD— THE COMMUNICATION, MOTIVATING EACH OTHER, LEARNING FROM EACH OTHER."

When König started thinking about going it alone in 1994, Logic once again helped him push forward. "Jörn Zimmermann, Logic's lawyer, put me in touch with the music scene in Hamburg. I did my first freelance job for Andreas Dorau, which led a Hamburg-based label, Motor Music, to promise me thirty assignments a year. This made my decision to go solo a lot easier. From there I went on to work for Inga Humpe of the band Ideal, Nina Hagen, Heaven 17, Robert Miles, and others."

König's work on the Zoran sleeve had been his first encounter with the computer: a machine with 64 MB of RAM, running Photoshop 2.0. Between the exponential improvements in equipment and working with gifted computer illustrators who were constantly pushing the limits of the machine, König mastered his skills quickly. In less than four years, he moved from the fairly conventional Zoran artwork to riding the wave of three-dimensionally rendered rave flyers to sophisticated vernacular aesthetic of projects like Dune and Heaven 17.

IT'S GOOD TO BE KÖNIG The time had come to name his new independent operation. König decided on Eike's Grafischer Hort—Eike's Graphic Play-ground. "The name is the mission," he says. "I could finally create a space and an energy that made me feel comfortable. I was living with my girlfriend and made the most beautiful room in the apartment into my office. We lived right by a nature preserve. Out the window I could see the top of a great birch tree that was full of birds and squirrels all year round.

1991   1993   1994   1998

Resistance D, record sleeves (opposite and above; left, middle, right) "We produced six different vinyls for the first single "You Were There" alone. The idea came from a typical email exchange when the client described his wishes for the artwork. It occurred to us that the description conjured up different images for everybody. That became part of the concept. On the three sleeves that went to DJs, we printed excerpts from our correspondence. The images those passages describe then appear on the commercial sleeves. For the final sleeve we shot all the previous covers hung in a gallery." *Translation of the sleeve to the left: "I like the idea, but you said it: the cost! Before we start this, I'll need an estimate from you! Is there an alternative to this idea? Because as much as I like a robo-dog..."*

Electro Star, record sleeve (right; top, bottom) "A Russian singer and two wild producers. It's a strong piece, reminiscent of Russian graphics, that lives by its wonderful illustrations. But it doesn't have a retro feel. We managed to build a bridge to the present. Ralf Hiemisch and Gaby Gerstner collaborated."

"I was on the road a lot—in Hamburg, in Frankfurt, in Munich. I slept in, worked nights, ate at random intervals. Eventually, it got on my girlfriend's nerves that couriers would be sitting in our living room at 8 p.m., watching TV, because I didn't have the work ready in time."

Ready and eager to expand, König rented a space in Frankfurt's north end—"a sunny nest above the rooftops"—and took the big step of hiring Ralf Hiemisch, a 3-D illustrator he had worked with in the past and who had made an impression on him with his unconventional, complex work. "For the past few years I had been making fantastic amounts of money. It was the golden age of the record industry. I had nothing to lose. Today I know what an employee costs. It was a big step in the right direction, even though I never made as much money again after that," he says, smiling. "But it was worth it. The daily exchange is worth its weight in gold—the communication, motivating each other, learning from each other."

By König's reckoning the two had completed more than 100 projects together by the time Hiemisch moved to Berlin. The two remain close friends, and König continued with a new designer, Martin Lorenz, who is now part of the core Hort team.

1999 28

2000 29

2001 30

2002

2003

NOW

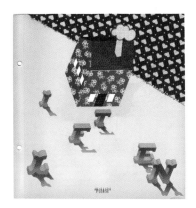

Enric Miralles, catalog "The cemetery designed by the Spanish architect Enric Miralles: A photographic encounter without words. Through the eye of the camera I'm experiencing one of this architect's greatest designs, a space for communication between life and death, heaven and crumbling earth, heaviness and light."

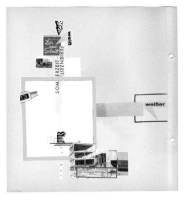

Sketchbook pages "These are excerpts from my personal sketchbook. It's something I always refer back to." About the image with the black cross König says, "It's my way of processing my experiences with artists and musicians."

TYPECASTING Over the next few years, the studio continued producing designs that reflected König's desire to create artwork that would hold up to a higher standard, going beyond the obvious. "The direct translation of a theme into the visual realm can be the simplest solution but also the most boring. Red doesn't always have to be red. Everything you're taught must be questioned. I realized that your own ways are better, that having the courage and the will to fight for your own ideas marks the biggest steps forward in my life."

His work quickly gained recognition and made Eike König a household name in the European music and design communities. In fact, his sleeve designs received so much attention that it started becoming a hindrance. "Suddenly, we were the cool record sleeve designers who make pretty pictures and are always on the edge with their visual language. We couldn't get out of the drawer in which they had placed us. There is so much more behind our work than that. We develop visual systems—the media are interchangeable. We are aware of our qualities. We want to build systems for museums, illustrate magazine spreads, books—you name it— but nobody dared to approach us, because we were the music business guys."

Faced with being typecast, König and Lorenz decided to create a separate brand. Eikes Grafischer Hort would continue as the home for music projects; all other work would be billed simply to The Hort. "Hort is meant to represent us as graphic designers in general—available for all kinds of work. It should also be easier to pronounce in English."

WHEN THE GOING GETS TOUGH König's rebirth under the Hort banner is a reflection of his desire to branch out and of the necessity of creating a broader client base in a tough economic climate. Times aren't easy for designers with vision—designers who have no desire to be merely executors of a client's whim. Looking at the trajectory of the design sector, König isn't happy. "The profession of graphic designer is rapidly losing its validity. The only thing that counts now is the estimate. Whoever charges least gets the job. It doesn't matter whether that's good for the product or not. 'We won't get the results back until later, but I have to explain the cost of the graphic designer now.'

1991 1993 1994 1998

A Tribute to RMB and Friends, poster For a record commemorating the label RMB's ten-year anniversary, König created a series of installations. "The interesting thing was seeing the cover as mere packaging and to elevate the importance of the content. The typography was die-cut, so you could actually get a look at the content."

We are no longer trusted, and suddenly every project manager knows better. We often hear questions such as 'Could you change it to blue and move the type to the left a little?' I always tell them: We went through a design process. What you're looking at is the result of our skills, our experience. Trust us: This is the best of all possibilities at this moment. But they insist, so we do it again. They see the result and say 'Oh, you're right, the other way was better.' What do you do at that point? It's a *Zeitmülleimer*"—a time trash can.

Of course, there is always the option of selling out, but it's clear that König isn't anywhere near that point. He's having far too much fun playing. "Making money is easy; having fun in the process is harder. So I go the way of fun and evolution, which in turn makes me unusable for some clients, because I don't want to be their idea-execution tool, the platform for their wishes." Taking a principled stand demands sacrifices, but König is unfazed. "I don't really see it as a sacrifice. I just prioritize my life differently. I draw incredible energy from what I do. I've created a space where I can be who I am, who I want to be, a place where I collaborate with people I respect and appreciate. For that, spending twice as much time at work is a small price to pay."

Hort Takes Control, spread For Nando Costa's book *Brasil Inspired*, we took control of ten spreads. We were introduced to topics such as plastic surgery, architecture, soccer, and the beach by a little bear."

"MAKING MONEY IS EASY; HAVING FUN IN THE PROCESS IS HARDER.
SO I GO THE WAY OF FUN AND EVOLUTION,
WHICH IN TURN MAKES ME UNUSABLE FOR SOME CLIENTS,
BECAUSE I DON'T WANT TO BE THEIR IDEA-EXECUTION TOOL.
I DON'T REALLY SEE IT AS A SACRIFICE."

From Hort to Heart, poster In 2004, König mailed out posters with his new motto. "This is our visibility campaign for the new year. The Hort is more than just a design office serving the music industry."

NEAL
ASHBY

Neal Ashby didn't wait for a lucky break. He cold-called the Recording Industry Association of America and talked them into creating a creative director position for him at the tender age of 25 and spent the next ten years creating work that continues to influence the people that influence you.

Every now and then a band becomes an overnight success. Its single races up the charts and its members are being interviewed all over the place. At that point, somebody in the band usually points out that they've been touring the country in an Econovan for the last ten years, playing songs from their first five albums for a small, but devoted, fan base.

Neal Ashby spent his ten years as the creative director of the Recording Industry Association of America in Washington, DC. There he created a stunning and substantial body of conceptually and aesthetically refined work. His RIAA annual reports were design show staples. Those who encountered the actual pieces in the judging process often ended up as fans. Still, the nature of his work for the association kept it from gaining a broader audience.

HIDING IN PLAIN VIEW Ironically, Ashby did have two huge crossover hits with a pair of logos that together have been reproduced literally billions of times: the enhanced CD logo and the redesign of the infamous Parental Advisory label. "I saw the advisory label project as a nuisance, really. Just like with the enhanced CD logo, I didn't see it so much as design in its highest, most artistic form, but design in its most basic, communicative, utilitarian form. I think both of them were done within an hour or two, in between other projects." Having produced thousands of pages of exquisite design over the years, Ashby realizes the irony of being recognized for these two very basic pieces: "It doesn't impress me as terribly good design. But it does have the currency of its own fame, and most people tend to be seduced by fame much more than good design."

SOMETHING FROM NOTHING Again and again, key moments in Ashby's career show his knack for recognizing moments of opportunity and seizing them. While getting his degree in advertising design at the University of Maryland, he regularly saw hundreds of college kids queuing up for $3 pitchers of beer at a local hotspot called The Rendezvous Inn or "The Vous." Surely some of these people would love to have a souvenir of their favorite bar. So Ashby designed a poster: "I saved up the money for printing, got a lawyer to set up an agreement between me and The Vous, hired a photographer, and actually printed 10,000 of these things."

1987   1994   NOW

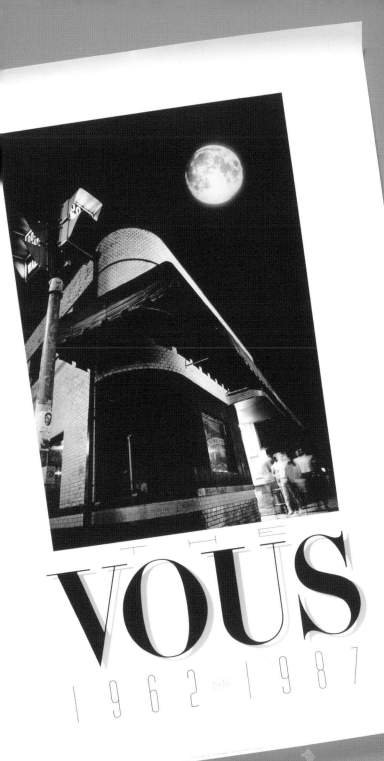

09

The Vous Ashby's first big success in design arrived in the form of this poster for a popular Maryland nightspot called The Rendezvous, also known among its patrons as The Vous. Ever the enterprising individual, Ashby noticed the long lines of students queued up for $3 pitchers of beer and decided that more than a few of them might like (or need) a stylish memento of their favorite college watering hole. He saved up the necessary money, hired a photographer, and had 10,000 posters printed, which he then started selling out of the back of his car. More than 15 years later, copies of the poster can be found in the living room of Maryland Superbowl quarterback Boomer Esiason and, as all things in life, on eBay.

The World Is Listening, annual report (below, left) This is Ashby's first annual report for the Recording Industry Association of America after assuming the post of creative director. Receiving creative counsel from William Claxton, Ashby displayed his love for the jazz album covers of the 1950s with the help of illustrations by David Plunkert.

Listening For Tomorrow, annual report (below, middle) Inspired by the simplicity of a 1960s annual report, the 1993 annual report for the RIAA contrasts the old way of listening to music with the new, outfitting a '60s woman of perked ear with retro-futuristic cyborg head gear. For his RIAA sophomore effort, Ashby once again enlisted the help of David Plunkert, as well as that of photographer Steve Biver. Staying with the "old vs. new" theme, Ashby used only two fonts throughout the piece: New Baskerville (old) and Matrix (new).

(r)evolution, annual report (below, right) "In terms of the evolution of my work with the RIAA, it was the first major piece that started to turn away from purely "retro" work. Other early work was fun looking, but was based on the idea of representing itself as actually being from the time period; it was a form of parody. With the Revolution annual, there was the first conscientious attempt to utilize retro elements (or retro-styled elements like Suzanna Licko's typeface Dogma), but to put to put my own contemporary stamp on the design."

I designed it to make the bar look very sexy and retro, shot it in black-and-white. I called them 'limited lithographs,' and charged $15.00 a piece." Its quality advertised by its steep price tag—five pitchers worth of beer, after all—the poster became a runaway success and was soon on sale in Washington, New York, and Baltimore. Even pirated T-shirts with the Vous image started popping up.

"BEING THE ONLY CREATIVE PERSON GAVE ME A LOT OF OPPORTUNITIES TO USE MY OWN VOICE,
BUT IT ALSO MEANT I WORKED SEVEN DAYS A WEEK, JUST TO KEEP UP."

LOBBYING By 1992, Ashby was working as a junior designer at Clark Keller in Annapolis when the RIAA commissioned the studio to design a party invitation. "When I learned they farmed out all their design to small firms, it gave me an idea: why not suggest to them the idea of an in-house designer? I showed them the benefits on paper using my best guesses about their budget—how they could save money, have better design, and more control over the image of their company. Somehow, they agreed, and at the relatively young age of 25, with very little to no experience in print production and computers, I became the creative director, designer, creative writer, and production artist for the RIAA. For the 10 years I was there I was the only creative person on staff, with no assistants."

Enhanced CD logo
Ashby's logo is the official mark placed on all CDs that carry digital content beyond music.

Parental Advisory logo redesign "In 1993, every hip hop CD seemed to have a different Parental Advisory logo. I made the argument that it needed to be treated like any other corporate brand, it had to be nurtured and taken care of. We determined that an official, definitive logo needed to be created along with usage guidelines. And then we had to make it available to all record labels in digital form."

1987 · 1993 27 · 1994 28 · 1995 29 · 1998 32

TechnoLogyMusic, annual report "The '97 annual broke ground in that it was one of the first pieces of graphic design to be recognized that incorporated the austere, ultra simple use of Helvetica Neue. Everyone was doing deconstructed/distressed type via the David Carson method. In that particular year, using centered Helvetica Neue, in a reverent, straightforward way was groundbreaking. A few other design firms had tapped into the same consciousness as well that year, including Cahan and Associates. I think it was the natural reaction against the style of decontructivism. Of course, now it is the current look that everyone is using as style, rather than an integral part of the overall concept."

AIGA Design for the Fun of It, poster Ashby's used the freedom of this AIGA DC poster assignment to add some humor to his always clean and stylish graphics.

Having generated the position for himself, Ashby single-handedly created the entire visual output of a national organization, starting with elaborate annual reports and ending with generating business cards for the new guy down the hall. "Being the only creative person gave me a lot of opportunities to use my own voice, both conceptually and visually. But being a one-person shop also meant I worked seven days a week, just to keep up."

Ultimately, Ashby was promoted to vice president. "I became more involved with not only crafting the look of the message, but the message itself.... It was a unique opportunity to be a part of something that was bigger than me, and yet be able to lend my own specific voice to it."

GOING SOLO So what made him strike out on his own after ten years? "The decision was really made for me. In early 2002, due to 9/11, the economy, and digital piracy from sources like Napster, the record industry was in a steady decline. Entire departments, like marketing, were cut from the RIAA budget. So I found myself trying to decide what I wanted to do with the rest of my life. I already had a steady stream of design consulting jobs, and was starting to make a little headway in getting some record label work, so it just kind of happened. My real passion is design education, and I had been on the adjunct faculty at the Corcoran College of Art + Design in Washington, DC for eight years. When they offered me a full-time position as assistant professor, I jumped on that. And while it's a bit of a juggle teaching full time and running a design firm full time, they really do dovetail nicely."

1999   2001   NOW

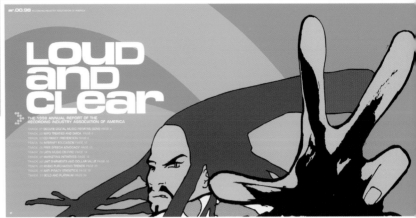

"DESIGN KEEPS ME INTERESTED IN LIFE. IT'S THE PRISM THROUGH WHICH I SEE JUST ABOUT EVERYTHING."

THIEVERY CORPORATION The work that has brought Ashby his greatest exposure so far found him in another seized moment when he was approached by Eric Hilton of the DJ duo Thievery Corporation while still at the RIAA. "He wanted to use a photo I had art directed for an annual report for the RIAA. I said 'yes' but joked with him that I'd only let him use the picture if he'd let me design the CD package. He took me up on it, and we've been working with each other ever since."

Hilton made Ashby the de facto art director of his label ESL (Eighteenth Street Lounge) and gave him the opportunity to forge Thievery Corporation's visual identity with the design of their CDs *Abductions and Reconstructions, The Mirror Conspiracy* and their latest, *The Richest Man in Babylon.* It is this work that has finally exposed the general public to the subtle elegance of his work.

GETTING YOUR PRIORITIES STRAIGHT "Design keeps me interested in life. It's the prism through which I see just about everything. What motivates you changes over time. It's ten years from now, which of these three things would you want to achieve as a designer?

Thievery Corporation—*Abductions and Reconstructions, CD packaging*
This CD of remixes features a vintage eight-track player on the cover and throughout the package. The hole pattern of the speaker, in particular, pops up again and again, both in the abstract and as a collage of 59 miniaturized players.

1987   1993   1994   1994

Loud and Clear, annual report The 1998 annual report of the RIAA, titled "Loud and Clear," features a series of striking illustrations of musicians and fans by Kristian Russell. "I wanted to do something with a set of cartoon characters inspired by some of my childhood heroes and icons: Dr. J, Fat Albert, the Saturday morning version of the animated Jackson 5. The trick was finding just the right illustrator and a way of using that vernacular to tell a story relating to the record industry." Ashby chose a group picture for the cover, but silhouetted everyone except the girl with the very loud, very clear pink afro (far left). The full illustration is revealed in an inside spread, providing a visual payoff (near left).

RANK THEM FROM ONE TO THREE:

1 → YOU COULD MAKE A LOT OF MONEY.

2 → YOU COULD BECOME FAMOUS, RESPECTED AS A DESIGNER BY YOUR PEERS.

3 → YOU ARE CONTENT. YOU HAVE A SHORT COMMUTE, YOU WORK WITH NICE PEOPLE, AND WHILE YOU'RE NOT SETTING THE WORLD ON FIRE WITH DESIGN GREATNESS OR MAKING A SHITLOAD OF MONEY, YOU ARE CONTENT.

"No one gets it all. There are choices to make in life, and priorities to establish for yourself. Don't say that making money is the most important thing in your life, and then torture yourself when you aren't doing award-winning work. Don't say that doing award-winning work is the most important thing and then expect to make a lot of money, and have a nice boss, and..."

"In my life, I've been all three. I started out as a two. I wanted the fame. I wanted to be in books and win awards. Then after a few years I became a one. I wanted to make money and buy a house and get a BMW. Now, I want to be with my baby in the morning, and teach, and slow down and look at life. I'm a three. And I miss one and two. But not like I would miss seeing my son grow up."

Art Directors Club, poster This poster for the Art Directors Club of Metropolitan Washington shows Ashby's deft touch in creating simple, eye-popping icons to draw the audience in toward the information, in this case a call for entries for the ADC's annual design competition. "Starting in 1998, as a way to stay motivated and energized about my design work, I wanted to find a way to integrate personal inspirations into my work. The popsicle poster is an example of this."

1998

1999

32

33

2001

NOW

THIS CD HAS MILLIONS OF SONGS

EARLY INSPIRATION AND LASTING PASSIONS

Having always used drawing as a way of expressing himself during his own shy, quiet childhood, Ashby's eyes first opened to a career in art when he was handed a booklet called *Careers In Art* by his art teacher when he was thirteen. "I read the description for art director and it was like the heavens opened up and angels were blowing horns, and, well, it wasn't really like that. But you know what I'm saying. It was a transcendental moment and I knew it."

This new dream soon fused with other burning teenage passions: "My biggest influences artistically were air-brushed murals on the sides of vans and pinball machine illustrations of impossibly proportioned women. And it's true in a way, those things really made me want to draw. But I found I was also drawn to letterforms. I was particularly adept at re-creating the logos of Aerosmith, AC/DC, Foghat, and most NFL teams, usually on the reversed brown paper grocery bags that served as schoolbook covers. Nothing feels better than a ballpoint pen sinking into kraft paper.

"But what really made me want to be a designer were the ten Led Zeppelin album covers. As if I didn't love Zep enough, their albums covers are all understated masterpieces that added to their aura. I think back now to the spinning wheel

Music Matters, annual report The annual report of the RIAA 2000 focused on the revolution brought on by downloadable music. Instead of providing the usual music sampler, Ashby gave RIAA members a CD with millions of songs: it contains links to music available online. For the inside spreads, Ashby chose a series of photographs featuring musicians and removed the key elements—one of Elvis Presley's gold record, the Beatles performing on the Ed Sullivan Show—to illustrate the chilling effect music piracy has had on the recording industry.

board

1987   1993   1994   1994   1998   1998

"I READ THE DESCRIPTION FOR ART DIRECTOR AND IT WAS LIKE THE HEAVENS OPENED UP AND ANGELS WERE BLOWING HORNS,

AND WELL, IT WASN'T REALLY LIKE THAT. BUT YOU KNOW WHAT I'M SAYING, IT WAS A TRANSCENDENTAL MOMENT AND I KNEW IT."

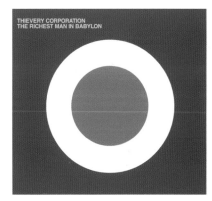

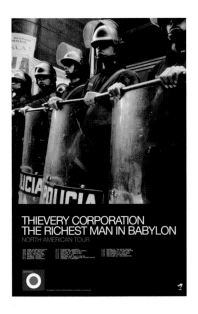

Thievery Corporation, CD packaging The icon on Thievery Corporation's *Richest Man in Babylon* album is Ashby's "take on what I thought might be a generic Central American freedom fighter symbol," thus setting the scene for the photography in the accompanying booklet—images of freedom fighters shot by photo journalists Daniel Cima, Bill Crandall, and Hector Emanuel. These images also form the core of all promotional materials associated with the album's release, including the poster shown at left.

of *Led Zeppelin III, Led Zeppelin IV* with it's wordless cover, *Presence* with its poetry of the mysterious obelisk, *Physical Graffiti* with its grandiose layers of information, and *In Through the Out Door* with its brown paper wrapper, four different covers and viewer interactivity. I didn't even know it while I was doing it, but I subconsciously referred back to all of that in my first fifteen years of being a professional designer. I strived for understated complexity with a unique and simple visual poetry, all the things I thought made every Zeppelin cover a conceptual and graphic tour de force. I loved Led Zeppelin, but it was their album covers that changed my life."

BACK TO THE FUTURE It comes as no surprise then that Neal Ashby's wish for his creative future is this: "I hope one day I get to design some graphics for a pinball machine. Or maybe airbrush a killer mural on the side of someone's van. Or maybe, just maybe, Led Zeppelin makes one more album, and they need a designer." ✌

"I STRIVE FOR UNDERSTATED COMPLEXITY WITH A UNIQUE AND SIMPLE VISUAL POETRY."

Re.Republican Highlife, sticker This 1981 promo sticker for White's first company, Re.Republican Highlife, features his illustration of his friends Heather, Stella, and Carl.

Paul White is the man behind Me Company.
Best known for digitizing the Icelanic performer Björk,
his pioneering use of 3-D graphics has fascinated
a generation of young designers and launched
a million rip-off rave flyers.

Born in 1959 in South London, Paul White grew up the youngest of six children. Before he was old enough to enter elementary school, his parents moved the family to Crawley, a new overspill town in West Sussex. He remembers "living in a house surrounded by the music of older siblings—one brother a mod, another a rocker. I became obsessed with music and subculture. At the age of nine, I decided I wanted to design record covers for a living." White was particularly taken with the designs of Hipgnosis and London designer Barney Bubbles, who brought Russian constructivism and futurism to post-punk imagery. His influence on White's aesthetics is profound and particularly visible in White's early design work.

Academically average, partially dyslexic, "but good at art," White navigated the British public school system and entered art college at age seventeen. After four years of studying graphics and illustration at West Sussex College of Design on the south coast of England, he moved to West Hampstead in North West London, where he still lives today. He struggled to find freelance work but eventually generated enough business to rent a studio space, giving himself the company name *Re.Republican Highlife,* an ironic moniker he would use for the next eighteen months. He got his work banging on doors. "I got a break when my friend Ken at Kilburn Lane had too much work and let me operate as a kind of overspill. This led to working with Einstürzende Neubauten, which introduced me to Stevo, Rob, and Jane at Some Bizzarre," an independent record label.

Ken asked White to join him and his friend Kath in setting up a design company for the Virgin Group. Thus, The Clinic was born. "After eight months I decided that I didn't want to work in the mainstream, so I left to pursue freelance work."

10 **PAUL**
WHITE

1981

1996

NOW

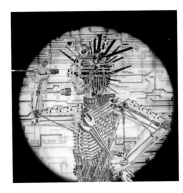

Einstürzende Neubauten, record sleeve
Working with singer Blixa Bargeld, White
created this sleeve when first setting up
shop in Kilburn Lane.

Fad Gadget, illustration White's
portrait of Frank Tovey, a.k.a. Fad Gadget,
shows an early attempt at turning
musicians into robots.

**Erasure, *Victim of Love* remix,
record sleeve** White explored a more
aggressive style of ink-bottle illustration
for this 1987 sleeve.

Flux of Pink Indians, record sleeve Created in 1986, this sleeve was one
of White's first collaborations with his future partners in the label One Little Indian.

ONE LITTLE INDIAN All the sleeves
for the early releases by Some
Bizzarre and its subsidiary label
K:422 were manufactured by a company
called Mayking Records. "I used to have
a regular fight with the owner over the
quality of printing and regularly had to make
them reprint. One such fight on a Swans
cover over the color red lasted for two days.
(We won, of course.) At the time I became
quite friendly with one of the producers, Sue
Churchill. She was also part of an anarchist
punk band, Flux of Pink Indians. They were
in the process of recording their album
Uncarved Block. Having relayed the story of
the two-day argument to her boyfriend
Derek Birkett and her co-band members,
Derek called me the following week and
said something like 'I hear you're the best
sleeve designer in London, and a right
bolshey bastard, too. We should meet.'

"The band was looking for a production and
distribution deal and needed someone
to design the cover for their album. At this
time, we had no plan to set up a label
beyond establishing the structure to release
this LP. I liked Derrick and the rest of the
band a lot, so I started attending the recording sessions and working on preliminary
ideas for the cover."

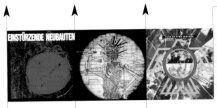

1981

1982
23

1984
25

1986
27

1987
28

1988   1989

The Sugarcubes *Birthday*, record sleeve This is the first record released by One Little Indian and the first sleeve White designed for the Sugarcubes. Note the beginnings of White's mid-'80s signature cartoon characters on the back, as well as the lovely touch of type reacting to the floating dot over the I.

"I PREFERRED SOMETHING THAT COMMENTED ON IDENTITY, SOMETHING COMIC AND IRONIC. *ME COMPANY* WAS PLAYFUL AND STUPID, AND AT THE TIME I WAS HAPPY TO EMBRACE THAT."

Me Sticker For his company's logo, White sampled the Golden Arches and the Playboy bunny and inverted the 3M logo to serve his satiric purpose.

"About two or three months into this period, some old friends of Flux got in touch because they were looking for someone to release a single they had recorded. This single was 'Birthday' and the band was the Sugarcubes. We discussed forming a label: Sue would handle mechanical production; Derek would guide recording production and management; I would look after the label's image and visual output; and Tim and Lu from Flux would handle press. Derrick, Sue, and I flew to Iceland to meet the Sugarcubes and to discuss releasing 'Birthday' and recording and releasing an album. That's how One Little Indian was born."

PAUL WHITE AND ASSOCIATES The stage was set for Me Company. "Derek and Sue tried to convince me that the OLI covers should be credited to me. I preferred something that commented on identity, something comic and ironic. Me Company was playful and stupid, and at the time I was happy to embrace that. Sometimes Me has made me cringe, but mostly I can't think of anything else I would have preferred. I would have consigned my body to a 1,000-foot plummet into freezing water before using Paul White and Associates as a name." White made sure that the Me Company logo reflected his disdain for self-important design studio identities: He created a mash-up of the Playboy bunny and the McDonald's arches and topped the whole thing with an inverted 3M logo.

The early days of One Little Indian and Me Company were a golden period for White. "I found myself with more creative freedom than I had ever had before. I was working with friends who were my partners in the label, and I really enjoyed that."

1990   1991   1993   1995   1996   2000   2001   2003   NOW

The Sugarcubes, *Life's Too Good,* DAT sleeve "I used to have a signature that was a character made up of just a face, legs, and a dick, so this is a derivation of that. The flat-color background is a continuation of the discipline started out on the two singles preceding the album, 'Birthday' and 'Cold Sweat,' born out of the need to keep the printing costs as low as possible. For this cover, I went a bit nuts, issuing it in five or six different fluorescent color schemes—yellow, pink, blue, and black. All production complaints evaporated when they were racked up together in stores, looking fantastic."

Jimmy Sommerville, *Mighty Real,* CD packaging White revived his trademark cartoon style for this 1989 solo debut by former Bronski Beat and Communards frontman Jimmy Sommerville.

"I was into the music and the artists with whom we were working and was excited by the work I was doing. I was getting good feedback on the work from the bands themselves and from people outside of the OLI organization. I felt that I had found a voice."

"ME COMPANY HAS ALWAYS BEEN ABOUT THE WORK WE PRODUCE, FORMING AND FOLLOWING NEW CREATIVE CHALLENGES— NOT THE MONEY.
HAVING SAID THAT, WE WOULD NOT HAVE SURVIVED THIS LONG HAD I NOT BEEN SAVVY ENOUGH TO GET THE BALANCE RIGHT (MOSTLY)."

STABILITY In 1985, White bought an apartment. "On the walls hangs a collection of Russian space program propaganda posters from the '60s and '70s, as well as art and photographs by friends." The fact that he stills lives in the same apartment today— resisting the urge to get the big house, the big yard, the big pool when business was booming—says a lot about White. "I am really lucky that I still love it enough not to want to leave." He talks about the need to balance artistic freedom with the need to pay the bills. "The adequate supply of money is a constant battle, and it always has been. There's never been a surplus of cash for grand, glitzy gestures. When I got money for my One Little Indian shares, it all went to a new computer kit. I remember the video card in my first mondo PC cost £6,000, the machine £14,000, a license of Soft-image £12,000, and Mental Ray render licenses £1,500 each. For years we really just operated at break-even plus a little bit. It's healthier now, thankfully."

"Me Company has always been primarily about the work we produce, forming and following new creative challenges—not the money. Having said that, we would not have survived this long had I not been savvy enough to get the balance right (mostly). I like Me Company as a niche organization. I'd hate it if it were big or corporate. I prefer actually doing the work rather than talking about it or, God forbid, wining and dining clients."

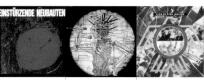

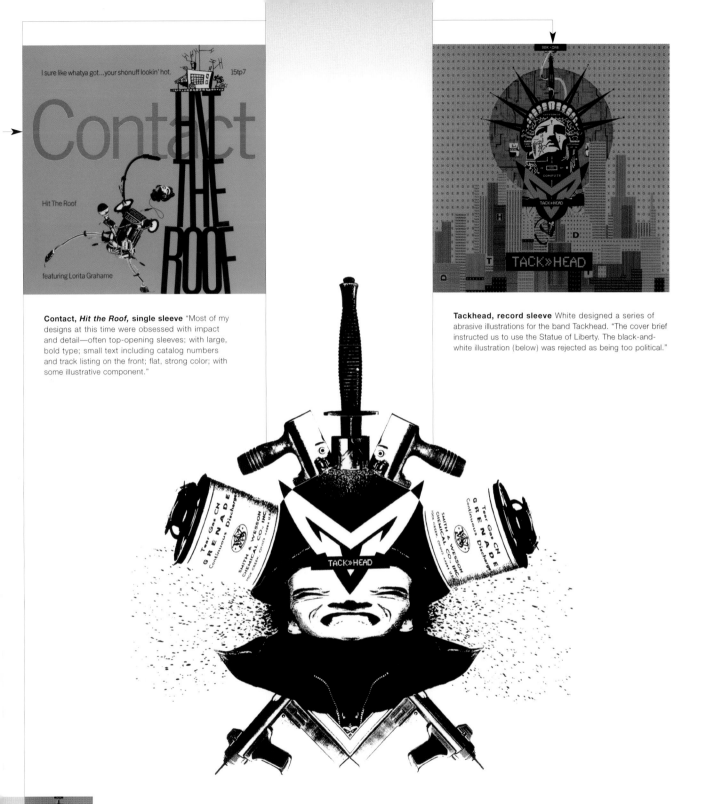

Contact, *Hit the Roof,* single sleeve "Most of my designs at this time were obsessed with impact and detail—often top-opening sleeves; with large, bold type; small text including catalog numbers and track listing on the front; flat, strong color; with some illustrative component."

Tackhead, record sleeve White designed a series of abrasive illustrations for the band Tackhead. "The cover brief instructed us to use the Statue of Liberty. The black-and-white illustration (below) was rejected as being too political."

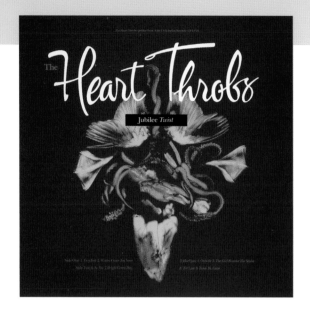

The Heart Throbs, *Jubilee Twist,* record sleeve (above and below)
White used the photocopier as a sampler. "Then and now, I remain
a vegetarian and support animal rights."

"I WAS FASCINATED BY THE POSSIBILITIES OF 3-D RENDERING.
SOFTWARE CASTING A RAY INSTEAD OF PHOTOGRAPHICALLY RECORDING LIGHT IN AN ANALOG WAY WAS ENTHRALLING."

MONDO PC Of course, that first mondo PC had a big
influence on White. It gave him the tools to properly explore
what would become his signature style. "I was fascinated
by the possibilities of 3-D rendering for years. Even conceptually,
the nature of software casting a ray instead of photographically
recording light in an analog way was enthralling. My very first
cheapo Mac 3-D software had my machine locked for hours playing
with the possibilities of surface and light. The pursuit of new,
interesting surfaces and structures has been a ceaseless fascination
ever since that first computer. Years on, I am still endlessly
challenged and inspired by it. So much of my new work explores
what's behind or beyond the surface. All of that is a direct influence
of rendering on the work itself, and, of course, it's this influence
that often irritates the hell out of critics."

Despite his track record, White still faces the Fear—fear of the
blank page, fear of getting started. "But I dance around it until it gets
bored or I win. I can spend a scarily large amount of my time
convinced that everything I do is shit. My successes can come
equally as easy as accidents than through hard bloody graft.
I can be guilty of clinging to a few technique comfort blankets when
things get too tough. In the end, I just do what I do and hope
that in 10 years' time, I can look back at some of what I have
done this year and find it interesting."

 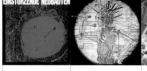

1981   1982   1984   1986   1987   1988   1989

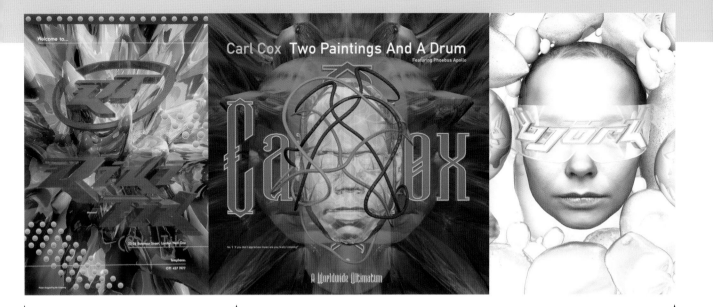

Riki Tik Bar, poster (above, left) "A popular misconception is that this logo copies the logo that we produced for Björk around the same time. Actually, this piece came before Björk, but both were derived from a typestyle that Craig had developed for a rejected logo we presented a few weeks earlier. It represents an early demonstration of a lasting fascination with surface, reflection, and refraction. I think it took about two days for my old Mac IIsi to creak through the render in good old Infini-d."

Carl Cox, *Two Paintings and a Drum*, record sleeve (above, middle) Often referred to as the best DJ in the world, Mancunian Carl Cox let White scan his face for the cover of this 1995 sleeve.

Björk, *Hyperballad*, CD poster (above, right) "The dislocated head at the bottom of the cliff—the brief said 'Something shiny, silvery, and like a pearl.' I still remember that rare moment on its completion where I actually kicked back and felt proud of the achievement, creatively and technically. I still love it today, although I cringe a little at some of the smaller technical compromises. Technically this was a nightmare—hours of rendering on poor, melting processors."

EVOLUTION Self-tolerance is an area that's been problematic for White. "I can get frighteningly close to destroying work under the ferocious conviction that it's not good enough. I have notoriously done so and started again. There is a Björk cover that no one will ever see. Only long experience has taught me that the moment of completion is the worst time to make a sound judgment. Now, reckless abandonment is the rule—followed by critical assessment from a distance and, when necessary, the rewriting of history."

Some designers pride themselves on not having an identifiable style, on assuming a new identity for every project. White's approach is evolutionary, his body of work closer to that of a painter than of a graphic designer. "Me Company lives a life of continual and ongoing reinvention. It's like the slow shedding of a skin on a multiskinned nonlinear snake. New ideas are born and we start exploring them until they, in turn, are no longer of interest to us and we move on."

In keeping with this, Me Company has all but abandoned design for the music industry. "I must have done about thirteen or fourteen years of working exclusively with music artists. I started to find the bulk of the commissions we were being offered pretty boring. The work had moved on to areas that started to feel inappropriate for a lot of the potential clients, and we started to get offers to work in new areas that did suit the work. Very soon Björk was our only music client."

1990	1991	1993	1995	1996	2000	2001	2003	NOW
31	32	34	36	37				

(Where), animation "Working the 3-D scenes as spaces, places to be navigated and explored, encouraging and planning for the accidental view— I guess I finally got sick of the shiny and reflective. These shapes built for the purpose of dissecting a space—a whole series of things I called twisters— with only the specular visible, scatter the space with soft, polygonal forms, like huge great chunks of dust. This piece is a direct link to a previous set of dust/pollen-filled spaces for Björk's records *Jöga* and *Homogenic*."

Cymbidium incorporalis, illustration Thomas Lenthal asked us to do some plants for an issue of Numero. We decided to focus on orchids. As studies, it was important to me that they be geometrically accurate as we could manage. I wanted to explore the ideas of plants viewed by insect eyes, x-rayish with a graphical xylem and phloem. The way insects see UV is the inspiration for the bright color.

Kenzo Autumn/Winter 2001, advertising image "Japanese autumn mixed with the northern European. The significance of autumn in Japanese culture, references to death and finally rebirth. Gender identity. I had this idea of a girl and her twin brother, now dead. Memory and loss in an autumn garden, abstract and wild. The model An Oust was cast as the girl, and we organized a male and female body double to shoot with her: First, shooting An as a girl with the guy body double, then shooting An as the brother with the female body double. The images of An as Stan would then be morphed and retouched to change bone structure, add a beard, and change skin texture to create a believable twin."

"IF MAKING A LIVING WERE NOT A CONCERN, I WOULD SLOW THE PROCESS DOWN AND THINK AND PLAY FOR MONTHS."

ME GALLERY Today, Me Company's work can be found in galleries as well as in the commercial realm. "I am intrigued by the boundaries of the relationship between our work and contemporary art. Over the last few years, the physical recontextualization of some of the work into gallery spaces has been extremely interesting because it lets me reassess some of it. It often leads me to be even more critical of the pace at which we work. If making a living were not a concern, I would slow the process down and think and play for months.

"Deadlines are (almost always) king. We push as hard as we can to maximize the time a client grants us. Sometimes we have to renegotiate that deadline along the way, but when push comes to shove, the job is delivered on the agreed date. This often means that to a certain extent the work is abandoned and isn't ever completely finished. Maybe this is why I am so keen to explore the work as often as possible after it's delivered and supposedly finished. In an ideal world I would take days off from projects to consider what's creatively occurring. I'd spend much more time exploring materials and forms, never multitask like crazy as we often have to, never rush something to hit a date. I would hit the galleries more. I'd research and think more. Actually, all the real-world shit—let's bin it! Let's move off into fantasyland and stay there forever.

"Being creative is like running in someone else's trainers. You don't know where you're going all the time. You don't think about thinking. The synapses fire and you feel possessed—you're speaking in tongues. We tap into the vibrations of the superstrings. We become one with our maker!" ✌

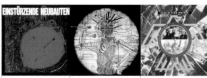

1981   1982   1984   1986   1987   1988   1989

Snowflake, illustration "From a series of six snowflakes for the December 2003 issue of *Numero*. One of the hardest parts in the process of developing the ideas for the flakes was getting the geometry to visually communicate a melting crystalline structure of a snowflake and, at the same time, for it to be idealized and perfect. Once we had the look right, Jess, Ross, and myself could have continued for ages playing with the possibilities."

1990

SHAMEN
EN-TACT

1991

1993

1995

1996

2000
41

2001
42

2003
44

NOW

91

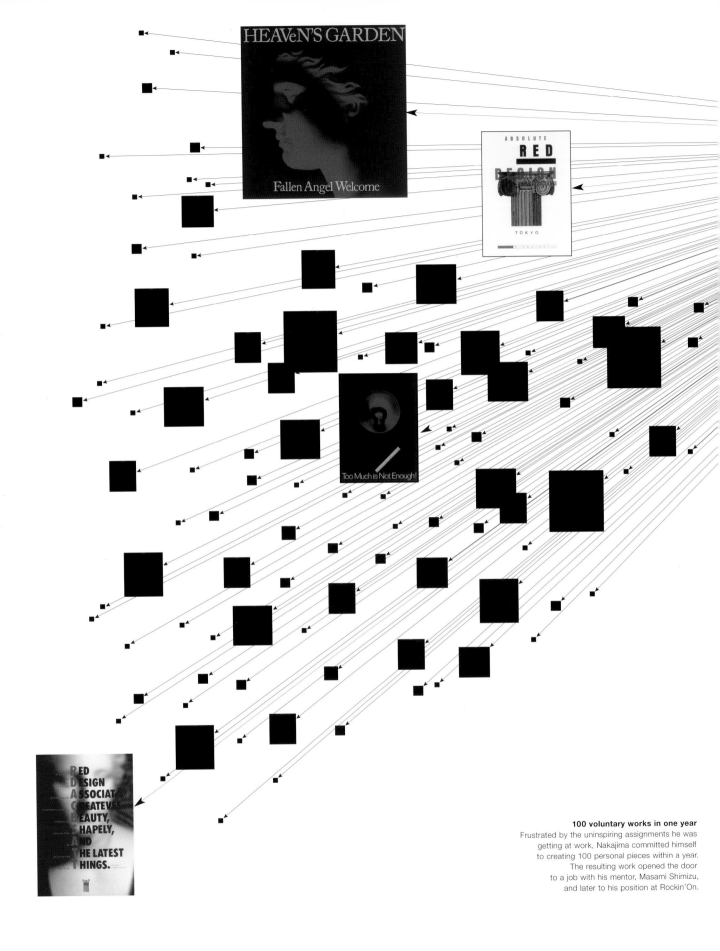

100 voluntary works in one year
Frustrated by the uninspiring assignments he was getting at work, Nakajima committed himself to creating 100 personal pieces within a year. The resulting work opened the door to a job with his mentor, Masami Shimizu, and later to his position at Rockin'On.

HIDEKI NAKAJIMA

11

Finding his love for graphic design via Ultraman and the record sleeves of Peter Saville, Hideki Nakajima has made a career of creating subtly lavish and elegant designs that astound with every closer look.

Hideki Nakajima was born in 1961, in the mostly agricultural Saitama region of Japan. The son of a kimono tailor, he grew up in a home that was open to the arts where he quickly discovered his love for drawing. An early visual influence came in the form of Ultraman, a 40-foot (12 m)-tall silver robot in the mold of Fritz Lang's *Metropolis*, dressed in the brightly colored superhero fashions of the day. Ultraman's sleek, futuristic styling and metallic good looks became part of Nakajima's aesthetic foundation and a regular character in his drawings.

Nakajima continued honing his drafting skills throughout his teenage years, but a trip to the record store soon turned him toward graphic design. He now describes it as the most dramatic event of his life, a moment that changed his destiny. "When I was a teenager, I wanted to be an illustrator. But after seeing the jacket of an OMD (Orchestral Manoeuvres in the Dark) LP, designed by Peter Saville, I changed my mind and decided to be a graphic designer."

100 **PIECES OF ART IN ONE YEAR** On entering the professional world, he immediately felt its artistic constraints. "My twenties were the darkest period in my life. During those ten years, I changed design companies seven times. Maybe I was very arrogant. My first design company fired me after just three months. At that time, I had strong pride, but that pride had no reason. In the real world, my ideal design was nothing. I didn't know how to persuade financial sponsors. Also, I didn't have the skill to make my ideas real. Somehow I decided to accept that reality and gradually came to think that I would be an art director after thirty, and that my twenties were training time."

Still, Nakajima was frustrated by the lack of freedom he found in his first jobs. He decided to find another outlet rather than let himself be stifled. "I decided that I would make 100 original works within a year, on my own time, which meant I had to make at least one piece every three days. In those days, we had no computers that could make artwork easily, so I made a lot of silk screens." The resulting pieces show Nakajima's admiration for Saville's album covers and modernist typography but move beyond mimicry in their subtle use of type, color, and photography.

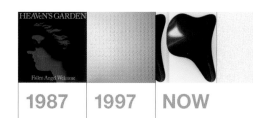

1987 | 1997 | NOW

Japan, **magazine cover** While fairly conservative overall, the use of the small red 3 demonstrates that Nakajima treated type and photography not as separate layers, but as one continuous space.

H, **magazine cover** Already more free-wheeling than the year before, Nakajima amps up this cover for *H* with bold type that accentuates the dramatic photograph.

Composit, **spread** A 1993 spread for *Composit* magazine shows an early example of Nakajima's flair for using typography as illustration.

"I WAS WORKING ALL NIGHT, EVERY NIGHT, AND NEVER CAME HOME. THOSE THREE YEARS WERE THE HARDEST OF MY LIFE.
BUT I THINK THOSE INTENSE DAYS WERE VERY IMPORTANT AND MADE ME WHO I AM NOW."

Included in this period of exploration are the first of what Nakajima calls his "typographies," three-dimensional typographic collages. "I started making typographies in 1987. I was just looking for something new but didn't think this could work well. Then I became the art director for *Cut* magazine and started making them again. This time I found great possibilities in this direction."

The 100 pieces led Nakajima to a job with Masami Shimizu, a man he admired and who would soon become his mentor. "I tried to be the ultimate assistant for him. I tried to do enjoyable works as much as I could, though I knew those works were beyond my capacity. I was working all night, every night, and

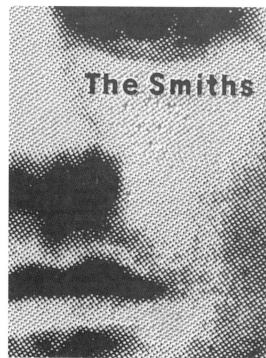

The Smiths, book cover What looks at first glance like a simple halftone image of the Smiths' frontman Morrissey reveals on closer inspection a tantalizing surface structure of tiny beads.

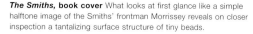

never came home. Those three years were the hardest of my life. But I think those intense days were very important and made me who I am now."

ROCKIN'ON Nakajima stayed with Shimizu until 1992, when he left to take a job at Rockin'On, Inc. Here he was put in charge of art-directing four magazines—*Japan, Bridge, H,* and *Cut.* Working on these titles gave Nakajima an opportunity to meet a great number of photographers, artists, and fashion designers. It also allowed him the freedom to experiment artistically.

Works & Friends, fashion catalog The *Works & Friends* catalog wraps a series of loose, oversize photo spreads into a cover adorned with a full alphabet (minus the W) set in a font created by Nakajima.

    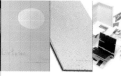 

1996　　　　　　　1997　　1998　1999　　　　　　2000　　NOW

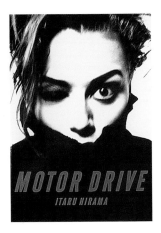

Itaru Hirama, *Motor Drive* (above, left) **Kurt Markus, *Dreaming Georgia*** (below) **books** Based on his work for Rockin'On, photographers started asking for Nakajima's help in designing their own volumes. The quite different styles of *Dreaming Georgia* and *Motor Drive* show Nakajima's sensitive treatment of the material. This talent for handling photography led to his first collaboration with Ryuichi Sakamoto on his 1995 photo book, *N/Y*.

Ryuichi Sakamoto, *N/Y (NO/YES),* book (above, right) This 1995 book of Sakamoto's photography brought together for the first time the four people who would later form the artistic collective CODE: Nakajima, Sakamoto, Sakamoto's creative director Norika Sora, and editor Shigeo Goto. Photographer Kazunari Tajima, who had brought Nakajima to the project, also participated.

Yohji Yamamoto, poster (above, left) **Mondo Grosso *Pieces from the Editing Floor,* CD cover** (above, right) Two pieces from 1995 illustrate Nakajima's fascination with type being present in a three-dimensional environment.

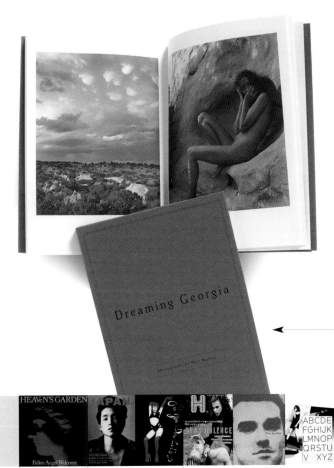

His most visible contribution to *Cut* was an evolving series of typographies that, paired with portrait photographs, served as opening spreads for the magazine's interview features. These pieces were formal explorations executed in various ways. Some featured type created as physical objects that were then lit and photographed. Others had computer-generated type inserted into photographs. Some were lavish typographic illustrations, executed either by hand or on the computer by one of his assistants. (Nakajima himself doesn't use a computer.)

The pages move from bold typographic statements to pieces of complete restraint that foreshadow his later output. His work for *Cut* soon caught the eye of design jurors around the world and earned him national and international recognition.

VIA BUS STOP

k.a.t., fashion catalog Using two unusual fashion photos by Mario Sorrenti, Nakajima created another memorable catalog cover with minimal typographic means.

Dune, magazine cover (above, left) This cover shows Nakajima going Vogue.

Via Bus Stop, poster (above, right) An otherwise fairly simple close-up of a model's eye is made strange and intriguing with the addition of colored beads to the tips of the eyelashes.

HE CREDITS EXPOSURE TO NEW COLLABORATORS WITH AN INTENSE PERIOD OF ARTISTIC GROWTH.

"THAT WAS THE SECOND BIG TURNING POINT IN MY LIFE.

I THINK MY TALENT BLOSSOMED BECAUSE OF THEM."

NAKAJIMA DESIGN By 1995, Nakajima had a number of design awards to his name and was ready to start his own studio, Nakajima Design. He left Rockin'On and was free to work with editors at other publishing companies and to collaborate with friends in the music and fashion industry. He credits this exposure to new collaborators with an intense period of artistic growth. "That was the second big turning point in my life. I think my talent blossomed because of them."

One of the first assignments paired Nakajima with clients who would become lasting collaborators and creative partners. On the recommendation of the project's photographer, Riyuichi Sakamoto and his creative director, Norika Sora, asked Nakajima to art-direct Sakamoto's 1996 photography book *N/Y (NO/YES)*. "Kazunari Tajima, the photographer, recommended that job to me. The editor of the book was Shigeo Goto. While making *N/Y*, our relationship got tight, as if we were drawn together like magnets."

Parco and Matsuda, posters (above, left and right) In 1996, Nakajima created two series of fashion posters for Matsuda and Parco, proving he was equally at ease with glamorous fashion shots as he was with a more documentary style.

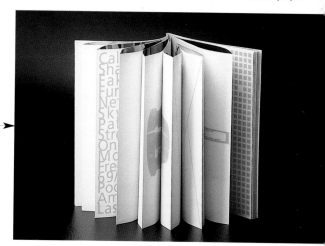

Light, book (above) Another iconic Nakajima project is *Light*, a book with a "flocky finish" cover design.

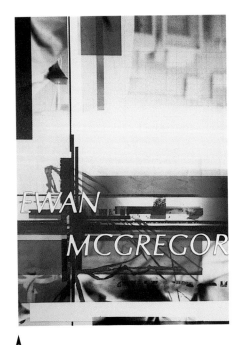

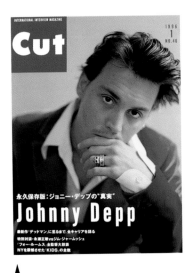

Following *N/Y*, Nakjima went on to design all of Sakamoto's record sleeves and CD packages. His design for *Playing the Orchestra 1997,* an homage to Peter Saville's OMD sleeve, brought Nakajima further acclaim in his own country and abroad. "I won a couple of design awards. Before then, I felt I was ranked lower in the public and had an inferiority complex." Back then, Nakajima says, he often felt that he had to prove himself. But now, accepted by his peers and admired for his work, he could breathe easier. "I felt very relieved and knew what I was doing was not wrong at all."

MOVING INTO THE FUTURE Of course, Nakajima was not content to rest on his laurels. "I can say that I had succeeded socially, but I was not interested in that. To me, it is more important to be satisfied than to succeed,

1987   1993   1995

Cut, magazine (all images at left and opposite, below) Nakajima's biggest early success came with the typographies he created for *Cut* magazine from 1992 onward.

Revival, book (right) Revival collects fifty-seven of Nakajima's typographies for *Cut* magazine in one silver volume, debossed with a skin of raindrops.

Ryuichi Sakamoto, *Playing the Orchestra 1997,* embossed record sleeve (below, right) Years after being turned toward graphic design by Peter Saville's sleeve for OMD, Nakajima paid homage with this sleeve for Ryuichi Sakamoto's album *Playing the Orchestra 1997.*

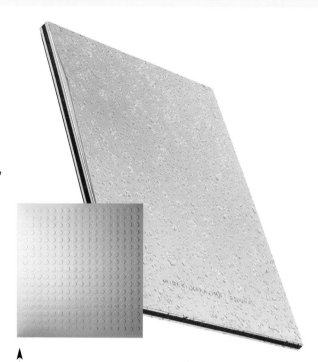

and I'm not satisfied yet. I will be satisfied if I can make a new form that nobody has seen yet. That is the definition of success to me." With this in mind, he has twice gathered collections of his work—*Revival,* a compendium of his typographies for *Cut,* and the monograph *Hideki Nakajima 1995–2001*—to organize his past and then move beyond it on his way to a more interesting future.

His recent pieces abandon the typographic playfulness that made him famous in the late '90s. Instead, they seduce with quiet elegance and effortless grace. What connects projects such as Sakamoto's *Sampled Life* box set and the completely abstract pages created for *IDEA* magazine with Nakajima's earlier work is his sure mastery of form.

Much of his energy now goes to CODE, a group formed with the original *N/Y* team of Ryuichi Sakamoto and Norika Sora. CODE's goal is to provide a space for experimentation

"TO ME, IT IS MORE IMPORTANT TO BE SATISFIED THAN TO SUCCEED, AND I'M NOT SATISFIED YET. I WILL BE SATISFIED IF I CAN MAKE A NEW FORM THAT NOBODY HAS SEEN YET. THAT IS THE DEFINITION OF SUCCESS TO ME."

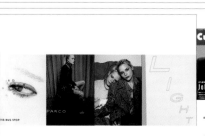

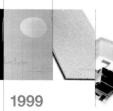

1996
35

1997
36

1998
37

1999
38

2000

NOW

**Ryuichi Sakamoto, *Sampled Life,*
CD box set** The 1999 box set accompanying Sakamoto's opera *Sampled Life*
was an unusually complex assignment
for Nakajima that had to be completed
in record time. "I can't believe that
I made this, even now. The schedule
almost killed me. Because *Sampled
Life* had a lot of tricks, we went through
many factories to manufacture it.
But, when we started, everything—
format, number of pages, tricks,
photographs, schedule—went right,
as if we had planned it from the
beginning. So, in the end, *Sampled
Life* was made by miracle."

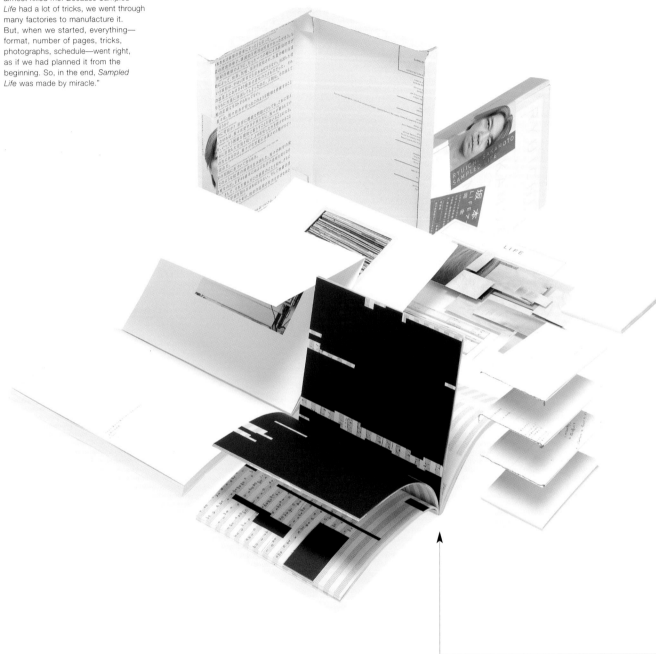

on survival in the creative field and to produce environmentally sustainable products. To this end, CODE publishes the magazine *Unfinished,* produces CDs, sells organic food, and organizes ecological tourism.

CREATING WORLDS Looking ahead, Nakajima sets out his next personal goal—to visually express "eroticism, the occult, and the confusion, all of which tend to be avoided in the graphic design world now. I think that's an ultimate purpose in my life as a designer. I always want to create the world that exists only in movies such as *Les Amants du Pont-Neuf* by Leos Carax, *Gummo* by Harmony Corine, or *Brown Bunny* by Vincent Gallo. Unfortunately, I can't see such a world in my own works yet. Whenever I see these movies, I can't help feeling jealous."

Though his artistic life has had a few clear turning points, Nakajima sees it as a constant evolution. "Every brick has been stacked one by one." Considering the beauty of his designs and what he has achieved, it is surprising and humbling to hear his view of his own work. "I still regret a lot. When I see the works I made three years ago, I feel very embarrassed. Maybe three years after, when I see what I do now, I will feel embarrassed. But embarrassment is important, because what is not embarrassing can't move people's hearts. I want to keep regretting." ✄

"I STILL REGRET A LOT.
WHEN I SEE THE WORKS
I MADE THREE YEARS AGO,
I FEEL VERY EMBARRASSED.
BUT EMBARRASSMENT
IS IMPORTANT, BECAUSE
WHAT IS NOT EMBARRASSING
CAN'T MOVE PEOPLE'S HEARTS.
I WANT TO KEEP REGRETTING."

Issey Miyake 2000, ad campaign "Before starting that campaign, I did a long interview with Naoki Takizawa, the designer [at Issey Miyake]. As a result, we decided that the whole concept was 'confuse.' We didn't choose one particular image but selected many perspectives. For example, we let people think, 'OK, this is Issey Miyake's image in this season' in one ad. Then, in another ad, we used completely different images. One of them was just a landscape photo. In another we used the close-up shot of the face, which had, if you looked closer, horns on the forehead. These complex images made it possible to be faithful to perspectives of Takizawa. After all, confused images can give us deeper memories."

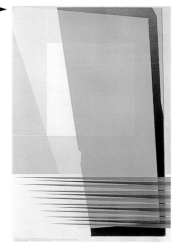

Unfinished #2–3, poster In recent years Nakajima has explored purely abstract, type-free compositions.

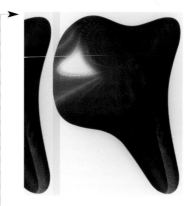

***IDEA* magazine, cover** Foregoing his signature typographies, Nakajima returned to magazine design with this abstract artwork for *IDEA* magazine. "I just wanted to express something that I didn't know. I am always looking for the next possibility of the design."

1996   1997   1998   1999   2000   NOW

RICK
VALICENTI

Rick Valicenti came of age in the American Heartland of the 1960s, and the experience left its mark. Having paid his dues the hard way, he built himself a design studio that has become an extension of his family—both personal soapbox and secret laboratory.

Rick Valicenti's story starts in a middle-class suburb of Pittsburgh, Pennsylvania. Born in 1952, "the oldest of three in a happy family," he describes his early years as "normal, normal, normal." However, his passion for art soon became apparent. "The code was inside me and evident at an early age. I learned it looking at album covers on my bed, guitar across my lap, headphones on, surrounded by paisley wallpaper. None of us knew who Milton Glaser was, but we had the Dylan poster or the early Syd Barrett's Pink Floyd, and Albert Lee's Love— killer type. My mother encouraged me by taking me to private drawing lessons and, on Saturdays, to the Carnegie Institute in Pittsburgh."

Despite his passion for art, Valicenti had more pressing concerns by the time he was ready to move on to college. "Back in the '60s, when I was finishing high school, no one imagined being a real-life artist. We just focused and fretted about Vietnam. We spoke out. I was in Ohio for school during the Kent shootings. Wearing an armband seems like a silly graphic device in hindsight, but it did leave an indelible bruise on my attitude toward trust and authority." It was a bruise that influences Valicenti's work to this day. "Most of my career, I have used both commercial and professional opportunities to comment on culture and design as culture's voice box. My approach has been consciously steady and subversive. I can do more from the inside than I can as an outside agitator."

WORKING AT THE STEEL MILL Valicenti graduated from Ohio's Bowling Green State University in 1973. "I returned to Pittsburgh with a portfolio of nudes and abstract paint-ings. I tried to have a go at the studio world. Back then it was a service to bring art direction to a print-ready state. Needless to say, I was underqualified." But money was tight, and unemployment not an option. "I went to work as a steel worker in the world's largest stainless-steel mill. I was a hardcore, steel-toed shoe and hardhat guy. I bought a small pickup truck and a 2¼" (5.5 cm) camera—there was money to burn at this job. I would sneak the camera into work in my lunch box and shoot the other older workers. With a little more money, I bought a darkroom outfit with a kick-ass Omega enlarger and East Street studio print washer—I was in the game and bored at work, so I decided to apply to grad school and went."

1973   1989   NOW

103

ZOTOS

Quadrant, logos (above left, middle left, middle right) "A Chicago retail identity. 'Rewards' was a sub-identity for a department within the store. These graphics are from the pre-Mac daze. I remember cutting both identities from Rubylith. Those were the days, indeed."

Zotos, identity (above, right) "In a post–Neville Brody period this Japanese hair care division of Shiseido required a new icon identity. I remember calling this the 'creation of beauty' and using an organic new growth as a point of departure for the formal design. The symmetry of the word was also mirrored with the Zs. Given the salon context, the mirror was a good subtle reference."

The New York Erotic Film Festival, poster "This was my first illustrative design assignment. It was a project for an Intro to Design class I took while at Bowling Green State University. Press Type Deluxe!"

***Blue Devil Gazette*, newsletter** "The first commercial work that excited me! I designed it while I was employed as newsletter and form designer for the Washington National Insurance Company, Evanston, Illinois."

"SUCCESS DOES NOT JUST HAPPEN. IT IS AN ACT OF PLANNING AND DESIGN.
I TOOK THE MESSAGE TO HEART AND KNEW THAT I WOULD APPLY IT NOT SO MUCH TO WORK BUT TO LIFE IN GENERAL.
HOW WAS I TO GET HAPPY AND STAY HAPPY?"

After receiving a masters of arts and a masters of fine arts in studio photography from the University of Iowa, Valicenti headed for Chicago to find work but was disillusioned with the options before him. "I looked at the photo scene and saw shots of hot dogs, cereal, and beer—that was not for me! I rented a studio space over a small vintage movie theater and set up a darkroom studio.

"I worked on my own things and did silly keyline in the daytime. That was my first exposure to the fringe of design—doing paste-up in an ad agency doing recruitment ads: 'accountant,' 'plant manager.' The format still exists today, but at that time the radius corner borders were inked and the type was set on an IBM Selectric and rubber-cemented to illustration board before making a Photostat." Though the job brought a measure of financial security, it came at a price. "I was just a specifier: This type, this photographer, this idea. Nothing seemed to come from within.

"I quit the ad agency after six months and was unemployed for two. In that time I finished a new series of photo collages and had a one-person show in Chicago. But I was broke, so I answered an ad to replace a woman on maternity leave at an insurance company. Graphic skills were required. Well, skills I had! I had to teach myself over a weekend how to expertly use a ruling pen and magic marker on tracing paper. Fortunately, I could draw, so the learning curve was not so steep. I showed up on Monday with examples in hand and pleaded for the job."

1973
21

1978
26

1986
34

1987
35

1989
37

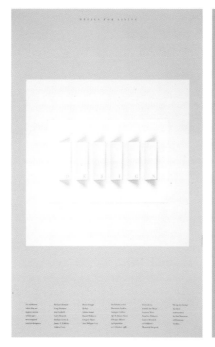

Harry Caray's Restaurant, coaster (above) "The Chicago broadcast icon Harry Caray opened a high-end themed restaurant. My identity spoke with fused vernaculars of baseball and Budweiser."

Design for Living, poster (near, right) "A poster announcing the first Design for Living fund-raising exhibition supporting the Children's Memorial Hospital pediatric oncology research. The event featured custom room vignettes designed by well-known Chicago interior designers."

DESIGNING SUCCESS The inspiration for change came from a colleague. "In one of my first experiences with a savvy designer in Chicago, we were gossiping about the successful office and lifestyle of one of his colleagues. He told me that this designer had actually designed his office. Well, I responded with my customary, 'Huh?' I was enlightened by our continued discussion about how success does not just happen. It is an act of planning and design. I took the message to heart and knew that I would apply it not so much to work but to life in general. How was I to get happy and stay happy?" So motivated and with the birth of his first son upon him, Valicenti started his own studio, R Valicenti Design, in 1981.

Now free to pursue more creative assignments in his own way, he embraced his love for the design process and took control of all aspects of the work, developing a playful, experimental style that has since become his signature. "I like the early moments of discovery. For example, for my first commemorative poster for the Lyric Opera of Chicago, I decided to take the picture myself. Perhaps it was because I was late in the process or the budget was low, but the DIY attitude grew from there."

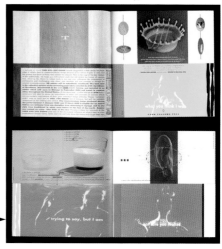

Feel Stupid (It's OK), poster (above, top) The disarming line on the poster for the 1989 STA Student Design Conference originated at the Valicenti home. "I discovered that some of the best ideas didn't come from me but from my kids. The best line that came from the kitchen table was 'Feel Stupid (It's OK).'"

***Enter,* booklet** (above, bottom) Valicenti created this STA 100 call-for-entries booklet for the Society of Typographic Arts, later known as the American Center for Design. "The typography and photography blended in an unexpected manner that delighted me and confounded the STA membership."

ZOTOS

1990

1999   2001   2002   2003   NOW

105

"GOOD COLLABORATION IS A RUSH. I DO NOT REALLY DO ANYTHING ALONE.
EVERYTHING UNDER THE BANNER OF THIRST IS A COLLABORATION."

"This attitude enlarged to the point of liking the idea, of crafting every form in the message—type, image, idea. Today, even if the work sucks—and much of what I do tries hard not to suck, but somehow sucks anyhow—it's at least all made within the studio. The words, the ideas, the letterforms, the imagery—and sometimes the paper—is our design as well. Ego? No. Fascination and curiosity? Yes."

WOULD YOU LIKE BREAKFAST? In 1989, Valicenti changed the nature of the staff and the client focus. R Valicenti Design became Thirst. At all times, Valicenti was careful to choose both the right employees and the right clients to invite into his sphere. "A life and career in design is not always easy. The pressures of the process and finding balance between providing service and being strategically creative often conflict. So how does one plan for success in design and happiness in life? One way is to enjoy the process and the people you work with and serve. I have used a simple qualifier to make it easier for me. If I would want them to wake up in my house for breakfast, I would probably enjoy working with them. That is not to say that every client and collaborator is from the same definition of *hip*. On the contrary, it suggests for me that they be honest, interesting, supportive, often dynamic, and always genuinely nice people. Each of us obviously has our own personal evaluation for the breakfast table guests.

"The same can be said for the collaborators and coworkers with which you surround yourself. Every day is not a good hair day, so the people in your (work) life should be loving enough not to make it an issue, if you know what I mean. I use a version of this barometer to make

Digital Petroglyph, film (above, left) Valicenti created a fifty-two-minute film for Herman Miller's Neocon Exposition in collaboration with Matt Daly and Vello Virkhaus. "All aspects of the film's movement are directed by the code captured by monitoring two dancers moving, dancing, and so on. The breakthrough was human presence."

Just My Type, animation (above, right) Produced in collaboration with Gregg Brokaw, *Just My Type* is "an animated series of stills captured from a pay-per-view Internet site of Alice World."

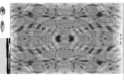

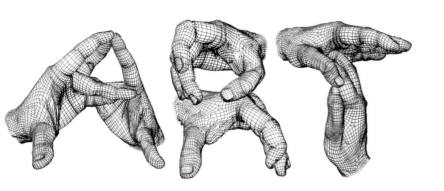

"HEY, RICK, WANNA GO OUT TONIGHT?"

"AH, I THINK I'M GONNA STAY IN THE STUDIO."

"HEY, RICK, WANNA GO OUT TO A NICE HOTEL FOR THE WEEKEND?"
"AH, I THINK I'M GONNA DO SOME WRITING."

"FUCK YOU, RICK, YOU'RE SUCH A SNORE!"

work feel like a conceptual extension of home." Having taken such care to grow his creative home, Valicenti can truly enjoy the work he produces with his team. "Good collaboration is a rush. I do not really do anything alone. Everything under the banner of Thirst is a collaboration."

WORKING AT THE FAMILY STORE The line between Valicenti's professional life and his family life is happily blurred. "Raising a family was not a design act but rather a creative life; not conscious, just aware. Along the way, I discovered that some of the best ideas didn't come from me but from my kids. But, oh yes, I sold them as if they were mine! My daughter gave birth to a page in the MTV Awards annual on sexual harassment. She also once did a back page of *Émigré*. And Rudy [Vanderlans, the editor/publisher] thought I was Paul Klee. My son is currently engaged in a project for Thirstype along with some of his high school friends, and my wife, a non-designer, has shaped many an image and concept."

Despite his passion and energy, Valicenti doesn't deny that his choices demand sacrifice. He acts out a typical dialogue: "Hey, Rick, wanna go out tonight?—Ah, I think I'm gonna stay in the studio.—Hey, Rick, wanna go out to a nice hotel for the weekend?—Ah, I think I'm gonna do some writing.—Fuck you, Rick, you're such a snore!" But ultimately, he feels that effort pays off. "The rewards come in excess with time well spent."

ART (a font called Handsome), typeface
(above, left) Valicenti and Brian McMullen created this font with the modeling software Poser using "the convention of speaking with one's hands to a tech/comic end."

Fireorb, brochure
(above) Valicenti brought this eight-page B2C product introduction to life with the help of Chester at Thirstype and photography by W. M. Valicenti. "It speaks with visual and verbal poetry."

1999
47

2001
49

2002
50

2003

NOW

107

This is called **"myth"**

This is called "the direction here"

Shipwrecked sailor is walking down the beach.
Finds a beat-up old bottle in the sand.

Brushes it off to see what it says
and a hallucination pops out.
"Dwah-ha-ha-haaaaa!" the hallucination says.

"Remember when you were a kid
and you invented that whole game
in your back yard
where the grass was an ocean
and all the flower beds were continents?"

Sailor nods yes and thinks to himself
"Shit, I'm really in bad shape."

The hallucination says
"Remember how to get from the birdbath
to the barbecue grill?"

The sailor nods yes.
And the hallucination says:
"Guess what?
You're on a birdbath island right now,
you lucky son of a bitch,
and I just told you how to get home."

And the sailor followed the hallucination's advice and made it home.

"WHEN I GET
TO THE END
OF ONE PLATEAU
AND STARE UP
AT THE LEDGE
OF THE NEXT ONE,
I USUALLY SAY

'OH, SHIT, NOT AGAIN!'"

Valicenti freely admits that he works hard to have his point of view recognized. "I am a promoter but mostly in service to fueling the ongoing discourse within the profession. Promoters with nothing of value are snake-oil salesmen. The design community can smell them a mile away." As for the work itself, "if it is a good idea it will have a life outside of me and those who helped bring it to life."

Keeping those ideas fresh year in and year out is no mean feat, either. Valicenti describes his process of evolution: "When I get to the end of one plateau and stare up at the ledge of the next one, I usually say 'Oh, shit, not again!' This happens day to day, month to month, and year to year. Whether it is the learning curve for a new way of doing something or a new challenge—the request feels like a challenge, and a challenge is there for the taking."

SPREADING THE WORD With Thirst and its subsidiary type foundry, Thirstype, firmly established on the international design scene, Valicenti now guides the next generation of designers. "As I make a real long-term effort to engage with college students and design communities everywhere, I see many of the same professional promises made and ultimately unfulfilled. Students are exposed to rich, imaginative work of design's past, which is actually culture's artifact. The impression must be overwhelming and simultaneously seductive. As a result, it implies a promise that says, 'Yes, you too, young student of design, can contribute to this important canon.'"

1973   1978   1986   1987   1989

Faust

2003 **LYRIC OPERA OF CHICAGO** 2004

Myth, book (opposite) Valicenti worked with Chad Johnston and Rob Wittig to spin this "collection of images and stories that contemporize mythology through the convention of a familiar joke template. 'A man walks into a bar…'"

Faust, poster (left) "The commemorative season poster for the Lyric Opera of Chicago speaks to the past and present in a very new and old way." Rob Irrgang helped.

Arch.IIT.edu, posters (right, top and bottom) Valicenti turned to classic information design for the Illinois Institute of Architecture's School of Architecture, making their spring and fall 2003 calendars of events into usable tools as well as attractive posters.

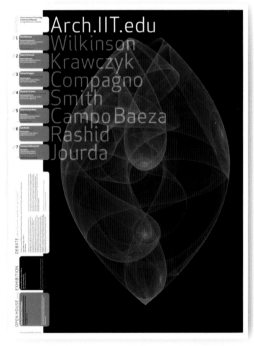

"Well, the canon's membership is proportionally small and, like professional sports, rather elite. There are enough reasons to fall out of love with design. What everyone needs to do is delight in the process of design and know that whatever they make as a result of 'time well spent' is of value first to themselves and to those who come in contact with it."

PHASE THREE Having passed through the student and the professional phase of his own life "with mostly blind enthusiasm and unbridled zeal," Valicenti now strives to move on to the third phase "with dignity and courage." All the while, his eyes are wide open, and what he sees explains the jubilant nature of his designs. "I see artists everywhere: kids, nature, inventors, stylists, musicians, everyone who is creative, anyone with innocence, vision, and courage." Two people currently on his mind are Apple founder Steven Jobs and one of his personal heroes, the late Saul Bass. "They were both, like many others, focused on giving back things that feed the soul and serve a day-to-day function. I like the push they applied. Along the way they inspired the shit out of those who were paying attention and made a little history—now that ain't a bad day at work, is it?" ✌

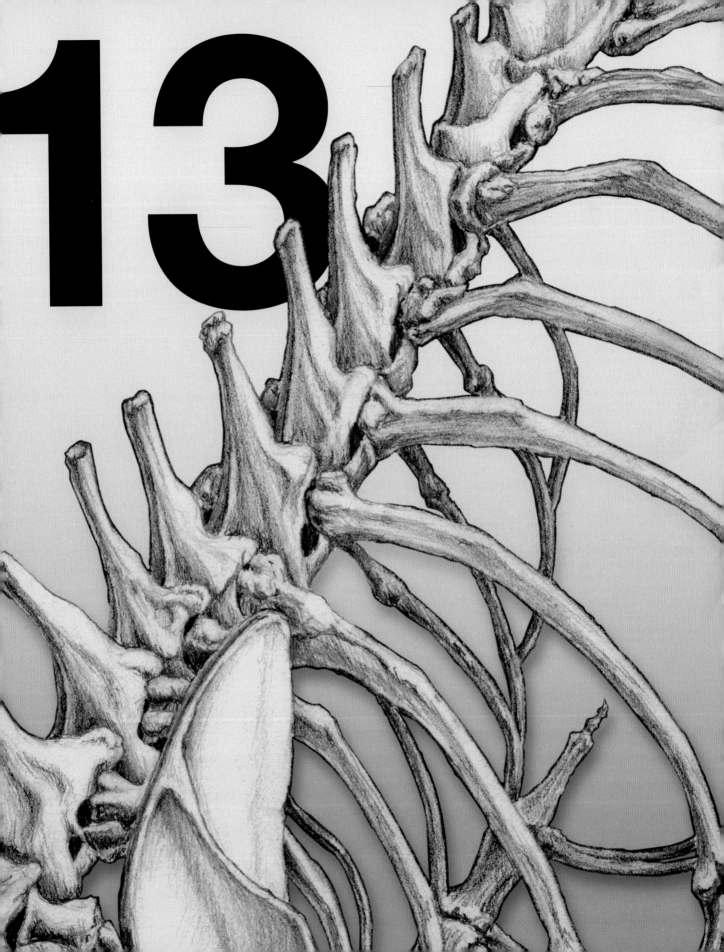

Bored with sitting in hospital basements drawing body parts, Margo Chase turned to graphic design. Dripping blood all over Francis Ford Coppola's posters and transforming Cher into a tarot goddess, she single-handedly invented high-fashion Goth design.

MARGO CHASE

Many designers come from backgrounds that make a career in the arts seem almost inevitable. Margo Chase is one of them: her late biological mother drew, painted, and made furniture; her stepmother plays bass viol with the Santa Barbara Symphony and studied calligraphy. Her grandfather was a photographer, and both aunts were painters. Even her father, an aerospace engineer by trade, is an accomplished jazz guitarist. Surrounded by so many artistic influences, Margo started drawing at an early age. "I got into trouble in elementary school for doodling and drawing horses all over my school papers. Most of my horses had heads that were too small and butts that were too big, but I kept drawing them anyway."

Surprisingly, nobody in Chase's family considered visual arts a viable career. So when it came time to pick a major in college, she enrolled in the biology department of Cal Poly, San Luis Obispo in hopes of later moving on to the School of Veterinary Medicine at UC Davis. "I loved studying biology. I was learning how living things worked. It was visually exciting to study all the life forms in comparative anatomy and learn about plants in plant taxonomy. I loved the classes where we looked at things under the microscope. I even loved dissection. I think my interest in organic form in graphic design carries over from my years studying biology."

SEEDS OF CHANGE It was an act of cold, hard calculation that eventually brought Chase into contact with graphic design: "Grades are extremely important for getting into medical school so I spent a good deal of time trying to figure out how to get my liberal arts credits without damaging my GPA. Drawing and painting classes were easy A's. I had already taken a few when I signed up for an illustration class that I thought would just be more figure drawing. It turned out to be a third-year class in the recently formed graphic design department."

1978   1992   NOW

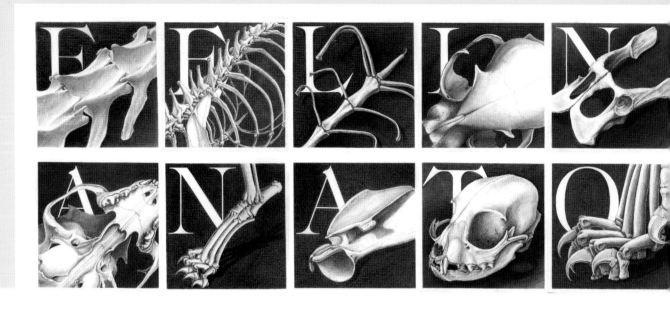

Human Foot, illustration This scratchboard illustration was a graduate project and one of the pieces Margo had in her portfolio when first trying to break into the graphic design field.

One of the first illustration projects was to pick a word and letters that expressed the word, and then illustrate it. She chose "Feline Anatomy" and rented a cat skeleton from the biology lab. "I had no idea what a typeface was. I'd copied the letters out of a book." Chase soon added a minor degree in graphic design to her biology curriculum. "The most exciting part was discovering that one might actually make a living doing something visually creative. Design was a revelation!"

Following the advice of one of her instructors, Chase signed up for the graduate program in medical illustration at UC San Francisco. "My parents were enthusiastic about the medical illustration idea. They were still sure I'd starve to death doing graphic design." But despite honing her technical skills, Chase was not thrilled by the idea of spending the better part of her life in hospital basements making drawings for medical textbooks. "I realized I hated it. I missed the creativity and openness of the graphics classes. I quit graduate school in 1981."

1979
21

1981
23

1984
26

1987

1988

1989

"MY PARENTS WERE ENTHUSIASTIC
ABOUT THE MEDICAL ILLUSTRATION IDEA.
THEY WERE STILL SURE I'D STARVE TO DEATH DOING GRAPHIC DESIGN."

Feline Anatomy, illustration "We were asked to choose a word and letters that expressed the word, and then illustrate it. I rented the cat skeleton from the biology lab. I brought the final drawings into class and one of the first questions was "What typeface is that?" Since I'd missed the first two years of Graphic Design, I had no idea what a typeface was. I said I'd copied the letters out of a book, which was true, but not the right answer. The instructor was extremely forgiving. By the end of the class I had figured out the typeface thing (it was Tiffany), and I did get an A."

GETTING A FOOT IN THE DOOR Times turned tough trying to scare up design work with a portfolio of anatomical field renderings and a drawing of a human foot. Eventually, she was hired to do production work for a small advertising agency in Long Beach, California. Any thoughts of a glamorous life in design were kept in check by having to do paste-up on plain wrap packaging for Ralph's grocery stores, the agency's biggest client.

Three months later, salvation came in the form of a small publishing company, Rosebud Books, where Chase had interviewed months before. Editor Rick Frey, acting on a hunch, asked her to design a series of tourist guidebooks. "I have no idea why he thought I could design books. I had nothing in my portfolio that suggested I could. He asked if I knew how to spec type. I lied. Then I went to the library and checked out everything they had on type and book design. Things didn't go badly and I loved the work." Rick Frey is now an executive at the WB television network and remains a Chase client to this day. "He gave me my first big break."

Olympic Arts Festival, catalog This catalog, one of Chase's earliest forays into graphic design, already shows her natural understanding of negative space and a lingering fascination with skeletal bones.

Lolita Pop, record sleeve (near left) For better or worse, the fate of album cover and logo designs are inextricably linked to the music they encase. *Lolita Pop* did not prove an enduring vehicle for Chase's artwork.

Virgin Records, record sleeve (middle left) Record companies ship advance copies of most records in generic sleeves. Chase created this design using overprinting for Virgin.

I, Napoleon, record sleeve (far left) Chase designed the logotype for this LP cover and then personally carved it from the living rock.

MAKING THE DIVA LIST Her work with Rosebud soon led to other opportunities: "My second big break was when Laura LiPuma, one of the staff designers at the publishing company, left and got a job as an art director at Warner Bros. Records. She hired me freelance to design logos for endless never-to-be-heard-from-again bands. She liked the work, so she recommended me to art directors at other labels like Virgin and Sony. When Laura was given all of Prince's releases to design, she asked me to design logos for *LoveSexy* and Prince's Paisley Park production company. "Once you design a logo for a successful artist, more work follows. I was hired by Laura's boss, Jeri Heiden, to design the logo for Madonna's *Like a Prayer*. Eventually I was able to talk my way into designing the full packaging, not just the logos."

A string of high-profile projects came Chase's way in 1991 and 1992: Madonna and Cher albums, divider pages for the first edition of *Alternative Pick,* and the poster campaign for the movie *Dracula.* "The music business was a fantastic place to work in the '80s and early '90s. I've been extremely lucky to get projects that were visible. They've propelled my career. I still hear 'Oh my God, you design for Madonna!' Her name is more impressive than the work, to most people."

Mac McAnally, *Finish Lines,* **logo** (above, left) The logo for the 1987 release *Finish Lines* by Nashville singer/ songwriter Mac McAnally shows just how far Chase had advanced her letter-form design in the eight years since her first attempt—*Feline Anatomy.*

Prince, *LoveSexy,* **logo** *LoveSexy* (above, middle) marked the aesthetic zenith of Prince's album artwork, fully expressing the Paisley Park aesthetic while retaining a clean, modern feel. It doesn't get better than this. And (graphically) it didn't.

Madonna, *Like a Prayer,* **logo** (above, right) "I've been extremely lucky to get projects that were visible." Madonna's *Like a Prayer* logo was one of the jobs that resulted in a string of high-profile work that came her way in the early '90s.

Cher, *Love Hurts,* CD packaging
(above and right) The special package for Cher's *Love Hurts* CD was the first project Chase tackled in Photoshop, a remarkable feat considering that the layers option was still several versions away from being introduced into the software.

Many of these projects gave Chase a chance to wrestle with infant versions of Adobe Illustrator and Photoshop. "I think the single thing that really created a breakthrough for me creatively was the computer. I was doing really complex, layered work using unusual methods and it took awhile for me to feel like the computer would actually help me do what I wanted and not force me to change the style of work I was doing to conform to the limitations of the technology.

"USING A MOUSE FELT LIKE DRAWING WITH A BAR OF SOAP.
BUT THE RESULTS WERE AMAZING."

"Before the computer, I drew every logo by hand, then revised it, redrew it, and finally inked it on Duralene. Every change or correction was agony. Adobe Illustrator was freedom! I remember, however, being extremely frustrated trying to learn to make smooth curves with those Bezier handles. Using a mouse felt like drawing with a bar of soap, but the results were amazing. I could duplicate shapes, flip things, rotate them, make changes, and print another, all without resorting to a stat machine. Incredible. I had always been interested in symmetry. The computer made it easy. My Lucigraph moved to storage and never came back."

The first job Chase ever tackled in Photoshop was a CD box set featuring a set of Cher tarot cards. This turned into a trial by fire. Creating a series of densely layered collages would be considered complex even on today's equipment. Add to that countless change requests from Cher in a time before layers became part of the software and you're looking at a truly Sysiphian task. Still, the effort paid off: The package was a hit and garnered Chase a Grammy nomination. "Prince, Madonna, Cher, Bonnie Raitt, Jody Watley, and others followed. Somehow I was on the diva list."

THE QUEEN OF GOTH The success of having a very identifiable aesthetic so widely exposed carries with it the need for change. "I got to be known for the style of work I was doing then, the Gothic thing. Even at the time, I knew that the sensation of walking into a record store and seeing several of my designs prominently displayed was an experience that wouldn't be repeated indefinitely. Fads change fast, but it was a lot of fun being 'it' in that world for a little while."

1991

33

1992

1997

2000

NOW

115

Germs, poster (above, left) **Incite Insight, poster** (above, right) Chase's posters advertising her lectures gave her a chance to explore dense layering effects that were necessarily missing from her logo work.

Bram Stoker's Dracula, poster (below) Chase made the typography for *Bram Stoker's Dracula* into an appropriately bloody affair, a device she would later revisit for the WB's show *Buffy the Vampire Slayer.*

Alternative Pick, tattoos For the divider pages of the first issue of *Alternative Pick,* Chase drew a series of tattoos. "The tattoos were designed to evoke a part of the body that I thought would tie in with the section title: illustration on the hand, support on the back, and of course, design on the head [not shown]."

One of the enduring hopes of designers everywhere is that recognition by your peers will make everything different. In 1993, Chase was featured in *Communication Arts* Magazine. "When it happened I was really excited. I thought it would change things, make getting work easier and maybe even make clients listen more to my opinions. It didn't. My strongest sensation after the article came out was one of anticlimax. I realized I hadn't planned what had happened, it had just happened, and I had no idea how to plan what to do next."

TEAMWORK Over the years, Chase has worked to expand her business. She took the big step of hiring her first assistant in 1985 and over the years, a number of designers have lent their talents to her quest. "I have a strong vision, so I have to be careful not to micromanage things. I look for people who have a strong vision that's different from mine. I think that helps to broaden the work and keep things from being stale and repetitious, not to mention keeping me inspired as well. I also look for designers who have strong hand skills and don't only think on the computer."

After learning how to lead creative enterprises came the need to face business realities. "I finally confronted the fact that I'm naturally terrible as a business person. I much prefer to be left alone with my creative team

"THINGS ARE STILL CHALLENGING AND DIFFICULT.
THE BIGGEST DIFFERENCE IS KNOWING THAT, NO MATTER HOW BAD THINGS GET,
I PROBABLY WON'T STARVE TO DEATH. EVEN MY PARENTS ARE CONVINCED NOW."

1979   1981   1984   1987   1988   1989

Matteo, product design (left) Expanding on her role as a graphic designer, Chase went beyond designing the identity and collateral for Matteo, a manufacturer of fine linens. She also tackled product and showroom design.

Perdu, banners and logo (right and below, right) When asked to design the stores for Lingerie Perdu, a retail store in Jeddah, Saudi Arabia, Chase was forbidden by local custom to show female bodies or this company's product. For two duratrans posters, part of the store environment, she translated the sexual allure of the lingerie into sinewy typographic abstractions using a font with both Western and Arabic character sets that she had designed for the brand.

to get the work done, so in the past the planning and finances always got left to manage themselves, which does not work well. It's been tough to find good support for the business side, but I've got two really strong business people working with me now. I couldn't live without them."

BEYOND GRAPHIC DESIGN By the mid-'90s Chase was getting bored working almost exclusively on music and entertainment assignments. She tried expanding into other areas, only to be faced once again with the drawbacks of a well-defined image: "Everyone thought I was the queen of Goth. They were afraid they would get something creepy if they hired me."

An opportunity presented itself in the form of Matteo, a manufacturer of bed linens. While she was initially hired only to design their logo and stationery, Chase's assignment soon grew to include packaging. "We were almost finished with that when their textile designer quit. The owner asked me if I'd like to take a stab at textile design." So Chase took a crash course in manufacturing: Matteo's owner sent her to visit the jacquard mills outside of Bergamo. "As usual I did as much reading and studying as I could to understand the process." Being thus prepared Chase ended up handling Matteo's product design for the next five years. In the end, she even took over the design of their trade show booths, display furniture, and Matteo's New York showroom.

Today, Margo Chase remains a powerful presence in the entertainment industry. While exploring ever further outside its borders, she continues to create products and environments that are seen the world over. When asked whether she feels she is successful now, she responds "I know that I'm successful, but it doesn't feel very different from when I wasn't. Things are still challenging and difficult in the same and different ways. I guess the biggest difference is knowing that, no matter how bad things get, I probably won't starve to death. Even my parents are convinced now. ❦

LINGERIE *perdu*

Cher, *Living Proof,* tour book Returning once again to one of her most famous clients, Chase designed the logo and tour book for Cher's Living Proof Farewell Tour 2002.

1991
33

1992
34

1997
39

2000
42

NOW

117

Charles Mingus, *Changes One, Changes Two,* record sleeves
"One of my first pieces to be produced, this was the first time
I worked with big wood type. It took me hours to do the mechanicals—
something that could be done in ten minutes today on a computer."

1974   1976   NOW

PAULA SCHER

After establishing herself early on as a designer of record sleeves—
and predicting that her epitaph would read "She designed the *Boston*
cover"—Paula Scher has taken over New York with her exuberant
and kinetic typography for the Public Theater and other cultural institutions.

Paula Scher is an East Coast native. "I was born in Virginia, then my family moved to Maryland.
I grew up in the suburbs, where every house looked the same." One of her earliest visual memories
was seeing the record cover for the 1949 Broadway cast recording of the musical *South Pacific*
in her parents' record collection. "I remember seeing this picture of an anchor, with Mary Martin's face
fitting perfectly into the anchor shape. I remember liking it." Scher always felt that she wanted to be
an artist, but it took her a while to rule out her other options. "I knew, but I didn't know what a graphic
designer was. I also wanted to be a singer-dancer-piano player-bareback rider."

It was her knack for drawing that soon led her to focus on art. "It was probably around the time I was
10 years old. I had always drawn by myself, off in my room. When I got to junior high, I became known
as the school artist. In the sixth grade, I did a transportation mural in a hallway at school. I had the
highways going backward, so my teacher teased me that I was British." Scher enjoyed the artist's life.
"I found it was the only thing at which I was really good. In junior high and high school, I took Saturday
art courses. I felt at home. The lifestyle was part of it, too. It was how I felt." Her art teachers recognized
her talent and encouraged her. Scher still remembers an early honor. "In high school one of my teachers,
Mr. Tucker, hung a 'Picture of the Week' in a glass display case—a lot of them were mine." During
this time she got more and more interested in graphic design and remembers being fascinated by great
album covers, "especially the Beatles' *Sgt. Pepper* and *Revolver* and Cream's *Disraeli Gears*."

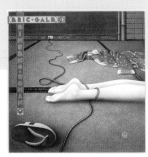

Leonard Bernstein, *Poulenc, Stravinsky,* record sleeve "For this cover, we produced and photographed an actual piece of stained glass fabricated by Nick Fasciano. Today, one would assume an image like this had been digitally manipulated in Photoshop."

Eric Gale, *Ginseng Woman,* record sleeve "The illustrator is David Wilcox. This cover was nominated for a Grammy Award and provided my first experience with politically correct interpretations of imagery after NOW cited it as an example of violent depictions of women. CBS was happy to point out it was designed by a woman."

Gary Graffman, *Bartók, Prokofiev, Lees,* record sleeve "In school, my teacher Stanislaw Zagorski showed me how to illustrate with type, and as an art director, I would follow the content by echoing it with typography. Most of the typographic covers I designed were for classical and jazz albums. They forced me to become adept at working in every period and style of typography."

Boston, *Boston,* record sleeve "Friends have joked that my epitaph will read 'She designed the *Boston* cover.' It's funny the way this image has resurfaced later in my career. A younger generation of clients and designers actually think this is cool, even if it's in an ironical sense."

LOVE IN THE TIME OF SWISS INTERNATIONAL Scher's transition into art school was seamless. "I went to the Corcoran School of Art in Washington, DC, for classes in junior high and high school, then I went to college at the Tyler School of Art in Philadelphia. In college I tried fine arts and crafts—pottery and sculpture—but I was bad at everything except graphic design. I had to take a general design course freshman year, and I learned about Basel and the Swiss international style, but I was too sloppy for it. Then sophomore year I took a graphic design course with a teacher named Steve Tarantel who showed me it was more about ideas than execution."

"In school I didn't understand type and rebelled against the Swiss international style. It felt like being made to clean my room. I did not have an appreciation or understanding for the nuances of ordered typography or the rules that applied to it. But I understood illustration, so a teacher, Stanislaw Zagorski, advised me to try illustrating with type." Zagorski was an eminent record cover designer, whose credit appears on such albums as the Velvet Underground's *Loaded* and Cream's *Wheels of Fire.* It's easy to see the influence of his work and his teaching in Scher's output in the years to come.

MAKING RECORDS Following graduation, Scher moved to New York and took a job laying out children's books for Random House. Next, she spent two years designing ads for CBS Records, before becoming an art director for Atlantic Records in 1973. "A year later I was offered a job as an art director in the cover department back at CBS. I took the job because there were more projects to design."

"THE GREATEST EFFECT MY EARLY EMPLOYERS HAD ON ME WAS SHOWING ME HOW TO GET SOMETHING MADE. WORKING IN A LARGE CORPORATION FORCED ME TO LEARN HOW TO DEFEND MY IDEAS TO THE PEOPLE WHO ACTUALLY HAD THE POWER TO GET THEM PRODUCED."

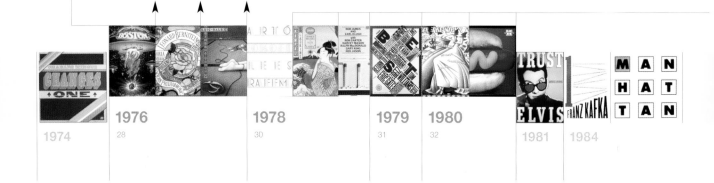

1974

1976
28

1978
30

1979
31

1980
32

1981

1984

Jean-Pierre Rampal and Lily Laskine, *Sakura: Japanese Melodies for Flute and Harp,* **record sleeve** "I actually prefer the back of this cover—graphically, it was unusual at the time because the typography is detailed, without any underlying image."

Dance the Night Away, **record sleeve** "This cover was one of my most successful integrations of type and image. In my covers, I liked to integrate typography into the image because it made the image look larger and more posterlike. The illustration is by John O'Leary."

Bob James and Earl Klugh, *One on One* (above, left) **Bob James** *H* (above, right) **record sleeves** "My record covers for Bob James and his Tappan Zee label were all simple American icons blown up to be larger than life. The most successful in the series was *One on One,* for which the matchbook became the entire package." Two of her covers for James received Grammy nominations—*Heads* in 1978 and *One on One* in 1980—bringing her total count to four, following her double nomination for *Ginseng Woman* and *Yardbirds Favorites* in 1977.

During her time working for CBS and Atlantic, Scher was responsible for hundreds of designs, and even the few examples shown here illustrate the mixed blessing of designing for a major record label: Every cover must be different. This dictum doesn't make it easy to develop a personal voice, but it opens up a great stylistic playground. Although the cover for the band Boston's eponymous first album has become a pop culture icon, thanks to adorning one of the best-selling records of all time, it would be hard to call it an aesthetic bellwether for Scher. Instead, her work on records illustrates her growing skill with expressive typography and iconic images. "I would follow the content by echoing it with typography. Most of the typographic covers I designed were for classical and jazz albums. They forced me to become adept at working in every period and style of typography."

Scher sums up this first part of her professional life: "I started in the CBS Records art department when John Berg was there. He showed me that you could do something of quality and have it be produced. The greatest effect my early employers had on me was showing me how to get something made. Working in a large corporation such as CBS forced me to learn how to defend my ideas to the people who actually had the power to get them produced. I still use this knowledge today."

The Best of Jazz, **poster** "For this poster, I organized wood type at angles and tangents in a Russian Constructivist manner and had it printed on kraft paper. At the time the design looked radically different, but it was eventually embraced and widely imitated and got me labeled a postmodernist."

1988   1994   1995   1996   1999   2000   2001   2003   NOW

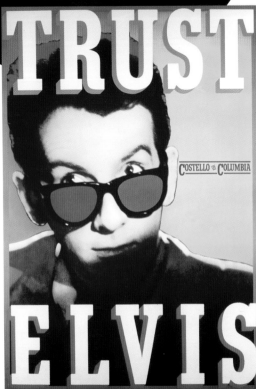

Great Beginnings, spreads from a promotional brochure for Koppel & Scher (above and opposite) "When my friend Terry Koppel and I went into business together in 1984, we believed our best asset was our expressive use of typography. To promote ourselves we designed this small book consisting of the beginnings of famous novels, designed in the style of the period in which the novels had been written. The piece was remarkably successful, but it inadvertently became a catalog of style for clients searching for one look or another."

KOPPEL & SCHER Scher eventually left CBS and, after a brief period of working as a freelancer, set up shop with her friend Terry Koppel, establishing the firm of Koppel & Scher in 1984. With her own name on the door, Scher continued to design for the music industry, but she now had the freedom to expand her canvas. Book covers were a logical extension of her earlier work, as was developing corporate identities. Her 1988 designs for the Swedish candy manufacturer Öola clearly carry in them the beginnings of her current work. She used the dynamic typography she had honed on countless record sleeves and translated into a range of packages. She even made letterforms part of the store architecture, with a giant Ö window, foreshadowing the large-scale environmental graphics she recently created for clients such as the New Jersey Performing Arts Center and the Cooper-Hewitt National Design Museum. "The client treated me like a full-fledged collaborator. From this project on I decided that marketing departments should work for me, not the other way around."

Manhattan Records, identity (above, top) "With this project I became interested in what a company's visual identity should look like in its entirety, not just the small corner that housed the logotype. In my research I came across the Mondrian painting, *Broadway Boogie-Woogie.* Apart from its connection to Manhattan, the painting's color blocks could easily be reconfigured for a whole program of collateral."

Trust Elvis, poster (above, bottom) "This was a fast, cheap poster that quickly took on a life of its own after Brett Easton Ellis included a description of it in his seminal '80s novel *Less Than Zero.* I hand-colored the glasses myself on a photo-stat."

1974   1976   1978   1979   1980

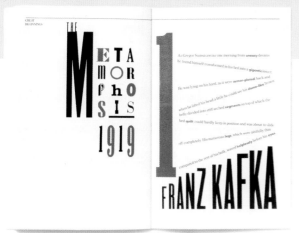

Öola, identity and packaging (below) "This was the first project to really show me what it was like to create a brand. I came up with the name for this Scandinavian candy company breaking into the U.S. market and designed the packaging and the stores."

Swatch Swiss campaign, poster "This poster was a visual joke—a parody—of a famous poster by Herbert Matter. But Tibor Kalman later identified it as an example of 'jive modernism,' and it became the focal point of the controversy over 'borrowed style' in the '80s."

Real Estate, **book cover** This early book cover shows how Scher experimented with truly illustrative typography, establishing another link between her record covers and her later poster work.

"I DECIDED THAT MARKETING DEPARTMENTS SHOULD WORK FOR ME, NOT THE OTHER WAY AROUND."

PENTAGRAM GOES PUBLIC Having established herself in the corporate arena, Scher took the next step in her career in 1991, when she accepted a partnership in Pentagram's New York office. Her move coincided with the desktop publishing revolution. "The act of designing became something you did on the computer. After this my work became less ornate—but quicker and more direct. I think this had less to do with the speed of the computer than with my impatience for the technology."

At Pentagram, Scher was hired to rebrand New York's Public Theater after the death of founder Joseph Papp. Papp's productions had been strongly identified with posters produced by Push Pin artist Paul Davis. The Public's new producer, George C. Wolfe, hoped to establish the theater's continued existence by presenting a provocative new look that caught people's attention. What followed was a hallmark collaboration between

1988   1994   1995   1996   1999   2000   2001   2003   NOW

The Diva Is Dismissed, **poster** "Designing for the Public Theater demands fast, instinctual solutions, which is how I work best. My identity and posters for the Public were initially designed to make it popular, to appeal to new audiences, and to make an impression on the street."

Him, poster Christopher Walken wrote and starred in *Him,* a play about Elvis Presley. Because Walken's only physical impression of the King involved adopting his iconic pompadour, that's what made the poster.

Bring In 'Da Noise, Bring In 'Da Funk, posters for the original off-Broadway production "The Public posters were designed to be sniped in multiple on the streets. Unfortunately, there was never enough of a budget to accomplish this, so most of the posters were seen →

designer and client that led to some of Scher's best-loved and most recognized work, such as her posters for the musical *Bring In 'Da Noise, Bring In 'Da Funk.*

Scher continues to work with the Public to this day and cherishes her relationship with the theater. In a way, creating diverse images for the various plays while staying true to an overall identity is a reprise of her early work for CBS and Atlantic Records, albeit in a more high-minded arena. "Designing for the Public Theater demands fast, instinctual solutions, which is how I work best. My identity and posters for the Public were initially designed to make it popular, to appeal to new audiences—to make an impression on the street. Over the years I've had to change the formula to make the most impact—some seasons the posters have gotten quiet when other advertising has gotten loud. My long-term collaboration with the Public's producer George C. Wolfe remains my best professional relationship."

CREATIVE GROWTH Over the course of her career, Scher has developed a way of treating letterforms in an illustrative way that is easily identified as hers, yet she dismisses any talk of a signature style. "I'm always disappointed at my own limitations. I have a limited talent. So what you're describing as a signature style—

1974   1976   1978   1979   1980   1981   1984

only at the Public. The exception was the campaign for the musical *Bring In 'Da Noise, Bring In 'Da Funk*. For a time the design seemed to be everywhere, and it became a kind of visual shorthand for Broadway and the city itself."

Dancing on Her Knees, poster After the frenetic typography of *Bring In 'Da Noise, Bring In 'Da Funk*, Scher went back to a simple, dramatic composition for the Nilo Cruz play *Dancing on Her Knees*.

Hamlet, poster Scher's poster for the Public Theater's production of *Hamlet* focuses on the essential, showing a pensive image of lead actor Liev Schreiber.

I think these are expressions of my limited talent, my klutziness. I compensate for the lack of talent by being obsessive, and that's what I've developed with my typography."

Interesting things happen when vision tries to move beyond the barrier of ability. "There is this point where you do something that looks weird and impossible and *right*, all at the same time. You're comfortable enough looking at it, but it didn't exist before. There's that tension. For me, it seems to happen when I'm doing something wrong." Yet these moments aren't a daily occurrence. "There are leaps of discovery, and then things level out. I go through six-month periods of no talent. It's happened throughout my career. I'll be dry for ideas or not happy with what I'm doing. I can usually make up for it with knowledge of design. It's safe work—no mistakes, but no breakthroughs, either. Fertile and fallow—it happens to everyone."

"THERE IS THIS POINT WHERE YOU DO SOMETHING THAT LOOKS WEIRD AND IMPOSSIBLE AND *RIGHT*, ALL AT THE SAME TIME. YOU'RE COMFORTABLE ENOUGH LOOKING AT IT, BUT IT DIDN'T EXIST BEFORE. THERE'S THAT TENSION. FOR ME, IT SEEMS TO HAPPEN WHEN I'M DOING SOMETHING WRONG

1988

1994
46

1995
47

1996
48

1999
51

2001

2003

NOW

New 42nd Street Studios/The Duke Theater, identity and environmental graphics (above, left) "Charles Platt designed a new building that contains a space housing rehearsal studios and a small theater, located just off of Times Square. I thought of the space as a 'factory' for performance. I made graphics inspired by De Stijl perform in the halls and stairwells of the building. Words start on the floor and run up the walls. The activity and bright color of the graphics is set off against the minimalism of the rehearsal studios."

New Jersey Performing Arts Center, Lucent Technologies Center for Arts Education, environmental graphics (above, right) "This school of the performing arts is located in downtown Newark, New Jersey. The building, originally a rectory, was drab and imposing. NJPAC wanted to project a warmer personality, but they could not afford a major architectural renovation. I covered the building in typography that describes what was going on inside. It quickly—and cheaply—gave the school a distinctive identity and turned it into a neighborhood landmark."

Inside Design Now **at the Cooper-Hewitt National Design Museum, installation at the National Design Triennial** Ellen Lupton, one of the curators, selected me for the exhibition and wanted to focus on my recent architectural work. She suggested I design signage for the show, which was split between the two floors of the museum. I decided to marry my painting with directional signage and drew graphics for directional rugs and the inside and outside of the elevator. My map painting, *The United States,* also hung in the section."

Henry V, **poster** "I've played with the format of my posters for the summer Shakespeare Festival in Central Park. The 2003 production was *Henry V.* I had already designed a poster using a big *V* when the festival presented the play in 1996. This time around I made it a giant *5.* The play is about war, so I used a passage from the text that resonated with the situation in Iraq at the time."

> " I'M INTERESTED IN ARCHITECTURE
> AND GRAPHICS AND IN MARRYING THE TWO
> TO CREATE A NEW KIND OF INSTITUTIONAL IDENTITY."

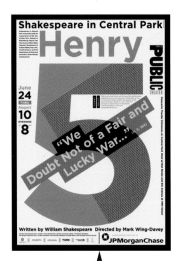

ARCHITECTURE AND CARTOGRAPHY In recent years, Scher has made another leap forward, expanding into environmental graphics, making her typography part of her clients' buildings, and creating some of her most impressive and joyful designs in the process. "I'm interested in architecture and graphics and in marrying the two to create a new kind of institutional identity." She has also invested herself in painting, growing intricate typographic grids into wall-size maps that can only be fully appreciated when one stands in front of them, reeling from the overwhelming amount of information and the thought of the time invested. The paintings are a monument to the power of obsessive-compulsive disorder, yet they also manage to stay light, open, and graceful. Scher explains: "The paintings are a reaction to the corporate work, the nature of which involves meetings and computers. In work like this, I frequently have little sense of being in control—there's no sense of touch, of that immediacy. So the paintings have become another outlet for me. They are emotional, spontaneous, and unplanned. They contain a ton of information, and I have total control. They don't have any pretense of being accurate. I find joy in their being wrong." Scher continues to evolve her work both in the context of Pentagram and in her personal artwork, discovering new ways of typographic expression. Her mission is simple and hasn't changed since her early days of making record covers: "I'm always looking for more to design." ✌

1974   1976   1978   1979   1980   1981   1984

Africa, **painting** Ever denser layers of freehand typography crystallize into a map of Africa in one of Scher's obsessive yet utterly elegant paintings.

1988   1994   1995   1996   1999   2000   2001   2003   NOW
                                            52   53   55

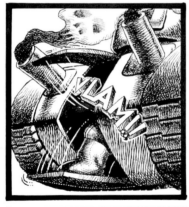

MIRKO ILIĆ

Coming of age in Communist Yugoslavia, Mirko Ilić used his work as a means of self-expression and political action that was simultaneously covert and highly visible. After moving to New York, he found that his time of resistance wasn't over.

Mirko Ilić was born an only child in Bosnia in 1956. His father served in the military; his mother worked at home as a seamstress. Ilić discovered his gift early and immediately realized its power. At the tender age of three, he used one of his mother's fabric markers to draw on the kitchen floor. She quickly discovered the unsolicited artwork; instead of yelling, she found a piece of carpet to cover up the drawing so she could show it to her husband. To this day Ilić remembers his parents standing over the drawing and talking to each other in a distinctly positive whisper.

A little while later, he drew a horse and carriage in one of his grandfather's books and found once again that he was praised for his transgression. He had discovered that drawing provided a way to express himself and get the approval he desired at the same time. From that point on, his talent was nurtured by his mother and by his teachers. "Between the ages of twelve and fourteen, I discovered that drawing was the easiest thing to do for me, so I went into that direction more and more."

RELOCATION His father's military postings forced the family to move four times over the course of Ilić's childhood. "I found myself in four different elementary schools, in different parts of the country, with different customs and ethnicity." Ilić was harassed for his accent and his heritage. Peaceful resistance was not a viable option. The only way to escape was to beat up somebody at each new school to immediately establish his position. He was thus forced to balance his artistic side with a tough attitude that would protect him in new surroundings.

Slikovnica Za Diktatore (Dictators Picture Book), **comic strip** *Dictators Picture Book* was the first comic Ilić ever published. "I was playing with sounds. Every image has some form of sound or noise. It was heavily influenced by the US underground comics."

1974   **1998**   **NOW**

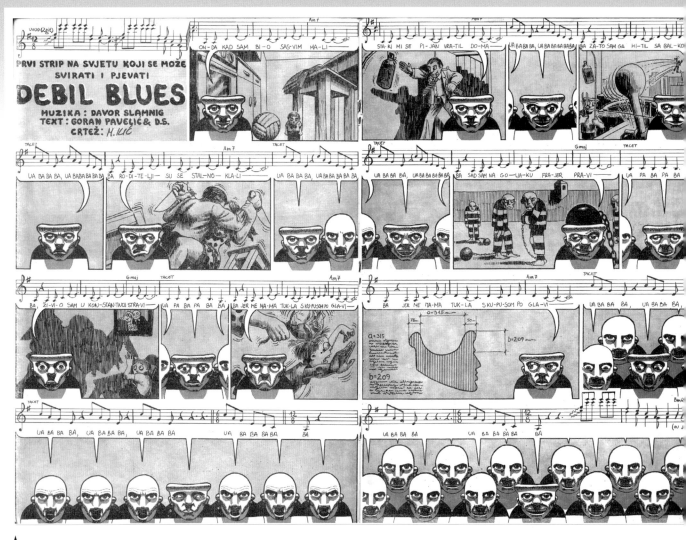

Debil Blues, comic strip "The first comics that you could sing and play along to," says Ilić of this 1976 strip. Again, he is preoccupied with sound but has evolved to a much higher level of sophistication in the two years since *Dictators Picture Book*.

" I BROUGHT THE EDITORS A BUNCH OF MY DRAWINGS AND LEFT THEM THERE. I NEVER BOTHERED TO SIGN MY WORK— EITHER IN THE FRONT OR BACK. TWO WEEKS LATER ONE OF MY DRAWINGS WAS PUBLISHED WITHOUT MY NAME."

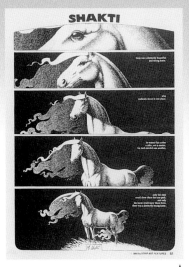

Ilić honed his skills throughout his teenage years and soon found a bigger audience. "The first time an illustration of mine was published was in a youth paper in Croatia. I was seventeen years old at the time. I brought the editors a bunch of my drawings and left them there. I never bothered to sign my work—either in the front or back. Two weeks later one of my drawings, of a mother with a child, was published without my name." After this first anonymous publication, he continued to place his work in youth papers and children's magazines and was paid for his art for the first time.

During his summer vacations and throughout his last semester in high school he interned at Zagreb Film, the home of some of Yugoslavia's leading animators, working on animations for TV commercials and corporations. "I spent most of my time there, working on projects instead of attending school."

ART SCHOOL After he graduated from high school, Ilić resisted his father's wish that he attend the military academy and instead enrolled at the School of Applied Arts in Zagreb. There he received classical training and honed his technique. By the time he graduated five years later, he was able to back his concepts with the masterful craftsmanship that remains one of the hallmarks of his work today. Looking at his work from this period, it is shocking to know that he applied to the graduate program at the art academy in Zagreb and was rejected. He was accepted by the Academy of Applied Art in Belgrade but never attended. He was ready to move on.

DISSENTING VIEWS After working as a freelancer for various magazines throughout his school years, contributing illustrations and comics, Ilić wanted to stretch his wings. "My first big achievement was in 1976, when I became an editor of comics and illustration in the youth paper *Polet*. The paper had quite a large effect on the society. Inside the paper I formed a group of comic artists called *Novi Kvadrat* (New Square). This put us on the map: We started getting awards and appearing on TV. In the process I became a local celebrity."

Shakti, comic (above, left) This 1977 comic about a "distinctly beautiful and strong horse" showed Ilić diving into the realm of fantasy comics with gusto and aplomb.

Consumer Pushed to Consume, illustration (above, middle) After seeing the work of illustrator Brad Holland in an issue of *Graphis*, Ilić felt he could have a bigger impact as an illustrator than as a comic book artist.

Narcissism, illustration (above, right) Ilić was twenty-two when he created this illustration of a man and his dog for *Start Magazine,* showing off his ever increasing virtuosity.

Prljavo Kazaliste/Dirty Theater, record sleeve (below) "The second LP cover I did. It was for a punk band. On this album, one of the songs was a parody of the song *Some Girls* by the Rolling Stones, called *Some Boys.* That's the idea behind the cover."

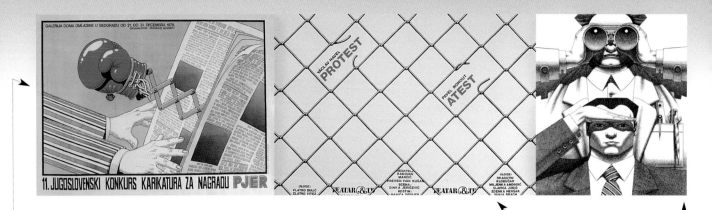

Jugoslavenski Konkurs Karikatura za Nagradu Pjer, illustration (above, left) Whenever Ilić managed to sneak a critical illustration past party censors, people would stop him on the street to offer him a round on them. However, he didn't drink alcohol.

Protest Atest, poster (above, middle) This 1979 poster showed Ilić becoming more openly political in his work, as well as more sophisticated in his use of typography.

Knowledge at Higher Prices, illustration (above, right) "This particular piece is a comment on the future of education. The man looking through the binoculars is looking at the future with a scientific approach; the other man is looking at it from a political point of view."

Buoyed by the recognition and inspired by artists like Roman Cieslewicz, Boris Bucan, and Brad Holland, Ilić began expanding his work from comics into illustration. His focus in both media became more and more political. After growing up directly exposed to the military and the country's political system, he saw it as his job to make sport of those in power—an attitude he maintains to this day. Tackling political subjects put him on the radar of government censors, and he had to tread carefully. "You had to calibrate your images. It would've been easy to end up in jail. The challenge was to make images that were on the edge—and to get them published. You could get away with illustrations as long as they could be explained in different ways." Due to this strategic ambiguity, illustrators were on a longer leash than writers, so Ilić felt that it was necessary for him and his peers to use their limited freedom to do political art—to register their dissent. Comparing his situation then with the challenges he encounters today, he draws this analogy: "In Yugoslavia, art was like hockey. Here in the United States, it's more like figure skating."

Ilić soon found an international audience. In the beginning of 1978, the Italian comic magazine *Alter Alte* ran the first Ilić strip outside of Yugoslavia. "After that, I started publishing work all around Europe in such magazines as *Metal Hurlant, 1984,* and *Epic*." Beginning in 1979, his work also appeared in publications such as *Pardon* in Germany and *Panorama* in Italy, and ultimately found its way into the U.S. underground comics cathedral, *Heavy Metal.* "I started getting offers for quite a lot of money, but this meant producing a certain number of pieces per month. What started out as a childhood dream and enjoyment turned into a job and a nightmare. I sensed that publishers wanted to get involved in my comics, even during negotiations. All of a sudden I could see that my work would be directed by them. That is when I decided to give it up. I did my last comic in 1981 or 1982."

Throughout the early '80s, Ilić kept busy designing posters for theater and film, as well as hundreds of record and magazine covers. In 1982, he and his colleague Luka Mjeda produced nearly 180 covers for the weekly *Danas* alone. Business was booming, but Ilić was restless. He had achieved a lot in Yugoslavia; now he was eager to compete internationally. "I wanted to see where I was in comparison to the real world." On March 26, 1986, he moved to New York City.

"IN YUGOSLAVIA, ART WAS LIKE HOCKEY. HERE IN THE UNITED STATES, IT'S MORE LIKE FIGURE SKATING."

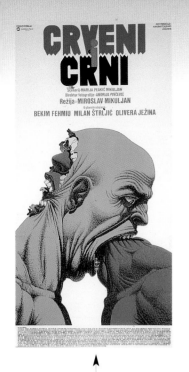

Rcrveni I Crni/Red and Black, **movie poster** (above, left) Ilić received an award from the *Hollywood Reporter* for this stunning 1985 movie poster. The international attention he received set the stage for his move to New York the following year.

Worrisome World of Work, magazine cover (above, middle) "This is one of many covers that I did for the magazine *Today* during the three and a half years I worked there. I was art-directing and illustrating the covers." Working in Communist Yugoslavia "you had to calibrate your images. The challenge was to make images that were on the edge—and to get them published. You could get away with illustrations that you could explain in multiple ways. The apparatchiks would ask me 'What does this mean?' and I'd give them a completely unexpected explanation. The explanation to the apparatchik (who was the editor): The issue celebrated May 1st, an important international holiday for workers. When they asked me what this cover meant I said the symbols of the hammer and sickel represent a smiley face with a cigar, the happy worker. In reality I was making fun of the symbols as being identified with the workers."

Terrorism and Mafia, magazine cover (above, right) Ilić art-directed this photo illustration by photographer Luka Mjeda with Franko Lefevre for the Italian magazine *Panorama.*

CHANGE OF VENUE Only one week later, Ilić went to meet one of his idols, Milton Glaser. The meeting had been set up by Gloria Steinem, who was a friend of Ilić's first wife and had worked with Glaser at the magazines *New York* and *Ms.* Glaser was impressed by Ilić's strong ideas, his political and cultural convictions, as well as his exceptional technical skills. Two days after their meeting, Glaser sent Ilić a list of art directors to contact about assignments. Glaser had marked the ones he had already called with a recommendation. Ilić and Glaser became fast friends and are currently hard at work writing their first book together.

Adopted by American design royalty, Ilić was asked to create a cover for *Time* magazine— not a bad first job for somebody who arrived on a new continent only the week before. Still, it wasn't necessarily a dream come true. Ilić was greatly surprised by the differences in the process in the United States: He had never been asked to supply roughs before. What shocked him even more was not that his illustration was rejected but that the editor had hired three illustrators to work up sketches simultaneously. The whole affair put him off balance, and he felt certain that he would never find work in New York. But his luck turned and his first scratchboard illustration appeared in the *New York Times* a week later.

The need to publish is a recurring theme for Ilić. He almost never creates artwork that wasn't commissioned, and if he does, he'll find a way to get it printed anyway. If he had to choose between selling an illustration for a lot of money and having it hidden away in a private collection, or accepting a tiny fee and seeing the piece published, he always prefers the latter. When I asked him where he hoped to go in the future, he replied "The Rich Man's Land." But it is clear that Ilić lacks the particular talent to sell out. By his own admission it's too late for him. "I couldn't do it if I tried."

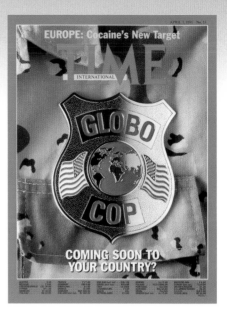

Time, **magazine covers** While serving as art director of the international edition of *Time,* Ilić introduced his conceptual, highly editorial covers to a global audience.

TYPECASTING During his first years in New York, Ilić firmly established his presence by contributing scores of editorial illustrations and cover designs to major magazines and newspapers. He initially executed many of them in his elaborate scratchboard method but changed to other styles when he felt that he was being typecast as "Eastern European Artist specializing in politics, doing scratchboard." Ilić isn't attached to any one style. He balances his perfectionism with a desire to find the shortest connection between the image in his head and the illustration on the page. When the Macintosh developed to the point of being a useful tool for him in the late '80s and early '90s, he eagerly embraced the technology. He now finishes most of his work digitally, though he still sketches out every piece first.

STANDING ON THE BIG SOAPBOX By 1991, Ilić's work had already made the cover of *Time* magazine numerous times when he was asked to take over as art director for the international edition. "The funny thing is becoming the art director at *Time International* was my first full-time job. I had never designed magazines until then, either. After three years of helping them with cover ideas that would sometimes be executed by other people, they asked me to work for them—not so much because of my technical and design abilities, but because of my interest and understanding of foreign affairs." It was a brilliant position for Ilić, but once on staff, he chafed at the office politics and decided to quit his post after only six months.

A few months later, the *New York Times* offered Ilić the job of art-directing its op-ed page. By then the war in his native Bosnia was in full force. "I took that job to raise people's awareness, to show that if this can happen in Bosnia, it can happen anywhere." Having learned from his experience with *Time,* Ilić accepted the job but told his new employer he would leave after a year and a half. He felt that it was enough time to explore the artistic possibilities and that remaining a visitor would insulate him from internal power struggles. Working for the *Times* also gave Ilić an excuse to work with some of his illustration heroes. "It gave me a reason to call them and talk to them on the phone. On the other hand, I also had the chance to assign jobs to young illustrators, giving them their first job and publishing them for the first time."

New York Times, op-ed pages Ilić served as the art director for the *New York Times'* op-ed page for six months in 1992 and 1993. These examples—"All You Do Is Just Sit Down" and "The Elements Defy Hungry Zimbabwe"—show his whimsical but graphically powerful use of the whole page as an illustrative medium. Milan Trenc illustrated the turkey; Ruth Martin contributed the Zimbabweans peering into the abyss.

"BECOMING THE ART DIRECTOR AT *TIME INTERNATIONAL* WAS MY FIRST FULL-TIME JOB.

I HAD NEVER DESIGNED MAGAZINES UNTIL THEN, EITHER."

1985	1990	1991	1992	2002	2003	NOW
	34	35	36			

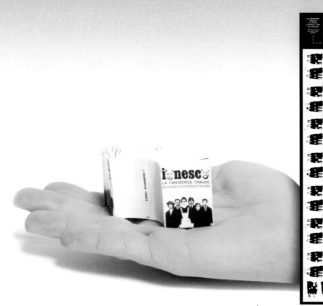

***Massin,* poster and book assembled from poster** "The poster's subject, Massin, designed *La Cantatrice Chauve,* which became his seminal work. This poster reproduces every spread of the book in miniature and includes diagrams on how to cut out and assemble your very own copy."

"EUREKA MOMENTS OCCUR RARELY. IT'S MORE LIKE AN ACCUMULATION OF EXPERIENCE. YOU THINK AND SOMETHING STARTS TO FALL INTO PLACE— A SUDDEN INSPIRATION."

FIGHTING THE GOOD FIGHT Following his stint at the *Times,* he opened Mirko Ilić Corp., setting up shop in Milton Glaser's building on 32nd Street. The pair have taught at Cooper Union together, and Ilić still conducts graduate classes in illustration at the School of Visual Arts. He remains a perfectionist. "When a client or printer does something wrong, I get upset, but the worst is when I do something wrong. Here I mean not something wrong as in experimental but plain, stupid mistakes—when you screw up because you overlooked something and did not pay close attention. Then I feel like chewing myself up alive. It is hard to face up to the fact that one is not perfect." Accordingly, he sees inspiration not as a divine spark but as a reward for time served. "I think eureka moments occur rarely. It's more like an accumulation of experience. You think and something starts to fall into place—a sudden inspiration. I don't think there can be any eureka moments for a person who has never designed before."

A unifying factor in Ilić's work is his need for resistance. Resistance, be it artistic or technical, corporate or political, ignites Ilić to do his best work. "I would like a society in which there is no need for design of dissent. That will be utopia." But he knows better. "I would probably have to consider a career change." ✌

1974   1976   1977   1978   1979   1980

Sex & Lies, illustrations (top row) In a puritan society, sex is political. Therefore, it comes as no surprise that Ilić tackled the subject in a series of more than thirty hypersexual illustrations. "It's an ongoing piece of work. Several of the images were published and used for various purposes."

Slobodna Dalmacija, **newspaper design and poster campaign** (bottom row) *Slobodna Dalmacija* is a daily newspaper published in Split in Dalmacia. In the late '80s, the formerly Communist paper changed its direction to reflect the country's changing political climate and even spawned a satirical supplement. Ilić gave the paper a major facelift in 2003.

2002
46

2003
47

NOW

137

1985   1990   1991   1992

WHO'S

NEXT?

2001

HARMINE LOUWÉ

Harmine Louwé's work manages the rare feat
of being incredibly sophisticated while staying
disarmingly friendly and approachable.
Her design is like a secret agent in a Saville Row suit
who suddenly starts throwing paper planes at you.
Over the years she has worked as a graphic ghostwriter
on some of the most visually advanced advertising
campaigns around. But her heart belongs
to the more cultural, ambitious work she produces
under her own name.

ONVZ, annual report The title of the report translates into *a year and
a life.* "It describes a year in the history of a Dutch health insurance
company and the whole life of a man. Photographer Bertien van Manen
went on a trip to France with the man we selected to be portrayed
in the report. He fit the description of average schooling, average income,
average weight/looks and so on. The photographer and the victim
were locked up together in a summerhouse for two weeks. Bertien
managed to take a series of very personal photographs of this man
who, of course, turned out to be anything but average." Louwé produced
this piece in collaboration with Kessels Kramer.

Harmine Louwé had a protected childhood: "I was born in The Netherlands in 1962. I grew up with my parents and two younger sisters in a small village in the middle of the country." As she got older she discovered her creative side. "During high school I became aware of my artistic ambitions. When asked about my preference for university-level education, my answer was 'art school' from the very beginning."

When Louwé got ready to go off to college, her choice of major was subject to intense negotiations with her father, who had doubts about his daughter's career choice. "Initially, I did not really know what I wanted to do; I just wanted to participate in all the arts. Later my dream was to become a sculptor. This is where my father stepped in: Art school was an acceptable choice as long as I would end up in a profession that would earn money. My father is not the type of man who likes to take risks. He thought teaching arts would be a good option, but I didn't, so we finally agreed on graphic design."

ART SCHOOL Louwé enrolled at the St. Joost Art Academy in Breda in 1980. "My first year there was a huge revelation. I learned to look at things in a completely different way; teachers were really interested in what I was doing—I loved it." During this time she moved in with her grandmother. "She was the only one who never doubted whether I would get somewhere with my art school diploma."

Louwé took her first step into the profession in 1984, when she interned at BRS in Amsterdam. "It turned out to be catastrophic. Several people told me I made the wrong choice, but I went ahead anyway. Unfortunately, they were right: The design firm worked only on huge identities for big corporations. I was bored to death. If this was to be my future I wanted to have nothing to do with it. Once I was back in school, however, it slowly became clear that it would be possible to work in design in a different way."

Back at St. Joost, she saw her work printed for the first time. "The school had a small offset press, so some of our assignments were printed. The first time my work was printed to be distributed to the rest of the world was when I was in fourth year. The fifth-year students asked me to make the invitation for their final exams exhibition. I don't think I have ever felt as honored again. It was also the first time that the object I made for the invitation was photographed and printed in full color. That blew my mind. I suddenly realized everything could be reproduced and printed. To this day I still get quite excited when my work gets printed, and I try to be at the press."

GOING TO WORK Louwé graduated in 1986, and landed a job working for Gert Dumbar. "It was almost a seamless continuation of being in art school. Gert would let me experiment and play around." She stayed with Dumbar for six years but faced unexpected resistance when she got ready to leave. "Gert openly questioned whether I would be able to pull it off on my own. And, of course, my father did the same thing: 'Why on earth would you leave a steady job? What makes you think you will ever be able to do it on your own?' My first 'eureka' moment came when PTT Telecom, the Dutch telecommunications company, asked me to design a set of phone cards for them, just weeks after I left Studio Dumbar. It was my first big assignment after starting my own business, and those cards put me on the Dutch design map."

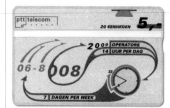
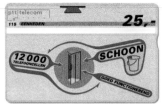
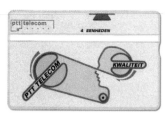

PTT phone cards "These phone cards were my first big assignment as an independent designer in 1992. The different services of PTT Telecom available to the public were to be the theme of these cards. I struggled with this idea for a long time. Finally, I decided to show the process that takes place to make these services work."

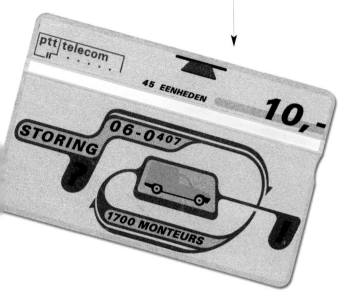

ON ADVERTISING As the years went by, Louwé found more and more work in the advertising industry. In 1994, she was airlifted to Wieden's Portland, Oregon, headquarters three times to work on a Microsoft campaign, and would continue to consult on the account on and off for the next several years. But Louwé doesn't see her advertising experience through rose-colored glasses. "In art school we were brought up thinking advertising was a dirty word. However, when my partner Robert Nakata was hired by Wieden & Kennedy Amsterdam, I realized they weren't necessarily the enemy. At a later point I was asked to do freelance work for Wieden & Kennedy, and I accepted. The money was great. It does take an entirely different attitude to work in an advertising environment, though. During the initial stages I enjoy the jungle of creative directors, art buyers, print producers, traffic people, and whoever else gets involved. At the same time, I hate the ongoing struggle to convince creatives in the advertising world that graphic designers can be more than just corporate beautifiers. I should point out, though, that working for a cultural client can be equally frustrating. Some cultural clients already know exactly what they want you to do, which doesn't differ much from what commercial clients want."

ON INDEPENDENCE In 1999, she decided to close her office and took a full-time position at Kessels Kramer. "I was tempted by the idea of being around other people again. Tempted by the thought of big assignments, big budgets, working with good photographers, and looking at the incredible portfolios of people who just walk into the church Kessels Kramer occupies." But once you've had your own studio, it's hard being an employee again. "I lasted only two months: I had to have my independence back." Louwé moved to Amsterdam in 2000, and is now working from home for the first time in her life. "It was lonely and depressing at first, but now it's wonderful." ✺

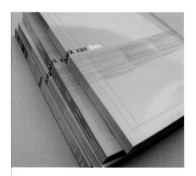

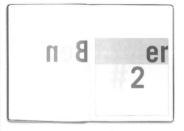

Ben, brochures Louwé created these promotional brochures for Ben, a Dutch mobile phone service provider, under the auspices of the Amsterdam ad agency Kessels Kramer. Please, take a moment to consider the materials you receive from your cell phone company, and think about how we stack up against the Dutch.

Four Seasons, stamps (left) "Since the Dutch postal service was privatized, its marketing department keeps coming up with new ideas to get stamp collectors to spend money. This time they started a series called the 'Four Seasons' stamps. I was asked to design the first set of four stamps in this series. It turned out that not only was the stamps' theme the four seasons but they had to be based on the Dutch landscape as well and, more specifically, on Dutch fruit. And all that on a few square centimeters." Please note the slice of strawberry pie in the top right corner.

Marjan Schoenmakers, poster (right) Artist Marjan Schoenmakers decided to spend time in the center of several roundabouts in Amsterdam with the thought that they can be seen as the eye of the storm. She brought a folding chair and table, photo, video, and audio equipment and collected material for four weeks. "The outcome of all that she dropped on my desk: She wanted to have 'something printed.' We decided that it should be a map of her experiences in the roundabouts. The 27" x 39" (70 cm x 100 cm) sheets are perforated so they can be taken apart into post-cards of 4" x 6" (10 cm x 15 cm). The posters were folded and packaged in pink plastic sleeves," as shown here.

"I WAS TEMPTED BY THE IDEA OF BEING AROUND OTHER PEOPLE AGAIN. TEMPTED BY THE THOUGHT OF BIG ASSIGNMENTS, BIG BUDGETS, WORKING WITH GOOD PHOTOGRAPHERS, AND LOOKING AT INCREDIBLE PORTFOLIOS, BUT ONCE YOU'VE HAD YOUR OWN STUDIO, IT'S HARD BEING AN EMPLOYEE AGAIN."

OpTrek, flyer (below, left) Transvaal is a lively, multicultural neighborhood in The Hague. Of its 17,000 inhabitants, 75 percent are of foreign descent. To deal with its many social problems, the city of The Hague decided to radically restructure Transvaal by means of demolition and new construction. OpTrek is a temporary organization that investigates the changes and consequences of this process. They also initiate and organize art projects.

Z004, cover (below, right) "This is the cover for an agenda that is published by two designers who own a small publishing house called ZOO. Every year they invite another designer to make this agenda. The size is given: 4" x 6" (10 cm x 15 cm), and the theme must relate to time. This Zoo agenda is about 'inner time'—time as we experience it: whimsical and elusive."

DNS
GONZALES
CRISP

Denise Gonzales Crisp went from a series of jobs that left her artistically unfulfilled to creating the visual identity for one of the world's preeminent art schools. She now leads the graphic design department at the University of North Carolina, shaping the next generation of designers.

Sci-Arc Lecture Poster

"Prior to designing this poster for the Southern California Institute of Architecture I had seen a great flamenco performance in San Miguel de Allende. The poster serves many functions for very little cost. In the spirit of the theme 'Transformations,' the four-color image was printed first. Then the fall series lecture information was added. In the spring, the poster was inverted and imprinted with new spring lectures and dates. The poster without the imprint got cut down into thirty-two different postcards with information on the mailing side. I produced all the photography and digital images."

Denise Gonzales Crisp was born in Hanford, California, in 1955, and spent her childhood in the Pasadena area. "My mom grew up in a migrant-worker family that ended up in California picking everything from cotton to peaches to corn. My father, who died when I was quite young, was from an immigrant family from Mexico. By the time I was born, the Gonzales family owned—and with its many children, staffed— a corner market. In my world, art was not an option. My parents supported my artistic bents, but nobody knew how to talk about it in terms of a practice or its earning potential. I painted sporadically, made ceramics, sewed, did crafty stuff, worked on the yearbook. But I was terminally undisciplined and unfocused." Design was clearly in her future, though. She remembers making pop-up greeting cards and family news-letters. "Imagine a 2" x 3" (5.1 cm x 7.6 cm), eight-page gazette with teeny, meticulously lettered headlines and careful lines representing blocks of text."

At seventeen, Gonzales Crisp enrolled at Chico State University in Northern California. "I majored in art for a short time. I got Cs in the few drawing courses I took and had my first experience drawing the nude. I realized I could draw, to my surprise. My stepfather was hell-bent on me going to college. I was the first on either side of my natural family to complete an undergraduate degree, and I'm the only one to have accomplished an advanced degree. My mom made it through the 11th grade and was the first in her family to have a desk job. It was her drive to improve her situation that set me on a better path."

MECHANICALS Her first real contact with graphic design came when she took a job as a front-counter girl and bookkeeper for Bee Line Printers in Reno at the age of twenty and learned to work with the company's machines. "I set type on an IBM compositor and a headliner machine. I became fascinated with what the guys were doing in the back—paste-up; making stats; exposing film; stripping, burning, and developing plates; printing on a little AB Dick 360. The place even had an old iron Kluge that they used to do sequential numbering and blind embossing. My love of design started with the mechanics. It wasn't until much later that I put the machine, the eye, and the conceptual together."

She continued taking classes in college. "I majored in art for only one semester. Other majors were psychology (didn't pass statistics, failed physiology twice), child development, and music therapy." She ultimately flunked out. Mind you, she never failed an art class. "I was just busy doing other (nonacademic) stuff." This was followed by some community college dabbling. "I knew I wanted something in the creative fields but wasn't sure what. I took a basic design course—boring!—a costume design course, one in interior design, and one in creative writing. It turned out that I loved interior design—textures, color, volume, themes— and creative writing the most."

ART CENTER After a few years of exploring her options, Gonzales Crisp was ready to get serious. In 1979, she enrolled in the illustration program at Art Center College of Design in Pasadena. "I loved the painting and drawing. A love of concept and content had been awakened in me. I also fell in love with literature. My basic design course at Art Center was taught by Gene Fleury, a thin, white-haired designer/painter tinted with nicotine. He talked about systems and made us apply them using a ruling pen and gouache, and lectured in such abstract language I thought he was poetic. It wasn't until I started teaching years later that I could appreciate what he was trying to sensitize us to."

Art Center Catalog 1999/2000, cover and spreads "This biennial catalog is Art Center's primary recruiting tool. The 1999/2000 edition is stitched in the center, which creates a structure that circles round and round, suggesting everything from the dot—Art Center's logo—to systems of random access, to a questioning of traditional hierarchies. It effectively eliminates the problem of relegating important information to the back of the book." Gonzales Crisp worked on the catalog with designer Carla Figueroa.

HACK JOBS Back in illustration school, Gonzales Crisp discovered the fine art department and absorbed as much of it as possible. "I aspired to make real art. I thought I would support my habit by being an illustrator in real life. When I graduated I rented a downtown loft with a friend who was a painter. I made some feeble attempts at painting and did my illustration work there. But in the final analysis I realized I couldn't sustain such a lonely— and courageous—existence." Illustration jobs, however, were rolling in. "But editorial doesn't pay much, and I'm not a good business hustler. I worked for *Playgirl, L.A. Weekly, Entrepreneurial Magazine,* and in-flight magazines. All lacked the pith of art, and none had irony."

She returned to printing and got a job as a paste-up artist for a four-color postcard house. From there she moved on to a larger printer before settling as a creative director in an in-house art department. "Just a string of hack jobs." Frustrated, she returned to Art Center for a year's worth of design training in 1989. "After that I worked in real design studios and did freelance work. I was on a standard path—and still not very happy with where I saw myself in ten years."

Her second turn at Art Center also brought Gonzales Crisp her first brush with design fame. Stationery she had designed for her business was recognized by the Art Directors Club of L.A. and was included in the Library of Congress collection. "I pictured my letterhead sitting next to the Constitution. Yea-huh!" Over the years it has become easier for her to get her designs seen. "I realize now that once you're in the network, your work is more likely to be recognized. It's still always an honor—I never take lightly when people value my work." ❧

***Artext* Magazine** Gonzales Crisp tackled the redesign of *art/text* magazine in 1999. She shortened the name to *Artext,* created a new logo system around four swashes, introduced type to the cover, changed the format, and designed a new grid structure. "I personally designed eight issues within two weeks' time each."

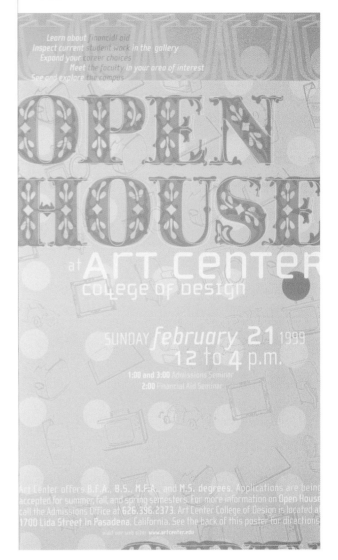

OVER THE YEARS IT HAS BECOME EASIER
FOR GONZALES CRISP TO GET HER DESIGNS SEEN.

"I REALIZE NOW THAT
ONCE YOU'RE IN THE NETWORK,
YOUR WORK IS MORE LIKELY
TO BE RECOGNIZED.
IT'S STILL ALWAYS AN HONOR—
I NEVER TAKE LIGHTLY
WHEN PEOPLE VALUE MY WORK."

Open House, poster "The poster invites high school and community college students to visit the campus. This reference to homey wallpaper creates a pattern representing Art Center's nine departments."

Art Center Catalog 2001/2002 "The 2001/2002 catalog disperses content over five forty-eight-page booklets that are stapled together. The use of patterns evokes diversity, craft, history, and technology, each an important part of visual education. The overarching concept for the catalog locates these aspects within the shared space of purchase and display, between storefront and cultural institution." Yasmin Khan and Ethan Gladstone helped.

Utopian Entrepreneur, book design "Published by MIT Press, this book launched the Mediawork Pamphlet Series. With this design, I established the format and feel for the series—small books targeting 20-something readers that focus on cultural and media issues."

"MY DEVICE OR TECHNIQUE HAS ALWAYS BEEN TO PUT MYSELF SOMEWHERE UNFAMILIAR."

In 1990, Gonzales Crisp started teaching night classes at Art Center and in the undergraduate design program at Otis, another local art school. "Three years later I was accepted to one month of study with deProgram: one month in Holland with Doug Kisor and Edward McDonald. We visited numerous studios, museums, and publishers. The trip brought into focus what was important to me about design. I had found my planet! I resolved to step up to my dream of doing more meaningful design." Within the year, she applied to the graduate program at the California Institute of the Arts.

SÚPERSTÓVE! After completing her degree, she shared studio space with Anne Burdick [p.16] and dubbed her one-woman firm SúperStóve! "It's pronounced SOO-pair-STOW-vay!" she says with a smile. But finding work was a struggle. "I supported myself teaching at CalArts and Art Center. I began writing for *Émigré* and a few other publications." A year later she started receiving freelance commissions from Art Center and was promptly offered the job of senior designer. "It was a great break. The work was constant and demanding. Within four years I had built a significant body of work." During that time she also designed eight issues of the magazine *artext* and other small book projects.

Influenced in equal parts by a modernist education and the visual culture of Los Angeles, Gonzales Crisp's style uses clearly organized information to anchor a skin of vivid color and high ornament. "My methods are unsound," she laughs. "My husband says I have a baroque imagination. Yet I'm very logical and rational. My head is always in at least two places at the same time. Some might call it schizophrenic, and I'm okay with that."

GOING TO CAROLINA In 2002, Gonzales Crisp was asked to head the graphic design department at the College of Design at North Carolina State University. "People have been kind to me, offered me opportunity and exposure. Now opportunities abound, and my home base has shifted. My scope is wider but more focused on particular design issues. I'm in the process of identifying what design research is and how it might manifest in practice, critical writing, teaching, independent production, and dissemination specific to my areas of interest. For instance, right now I'm working on a theory of the 'decoRational.'"

She acknowledges the influence that recognition has had on her life. "Had I not had a modicum of recognition I would not be in the position I am today, as chair of a nationally recognized graphic design program. That's what recognition affords you: opportunities not available to just anyone.

"My device or technique has always been to put myself somewhere unfamiliar. I gravitate toward situations that ask me to accomplish what I never imagined I could do, or would have the opportunity to do." ✌

"MY HUSBAND SAYS
I HAVE A BAROQUE
IMAGINATION.
YET I'M VERY LOGICAL
AND RATIONAL.
MY HEAD IS ALWAYS
IN AT LEAST TWO PLACES
AT THE SAME TIME.
SOME MIGHT CALL IT
SCHIZOPHRENIC,
AND I'M OKAY WITH THAT."

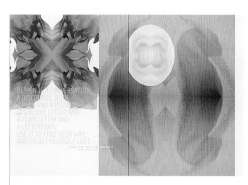

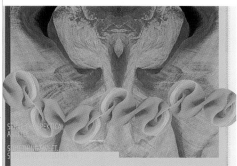

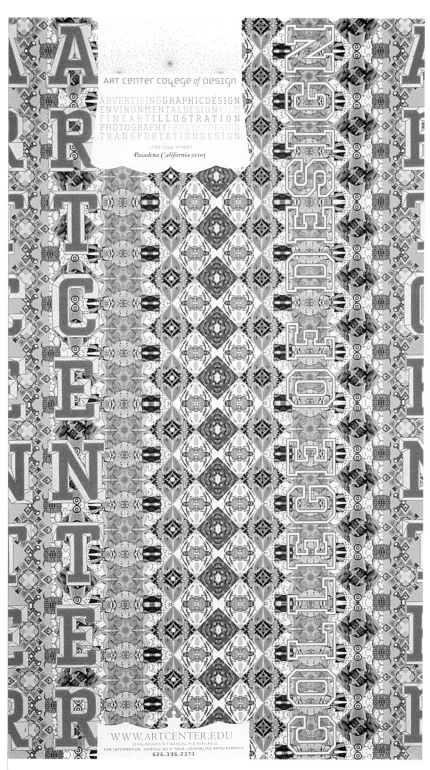

2001   **Creative Impulse 6, spreads** "These spreads promote my studio SúperStóve! for a book that covers international design. In addition to designing the spreads, I produced the photographic illustrations and wrote the text."

2001   **Art Center Recruitment, poster** "Another wallpaper poster, though this one literally works as wallpaper so traveling counselors can paper their booths with it. We developed a cheeky 'collegiate' typeface for the poster to associate Art Center with 'real' college." Ethan Gladstone collaborated.

Cottonmouth, Texas, *The Right to Remain Silent,* **CD packaging**
The packaging for this 1997 CD by spoken-word artist Jeff Liles illustrates the dark, densely layered style Vattanatham favored at the time.

Krausse, poster "This is a piece for a short story written by Jeremy Doss. I'm really proud of how I came to this perfect blending of the teeth for the toe bones."

Hubris, poster Hubris is "one of many images for *Tangible*," a magazine that uses each issue to focus and expand on one theme, such as videogames, sex, or traveling missionaries.

ART CENTER Returning to school, Vattanatham encountered three teachers who changed his views further: Roland Young, who "erased that line dividing advertising and design," and the master and apprentice team of Mark Fenske and Geoff McGann. "They taught me that advertising didn't have to be the formulaic 'headline + visual,'" Fittingly, this thought would become both headline and visual in an ad Vattanatham created for the school years later. "They taught me that advertising could be art. It could speak to people on a much deeper and true level." This insight formed the bedrock of Vattanatham's art, pushing him to go beyond the tried-and-true formulas of advertising and making each piece a true, personal expression of his insights into the project at hand— an approach that manifests itself in every piece of work he has done since then.

But as much as Vattanatham enjoyed flexing his wings, having to confine himself to a long-distance relationship with Valdez was beginning to wear on him. "I needed to get started somewhere and wanted to do good work right off the bat." But three years were enough. "I really wanted to move back to the West Coast to be with my girlfriend."

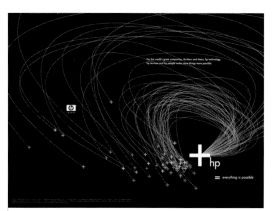

+hp/Hewlett-Packard, ad campaign
Vattanatham's work on the +hp campaign illustrates how his detailed personal aesthetic makes the jump into the realm of hyperclean technical art without losing its intricate elegance. "+hp was an initiative of Goodby, Silverstein & Partners to talk about Hewlett-Packard's important techno-logical relationships with other brands and entities. I worked with John Norman and Hunter Hindman to help launch this campaign."

Hostile, poster One of his personal pieces, Hostile shows Vattanatham blending vintage photography and silk-screen technique with sharp computer elements to convey his meaning.

Cocks and Pricks, book pages "These were part of a larger group of submissions by 86 the onions for a book titled *Fuck Off Typography,* which aimed to visually explore the expressive powers of swear words, insults, and offensive language." Shown are Dutch people whose last names take on a different meaning in English. The pages read *Hello. I'm Evert de Cock from Amsterdam.* and *Hi. We are the Pricks from Groningen.*

"MY INABILITY TO SETTLE DOWN AND DO JUST ONE THING HASN'T DIMINISHED.

I'M AN ART DIRECTOR, A DESIGNER, AN ILLUSTRATOR, AN ARTIST, AND MORE.
AND I DON'T SEE THAT CHANGING MUCH IN THE FUTURE."

PAST, PRESENT, FUTURE Vattanatham came back to Los Angeles, briefly worked at Ogilvy & Mather, then freelanced for several music clients. Later he pitched in at Goodby, Silverstein & Partners, an agency he had interned for during his school days, to help launch Hewlett-Packard's +hp campaign.

Now married to Valdez, Vattanatham has recently found a new creative home. "Many things have come full circle for me. I'm currently working at 86 the onions, a youth-and-entertainment brand communications collective run by Chad Rea, someone I met back at Pyro." Since then, Vattanatham has evolved: His work still carries the visual DNA of his earlier, more baroque period, but he now designs with a lighter, more refined touch that betrays an ever-growing confidence in his craft. Closing another loop, Art Center is now among his clients.

"Looking back at everything now, I can see that my inability to settle down and do just one thing hasn't diminished. I'm an art director, a designer, an illustrator, an artist, and more. And I don't see that changing much in the future." ✄

Art Center, ads (right) Vattanatham art-directed a magazine campaign for his alma mater, inviting advertising students and professionals to enroll in the school's advertising program. Written by Chad Rea, the ads feature a series of subversive manifestos demanding change within the current advertising model.

***Bionic Arm,* magazine** (far right) "This is 86 the onions' quarterly trade 'zine that showcases our international talent network, latest work, cultural and industry insights, plus a whole lot of nonsense. We have a lot of fun creating these and even more fun designing them."

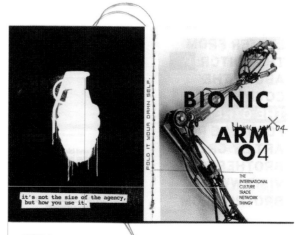

The Egg Code, book cover

"*The Egg Code* chronicles several family units, all linked to a corporation attempting to take over the infrastructure of the Internet. The baby managed to encapsulate both the awkward reality of family life and the birth of the Internet. The silhouette of the United States, which appealed to me initially for its suggestion of anonymous demographic data, began to look like a little toddler awkwardly hobbling eastward. It's a rebus that should mean something, but doesn't."

19EVAN
GAFFNEY

Raised on a diet of pop culture graphics and battle-hardened
from designing coupon ads for the *Pennysaver,* Evan Gaffney
has created book covers that are among the most elegant
and stylish designs to emerge from the post–Chip Kidd generation.

Born in Annapolis, Maryland, in 1969, and raised in the suburban sprawl of nearby
Severna Park, Gaffney discovered his interest in graphic design in one epiphanic
moment at the age of eight. "The day I found the row of white and green *Worldbook
Encyclopedias* was when I knew I wanted to be a graphic artist—not that I actually knew
what a graphic artist was." He wasn't content just to breeze through this information, though.
He wanted to absorb it. "I began my own atlas, copying the population maps one by one,
feeling empowered by reiterating someone else's charting of human settlement." Projects
such as this honed Gaffney's drawing skills, and his new talent found an immediate and
enthusiastic audience. "I drew for purely Pavlovian reasons. My parents indulged me
completely. Who would object to their kid holed up in his room copying encyclopedias?"

He grew fascinated by periodicals. "I inhaled my parents' magazines—*Reader's Digest, Popular
Science, The Baltimore Sun,* even *Good Housekeeping.*" Despite his young age, he displayed
a startling awareness of stylistic nuance. "I found the power of the printed word irresistible and
would spend hours reading articles of no relevance to me whatsoever. 'We Rate the Top Ten
Microwaves!' for example. I'd notice the subtle changes in typography and how the voice
changed with the content. I sensed the setting of priorities—for the magazine itself, and for
the culture at large—and wanted to understand how they were formed. For me they were as
much eye candy as a conduit to greater knowledge, a tapping-in to society's conversation."

As he got older, Gaffney continued to draw. "I was basically a human scanner. I eagerly took
on every art project high school could offer: drawing cartoons for the school paper, designing
the school arts magazine, painting corny murals, embellishing the backs of leather jackets
with logos of bands I had never heard of. I also conned my teachers into letting me present
reports as magazines and posters, so I could conceal my disinterest in the subject under
a layer of flashy graphics."

1999

Nothing Is Terrible, **book cover**
Gaffney chose an image that had no direct connection to the story. "The content of this book was so deviant I couldn't hope to capture it. It was best experienced without previous warning from the jacket designer."

2000

My Little Blue Dress, **book cover**
"A novel within a novel, *My Little Blue Dress* is a fraudulent history of the last 100 years told by a lovesick young man as a gesture for a disinterested girlfriend. It's a complete put-on, as much as any costume, so the image of a chintzy paper-doll dress was perfect."

2001

Masters of Death, **book cover** "*Masters of Death* looks into the psychology of the SS soldiers behind some of the worst atrocities of the Holocaust. The reader is asked to consider the Nazis as human beings, and the cover had to do the same. It was a challenge to both convey the grisliness of the subject without dishonoring the victims and to suggest the humanity of a Nazi soldier without appearing sympathetic. The solution was an inexpressive soldier caught in a fury of red brush-strokes: This world seen though distorted nationalism."

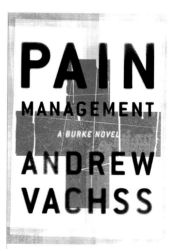

2000

New York Graphic, **book cover**
"I wanted the screaming energy of a tabloid on a little paperback, so my only recourse was to have the type break out of the edges of the cover. It was a great opportunity to use one of my favorite Weegee photographs, as well as pay homage to a favorite subway ritual, the *New York Post.*"

2000

Crazy, **book cover** "An exceptionally frank look at the wild years of adolescence written by a sixteen-year-old. My early attempts to be crazy were failures. In this case, the title didn't need to be illustrated so much as contradicted. The title type feels very clinical, until the misshapen y suggests a deviant streak."

2001

Crawling at Night, **book cover**
"This is a dark, erotic story in which a retired sushi chef and an alcoholic waitress meet, hit bottom, and ultimately pull each other together. Not a lot of visuals here, until you meet the sushi chef's long lost love from Japan, a nubile young prostitute. I wanted the cover to be brazenly sexual without turning into another pin-up. The model in this image by Robert Maxwell had the requisite sexiness but also a defiant gaze that rescued it from mere titillation. The stripes were the best way to cover the naughty bits in a way that didn't seem forced."

2001

Pain Management, **book cover**
"A gritty crime thriller involving a medical vigilante named, yes, Ann O. Dyne. The medical sub-plot was unusual for this author, and Knopf wanted to focus on that, without making it look like a medical thriller. I gave the red cross, a symbol of rescue, the feel of a corroded street sign, or even a wound."

HUMBLE BEGINNINGS Toward the end of high school, Gaffney, looking to earn money in any way not involving a spatula, took a job at the local edition of the *Pennysaver*, the coupon-filled pulp rag that clogs millions of mail slots every week. "I naively applied for a paste-up job with an oversized portfolio of charcoal figure drawings and still lifes. I had no concept of clip art or photo conversions and assumed I would have to painstakingly draw the art that appeared in every gas station and hair salon ad."

Gaffney went on to pursue a fine arts degree at Maryland Institute College of Art. "Even though I had enrolled in fine arts, I inadvertently made for myself a parallel design education based on the work of artists who were essentially creating graphic design without clients. I dropped the notion of being a fine artist the minute I graduated, knowing I could never be content with articulating my own ideas exclusively."

NEW YORK It took only one phone call to prompt Gaffney to head to New York shortly after graduation. A friend and former employer named Craig Winkelman, taking a break from the urban grind, offered both his apartment and job, starting immediately. Gaffney became the art director of an early incarnation of the tabloid weekly, *Downtown Express*.

"Craig had a lot more faith in my abilities than I did. When I took that job, I was twenty-two and so green I made Mary Tyler Moore look like a jaded crone." Filling such shoes proved inspirational: "There was no time, no money, and only a battered Mac Plus to make it all happen. I took his talent for improvisation and example of self-reliance to heart.

"A new editor had been hired named Jan Hodenfield—a publishing veteran who had worked at *GQ, Rolling Stone,* and the *New York Post* before landing at the *Downtown Express*—who terrified me with his imperious manner. We couldn't have been more different—he was slumming at a local weekly and I was in over my head—but we bonded because both of us had little business being at that paper at that time." Hodenfield gave Gaffney a piece of direction that still guides him today. "He would can my layouts and issue a mantra: 'Every picture needs a verb.' It finally sunk in that aesthetics and communication were different things. Meaning had to be put there—it wasn't inherent to the process. I learned to prioritize the narrative and to leave my aesthetic interests out of it."

CUT TO COMMERCIAL In the spring of 1992, Gaffney left *Downtown Express* and took up residence as a junior designer at Penguin USA. Despite its marquee name, Penguin didn't immediately allow him to shine. "My boss at Penguin was very old-school—black mock turtleneck, ponytail, martini lunches—who wasn't about to stoop to learning QuarkXPress. He hired me to be his technical assistant but as a practical matter let me design covers, because standing over my shoulder got boring. Between phone calls to his stockbroker he would order me to crank out designs 'like shit through a goose,' then casually dump the designs he disliked in the trash, right in front of me. No concept was commercial enough for him, no type large enough. As aesthetically limiting as that was, I respected his hunger—I had it, too. But unlike him I could distinguish between a high note and a primal scream." At that time, many major trade imprints were just beginning to understand the value of the unusual work being produced by Carol Carson and her staff at Knopf.

"I LOVED DESIGNING BOOK COVERS BUT COULDN'T BEAR THE DAILY INPUT FROM THE EDITORS AND PUBLISHERS, ALWAYS TRIPPING OVER THEIR OWN AMBITION.

GOING FREELANCE WAS AN ACT OF PSYCHOLOGICAL SELF-PRESERVATION."

2001

***Twelve Fingers*, book cover** "*Twelve Fingers* is a fraudulent biography of a man who stumbles clueless into the major political events leading up to WWI—the Forrest Gump of assassins—and whose gaffes almost—but never quite—change the course of history. The portrait in the background is from a flea market, and the photograph of the book is my own, pulled from the massive scrap heap of killed book cover designs. It's meant as a failed disguise."

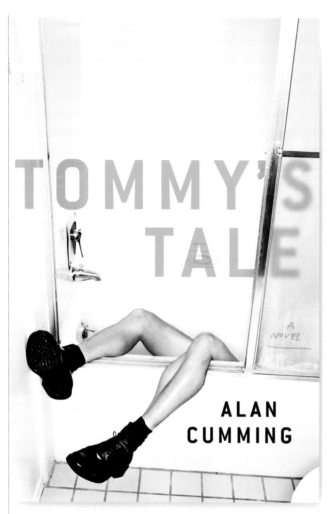

> "I WOULD COMPARE
> MY PROCESS
> TO METHOD ACTING:
> THE EXECUTION IS BASED ON
> WHATEVER THE ROLE REQUIRES,
> WHATEVER CONVINCES.
> I LIKE THE COMBINATION
> OF SHOWMANSHIP
> AND ANONYMITY."

Gaffney's work combined this new breed of imagery with the dapper typography of one of his mentors at Penguin, Michael Ian Kaye "who designed everything with an incredible degree of discernment and precision."

A year later, Gaffney switched to St. Martin's Press, a job that would eventually push him toward establishing himself as a freelancer in the spring of 1994. "Editors would descend from their offices to replace my cover designs with their breakthrough ideas, always a variation on an embossed gold icon in the shape of a heart/dove/mansion/ bullet/coin/what have you. I loved designing book covers but couldn't bear the daily input from the editors and publishers, always tripping over their own ambition. Going freelance was an act of psychological self-preservation."

ACCENTUATING THE POSITIVE As an untested freelancer, Gaffney was hired for less-than-coveted assignments: "Projects that designers hate: self-help books, military thrillers, romances." The lack of inherent glory triggered Gaffney's ambition. "I enjoyed rescuing a project that seemed doomed to tackiness. My covers would be fast, insistent, strident, and direct. My style is 'Whatever It Takes.' I would compare my process to method acting: The execution is based on whatever the role requires, whatever convinces. I like the combination of showmanship and anonymity," he explains.

Now an established presence, Gaffney is giving back. He joined Gabriele Wilson, his first-ever employee and currently a designer for Knopf, in teaching a continuing education class on book cover design at Parsons. Both in his class and in his practice he stresses the need for design to get out of the hothouse. "I love design that is out there participating in the culture. Designers are so trained to think outside of the box they design *around* the projects rather than for them."

Gaffney strives for designs that are unassailably appropriate to the task at hand. "My goal is for my designs to be distilled down to their most essential parts so that their effect is inevitable— not minimalism, but pragmatism." ℑ

2002

Tommy's Tale, book cover "The Tommy in the novel is a pansexual pill-popping manslut (nothing in common with Alan Cumming, of course) who undergoes soul-altering revelations on the eve of his 30th birthday. For this dirty book with a happy ending, the cover had to straddle the line between sweet and smutty. My favorite part is 'a novel' written on the steamy surface of the shower door."

2002

The Devil Wears Prada, book cover "*The Devil Wears Prada* was to be a serious payback for a notoriously cruel fashion magazine editor—and I was thrilled to join the crusade. The stiletto boot summed up things nicely—enormously popular among the chick-lit demographic and de rigueur for any dominatrix."

The Hipster Handbook, book cover "A style manual parody in the spirit of *The Preppy Handbook.* The harder you work to be hip, the more you'll fail. Therefore, tarting up this book with Urban Outfitters-style 'edge' was the quickest way to assure its doom. The cover is meant to look conspicuously ordinary, so its hipness would be assigned by the purchaser. The publisher not only understood the design but drastically improved it by removing all copy but the title."

2002

John Adams, *Naïve and Sentimental Music,* **CD cover** Occasionally, Gaffney takes a vacation from the publishing industry and goes slumming among CD designers. This package for a recording by Essa-Peka Salonen and the L.A. Philharmonic proves that his style translates.

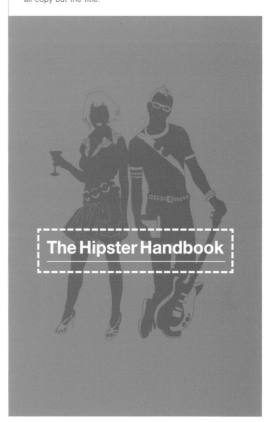

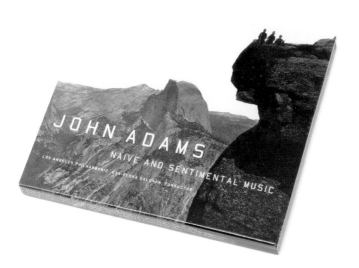

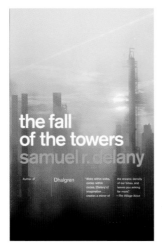

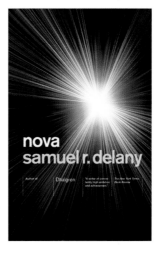

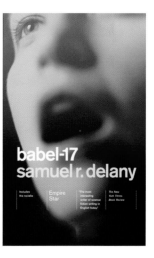

2003

Samuel R. Delany, series of book covers "Unlike many sci-fi authors, Samuel Delany is highly regarded by the larger literary community, yet his books have been packaged with shop-worn science fiction clichés. The publisher was eager to shake off the clichés but wanted to maintain and expand the audience. Like science fiction itself, the covers are meant as different forms of immersion, like suffocating in a haze, sinking in a pool, or speeding into a new world."

HJALTI
KARLSSON 20
JAN
WILKE

LONG PILLOW FOR TINY PEOPLE.

CAPTURED HOURGLASS FUGITIVES.

HELP. IT'S DARK IN HERE.

THIS IS WHAT HAPPENS TO NAUGHTY LITTLE TREES

EL DINER

EL MIKADO

TWENTYFOUR OURS.

DENTISTS MAKE ON AVERAGE $120,000 A YEAR

I'M YOUR DAD'S COMPUTER

CHOPSTICK THAT WRITES

BREAKFASTLUNCHDINNERBREAKFASTLUNCHDINNERBREAKFASTLUNCHDINNERBREAKFASTLUNCHDINNER

FRESHMANSOPHMOREJUNIORSENIOR5THYEARSENIORGRADSTUDENTEMPLOYEEPROFESSORHAPPYLONELYDEAD

2001

EL DINER, restaurant signage and artifacts
karlssonwilker developed a complete identity around a set
of seven metal letters the owner found at a flea market
and arranged to spell El Diner (versus *Red Line* or *Lie Nerd*).
They created a complete font—El Font—to match the logo
and proceeded to decorate the entire joint, including pencils,
sugar packets, and toothpick wrappers.

EMPLOYEES MUST WASH
THEIR OWN HANDS

ROne coming from Iceland, the other from Germany, Hjalti Karlsson and Jan Wilker met in New York and decided to start a company together. Relying on clean yet quirky designs and on the power of English as a second language, they are making the world a little safer for designers with a sense of humor.

KARLSSON Hjalti Karlsson came first. Born in Reykjavik, Iceland, in 1967, he was raised by his father, an executive with the National Icelandic Bank, and his mother, a painter. "She always encouraged me to draw and take life drawing classes, but I was never good at either."

After spending his first year in college studying physics, he soon transferred to the Reykjavik School of Visual Arts. Upon graduation he took time off from art and worked as a driver, distributing candy. At one drop-off, he bought an instant lottery ticket and suddenly found himself with an extra $13,000 (US) to spend. He decided to use this seed money to apply to the Parsons School of Design in New York. He made the move in 1989, and completed his bachelors of fine arts degree three years later.

WILKER Jan Wilker, born in 1972, grew up in Ulm, Germany, home of the storied Hochschule für Gestaltung [the Ulm School of Design], founded in 1953 as a school for radical modernism. By the time it closed in 1968, it had already infused the city with its energy, providing an early but lasting influence on Wilker.

Following high school, Wilker joined forces with a friend to start the Büro für Alles Kreative und Verrrückte—the Office for All Things Creative and Crazy. "We had all these ideas, so we rented a very cheap place, bought a phone, a fax, and a Xerox machine, and started going there every day. We did it to have a room and an address for our ideas." Wilker had created a prototype for his later collaboration with Karlsson. "We represented musicians, took part in architecture competitions, organized events, and designed a movable bar and a fitness obstacle course. We eventually designed logos, posters, and CD covers as well as many, many more things." Two years later, he decided to get a serious education and enrolled in the architecture program at the Technical University of Stuttgart. "I thought architecture would combine all the design fields, but it didn't." He transferred to the State Academy of Fine Arts, majoring in graphic design.

SAGMEISTER Meanwhile, Karlsson had wrapped up his degree at Parsons and entered the work force, first as a designer at the mature-women's magazine *Longevity,* then as a freelancer. In 1996, he landed his dream job: He went to work for Stefan Sagmeister [p. 42], who quickly became a mentor to Karlsson. They would be a team for the next four years, riding the growing wave of Sagmeistermania together.

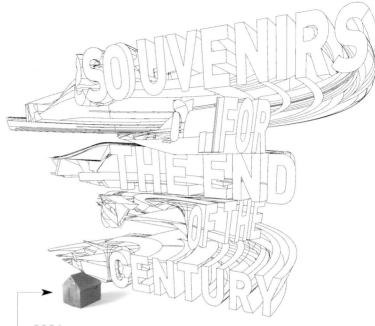

2001

Doglamp, object karlssonwilker turned this dog on his collar and made him into a one-of-a-kind lamp as a contribution to a charity action. "We had the idea for three months but couldn't get our asses up and had to do it in three days. We would like to have one for ourselves."

2001

Souvenirs for the End of the Century, catalog spread Constantin Boym asked karlssonwilker to design the catalog for his infamous souvenirs—nickel miniatures of famous structures where tragic or terrible events took place, in this case, the Unabomber's cabin.

"IF YOU WANT TO HAVE SOMETHING DONE
THAT IS NOT THE NORM, YOU HAVE TO PUT A LOT OF TIME IN IT.
IN OUR FIRST TWO YEARS, WE WOULD ALWAYS BE SO WORRIED AND STRESSED OUT ABOUT EVERYTHING
THAT OUR PRIVATE LIFE WAS KIND OF COMPLICATED, TO SAY IT MILDLY."

2000 / 2001

CRI/Blueshift, CD packages Karlssonwilker designed all five releases the CRI/Blueshift label produced before its untimely demise. They used black-and-white printing on the booklet and inlay to offset the cost of solid colors silk-screened onto the individual jewel cases. Both sides of the *96 Gestures* CD package are identical, but silk-screened blue lines obscure different lines to establish cover and back.

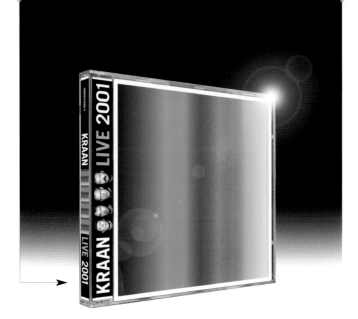

2001

Kraan, CD package For this CD sleeve, Wilker made good use of Adobe Illustrator's built-in color swatches and gradient presets. "Jan was switching from Freehand to Illustrator. It was done over a weekend," says Karlsson.

Back in Stuttgart, Jan Wilker was drawn to Sagmeister's work as well. His curriculum required an internship, so he decided to go for the gusto and landed a three-month stint at the firm in 1999. Karlsson and Wilker now worked side by side at the same office. They didn't immediately become fast friends but stayed in touch when Wilker returned to Germany to finish his degree. In the course of their correspondence, they hit on the idea of starting a studio together. When Sagmeister began his "Year Without Clients," the two decided to go for it: Karlsson started scouting for office space while Wilker persuaded his professors that opening a design studio in New York was a valid subject for his masters thesis. In the summer of 2000, straddling a 6th Avenue Dunkin' Donuts franchise, karlssonwilker opened its doors.

EVOLUTION Hewing closely to their mentor's philosophies, karlssonwilker are undeniably Sons of Sagmeister. Like him, they pursue design that is driven by ideas—often funny, based on a foreigner's view of the English language—as well as by a clean aesthetic and a no-bullshit attitude. Yet, they aren't simply Sagmeister II. Combining their unique backgrounds, playing off each other's quirks, karlssonwilker owe just as much to the underground energy of Wilker's earlier Büro.

Both men were keen to establish that they weren't out to ride on the coattails of their former boss. They decided to exclude from their portfolio all the work they had done for him—an admirable decision, considering that this meant leaving out CD designs for the Rolling Stones and Lou Reed, as well as the *American Photography* annual that had won just about every award there was the year before.

SACRIFICE The early days weren't easy. Work was scarce, money tight, and the team often found itself on the verge of insolvency. "If you want to have something done that is not the norm, you have to put a lot of time in it," says Karlsson. "In our first two years, we would always be so worried and stressed out about everything that our private life was kind of complicated, to say it mildly. We want to thank our girlfriends for their endurance!"

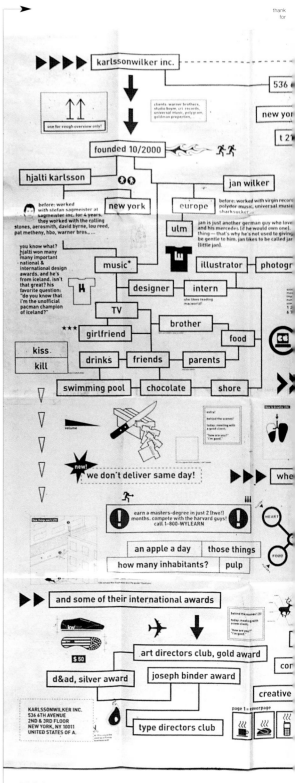

2001

karlssonwilker, self-promotion mailer One of the firm's now-famous mailers illustrates their aesthetic and gives a frightening glimpse into two European brains let loose on the Americas. "It's cheap newsprint, black and white by nature. Now we're black and white by choice."

2002

Curious Boym, book The first book the team designed under their new company name focused on the work of artist Constantin Boym. "The process was very enjoyable: No stress, enough time—we could do whatever we wanted. Mr. Boym would come by with beer and we would talk."

2002

The Vines, CD package Capitol Records tapped the duo for a major project: designing the packaging campaign for The Vines. The CD was the first major-label release to use printed shrink-wrapping. "One of the easiest jobs to work on so far: a shitload of work, one summer of joy."

2002

fuck all standards, shirt This promotional item is a fine example of the quiet dignity and reserve that permeates all of the firm's work. "A timeless polo shirt with a nice script typeface print on the back—our personal favorite T-shirt design."

"INSTEAD OF SHOWING ONLY THE BEST PROJECTS AND TELLING THE WORLD HOW GREAT YOU ARE, THE BOOK TELLS A STORY ABOUT A SMALL DESIGN STUDIO THAT NOBODY KNOWS AND TWO DESIGNERS WHO ARE TRYING TO MAKE A LIVING WITH DESIGN. WE TRIED TO BE HONEST. WE ARE NOT REALLY INTERESTED IN HIGH-GLOSS SUCCESS STORIES."

2002

Sverrisson/Gudjonsson Duo, CD package For an album of music inspired by family occasions, Karlsson and Wilker went through the musician's family albums and recropped old snapshots.

Luckily, karlssonwilker soon found that they had fans. Record companies allowed them to play, as did book publishers, restaurateurs, and other artists. All delighted in the duo's intricate, literate designs. Their self-promotion mailers and website still stand as the masterpieces of this early period, spinning basic black-and-white design elements into utter complexity, structuring layer upon layer of in-jokes, puns, and strange observations. The look is both homage to and parody of Modernist dogma, betraying the academic background of both men. Consequently, the end result displays an unimpeachable sense of style and elegance.

IN THE LIMELIGHT In 2002, Princeton Architectural Press asked them to document their journey so far, resulting in the book *tellme-why—The First 24 Months of a New York Design Studio.* Wilker explains: "Instead of showing only the best projects and telling the world how great you are, the book tells a story about a small design studio that nobody knows and two designers who, by opening their own company, are trying to make a living with design. We tried to be honest. We are not really interested in high-gloss success stories."

Following the book, they were invited to write and design a feature on inspiration for the *New York Times Magazine.* "We were not designers anymore," Wilker remembers. "We were writers or journalists or reporters for the magazine." Today the two men continue to divide their time between creating work for high-profile clients and cooking up a fresh batch of personal projects. On top of the Dunkin' Donuts Hjalti Karlsson and Jan Wilker are hard at work. Be afraid. Be very afraid. 🐰

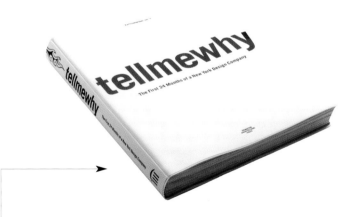

2003

***tellmewhy*, book** Together with writer Clare Jacobson, karlssonwilker chronicled the early days of their studio in this book, named for a Backstreet Boys song. "We did it in four weeks and learned a lot about ourselves. Now we have a nice photo album of our first years as business owners in New York." Check page 217 of *tellmewhy* for the thought that started this book.

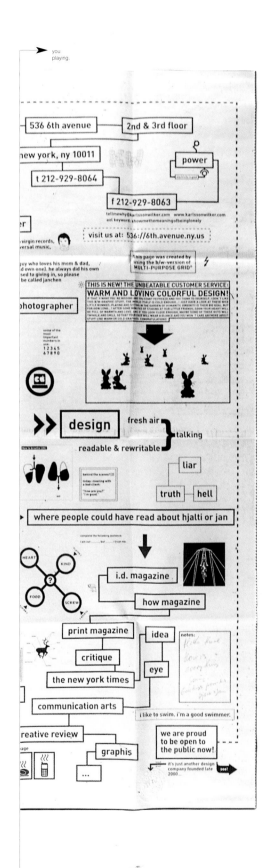

BIG
ACTIVE

Slightly twisted ideas simply and clearly presented distinguish the work of the London design group Big Active. Now they are pushing the idea of what a design studio can be by managing illustrators and photographers and developing their own mainstream product lines.

2000

Bleachin', record sleeve (above) *Bleachin'* is Jamaican slang for partying without sleep. "The album's lyrical theme centers around a fictional hedonistic jetsetter known as 'Bleach,' who lives the international luxury party lifestyle, existing only on a high-octane diet of disco powders, pills, and erotica. We made all of the packaging accessories to his lifestyle: For the limited-edition album we produced a mirror finish casing that contains a rolled-up bank note. Of course, you could use the vinyl version for rolling out reefer."

Simian, record sleeve (right) "The band wanted to do something that had the feeling of enchanted forests where mythical creatures exist. We remembered a taxidermist shop in Portobello Road selling weird stuff, such as fish with beaks. If these forest creatures actually existed they might have ended up exhibited here. Sadly the shop had closed down, but it reminded Mat Maitland of a series of taxidermy sculptures called Misfits by the German artist Thomas Grünfeld. Thomas liked our thinking and enjoyed the music. This campaign is a result of that collaboration. (Beware: These creatures sneak into your bedroom at night when you're sleeping!)"

simian
chemistry is what we are
(lp)

simian
mr. crow
(ep)

The members of the Big Active refer to themselves as a design-based studio that believes in creative networks. Says Gerard Saint, one of the founders, "We have always admired what we imagined Milton Glaser's Push Pin Studios to have been like. What makes our studio unique is that we also represent other artists. The wider picture of Big Active includes a number of associate image-makers—illustrators and photographers—who operate under the Big Active umbrella. Our creative management operation acts on their behalf to negotiate outside commissions and plan strategic development. Our artists also work with us on on Big Active commissions and projects, and vise versa."

RATHER THAN A BAND The original members of Big Active—Saint, Mark Watkins, and Paul Hetherington—met at the Berkshire College of Art and Design, in Reading, United Kingdom. "We were all into music," Saint remembers, "but rather than forming a band—which was my original intention—we formed a design company. We just figured it would be cool to start our own studio and see what we could do with it." Big Active first opened its doors in 1990. "There was no real plan as such—we just had tons of energy, being fresh out of college, and a desire to bag some real commercial clients and see our work in print."

The gods of real estate smiled on the young company, and they found a space that remains their home today. The group initially did a lot of corporate identity work but quickly migrated into music packaging, following the personal preferences of all involved. Their first music project was a series of remix sleeves for the band Soft Cell of "Tainted Love" fame.

"Our only agenda was to remain in control of our careers. At the time we were really influenced by the likes of Peter Saville and Assorted Images founder Malcolm Garrett, both of whose work we all admired. They had both set the agenda as far as we were concerned, and, although we came along a few years after, we still believed in a punk/new wave attitude of 'Let's do it ourselves.' Our philosophy has always been to produce work that is bold, spirited, and direct—design that makes you look. That attitude and a tight ganglike mentality remain true to this day."

Hetherington eventually left the group in the mid-'90s to work with Peter Saville on his new ShowStudio venture, so Saint and Watkins added a new voice. "In 1997, we were joined by Mat Maitland, who had originally been a designer with WEA Records in London." In fact, one of his first projects at WEA had been an album sleeve for Marc Almond, formerly of Soft Cell. "We hired Mat particularly for his empathy for record-sleeve design. His energy has become a strong influence in developing the graphic style we are best known for today." In 2001 Watkins left the group to form his own studio and Big Active brought in designer Richard Andrews to complete the current lineup.

MANAGEMENT "In the late '90s we were also heavily into magazine design." Saint continues. "I was art-directing a British fashion magazine called *Scene* (and later the re-launch of *Nova* and the redesign of *Viewpoint*). As art directors we've always believed in the collaborative nature of creativity and commissioning. Around this time we found ourselves working with many fresh new artists whose work we admired immensely—in particular Jasper Goodall and Kate Gibb. The close relationships they developed with these "like-minded visual conspirators" inspired the formation of Big Active's creative management operation.

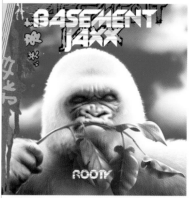

2001

Basement Jaxx, record sleeves "The band had asked us to come up with something along the lines of *Bitches Brew* or George Clinton's *Hardcore Jollies*. The initial demos of the album were charged with sexual tension. We suggested producing a series of kitsch '80s-style airbrush images of sexy girls that could be naively defaced as the basis for the style of the campaign. The Jaxx's Felix Buxton was at our studio one day and pulled out a postcard of Snowflake," the world's only albino gorilla, who lived at the Barcelona Zoo. "We all really liked it and thought an albino gorilla would make an even better cover star for the album. This led to the idea of creating an imaginary zoo and featuring other animals on the single covers. We asked airbrush artist René Habermacher to illustrate Snowflake and his friends. Later Mat Maitland and graffiti artist Rob Kidney defaced the slick pictures to form the designs. We did feature a girl on the 'Get Me Off' sleeve. I believe she was also wild and untamed."

2002

A, record sleeve "This is a campaign we have been working on with Big Active illustrator David Foldvari. 'A' is a skaterock band, and we gave the series a strong urban/street vibe."

2002

Acoustic, record sleeve "This idea was developed to work over a series of releases. So far there have been four, each using a different style of wallpaper, as if the cover has been redecorated each time."

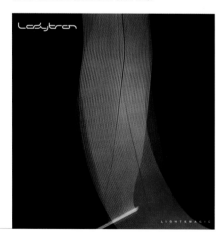

2002

Ladytron, *Light and Magic*, record sleeve As the title of the album suggests, we wanted to create something abstract using light. We shot this and many hundreds more images over a cold November weekend with the Scottish photographer Donald Milne."

2002

The Charlatans, record sleeve "This live CD is simply personalized with an adhesive nylon 'tour security' sticker. We presented the package as a homemade souvenir of the concert: The disc resembles a CD-R. There's a roll of photographic 'prints' inside the case, and the 'security pass' is adhered to the outside, as a memento. All the best shows are bootlegged by fans."

The cross-pollination between the designers and their stable of artists is immediately visible on signature projects such as the Basement Jaxx' *Rooty* and Simian's *Chemistry is what we are*. Their strong association with high-end illustration and photography has also helped the group to avoid the nadir of CD cover design: the supplied artist portrait with the name and title of the album in the upper-left corner. Even when they've gotten close to the formula, as on the *Strict Machine* cover for Goldfrapp, they managed to escape cliché by using intriguing, conceptual photography and giving it an illustrative treatment. The group's visuals are united not so much by any particular style or technique but by their visual crispness. The ideas are often left of center but always uncluttered and direct. "We have a straight-up attitude toward visual communication: If an idea can't be articulated simply and successfully over the phone, it ain't worth a fuck."

IN STORES NOW The desire for autonomy is at the root of Big Active. They realize that a bit of fame of their own gives them greater freedom to do the work they want to do. "Behind all the very best artists there are even better publicists. Instant recognition is really a matter of how visible your work is. We're quite lucky because many of the bands we work for command a high degree of visibility." And so the designers of Big Active have set their sights on using this visibility as a launch pad toward other areas beyond the design scene. "We are looking at producing

Pleasure, record sleeve "'Pleasure' is a collaborative project by producer Fred Ball. One of the featured artists is Big Active's Mat Maitland. Mat not only wrote and sang on two of the tracks but also designed and collaged the covers and appears on the front cover of the album."

Nio, record sleeve "The idea behind this campaign was to put the artist in the uncompromising position of having to endure many near misses with danger. Luckily, no one was hurt during Klaus Thymann's shoot!"

Goldfrapp, record sleeve "Children's fairytales and burlesque Berlin cabaret are some of the themes behind the imagery for Alison Goldfrapp's album *Black Cherry*. We asked Polly Borland to photograph Alison, inventing a number of evocative fairy-story scenarios for Alison to appear in. Mat Maitland got to work on the pictures— with a child's pair of blunt scissors—to produce the collages that you see on all of the covers."

Span, record sleeve "Span is a really cool rock band from Norway. We decided to create a campaign that was bold and simple with a bit of an agitprop feel. The band really liked the work of Big Active illustrator Dave Foldvari, so we collaborated visually to create the campaign."

a number of self-initiated projects with our imagemakers. The difference here will be that we're the client, so there's really no excuse for compromises!" The first outing of Big Active, the consumer brand, is Jasper Goodall's luxury bikini collection JG4B, which is now sold at the British department store chain Selfridges.

Saint admits that the members of Big Active don't have patience for the traditional divisions between design, illustration, advertising, and product design. "We have always tried to ignore these labels, particularly more recently by embracing the idea that a design studio can also be an agent to other creative individuals.

"Our first-ever business cards had *fuck off* printed on the reverse side. We found that not only did they work particularly well in getting rid of unwanted photocopier salespeople, but potential clients loved them. That sums up a lot of the attitude toward design that we still have to this day." ✄

"IF AN IDEA CAN'T BE ARTICULATED SIMPLY AND SUCCESSFULLY OVER THE PHONE, IT AIN'T WORTH A FUCK."

JG4B, deluxe bikini range Branching out into the mainstream, Big Active launched this line of high-end bikinis with illustrator Jasper Goodall and swimwear designer Louise Middleton.

KJELL EKHORN JON FORSS

22

Magazine design has, for the moment, turned its back on the mid-'90s explosion of Carsonic typography and is moving, at best, toward a safely simplistic modern style, and at worst, toward the graphic hodge-podge of "lad mags" in the vein of *Blender* or *FHM*. With their work for the British magazine *The Wire*, Non-Format, the Anglo-Scandinavian team of Norwegian Kjell Ekhorn and Brit Jon Forss, is forging a third way that combines clean, dramatic layouts with intricate details that reward the reader's attention.

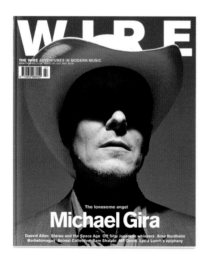

2003

The Wire, cover and spreads
Non-Format's work for *The Wire* shows their greatest strength of marrying classic layouts with modern photography and dramatic ornamentation.

oundations of virgin modernism are taken over by graphic wildlife. Like vines taking over a Frank Lloyd Wright building, delicate lines grow from bold magazine headlines. Massive numerals catch the wind and blow away as a mass of leaves and flower petals. And a minimalist magazine cover faces slow invasion by the encroaching underbrush of flash Internet style.

Both men were raised by artistic families. Says Forss, "My father is a furniture designer/maker, sculptor, and craftsman. Kjell's father used to be an architect. So our respective parents were a strong influence from a very early age. Both of us recall channeling our energies into art studies, and we have a common love of pop art, fashion photography, and Modernist architecture."

The early years of Ekhorn and Forss's careers are surprisingly similar but entirely separate. Both started their professional lives in advertising but were soon frustrated and left to pursue a better life in graphic design. "Kjell and I started out in graphics by working in advertising, but we both left that field at about the same time. We both then got into designing for the publishing industry—book jackets. We spent quite a few years pursuing this—in my case nearly a decade. We both really wanted to be doing something else." A mutual friend finally introduced them in the late '90s. "We quickly realized we had a similar approach to design. We enjoyed the same kinds of idea-based work."

They joined forces almost immediately and decided to seek work in the music industry. Forss had already designed CDs for Jon Tye's Lo Recordings and Tony Morley's Leaf Label. "I wanted Kjell to be involved straight away. We started working together on music packaging, then set up EkhornForss." Assignments for EMI, Mute Records, The Leaf Label, and Lo Recordings followed, as did book covers for Granta, Orion, and Random House. In 2001, EkhornForss gave themselves a new name: Non-Format.

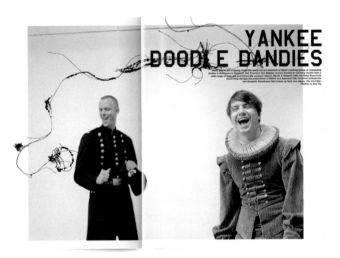

Asa-Chang & Junray, record sleeve (above) For artists Asa-Chang and Junray, Non-Format overprinted a field of four-color flowers and foliage with a coat of gold ink. The inner bag is printed in black ink with a similar foliage design.

Creative Review, **cover (front and back)** (right and opposite, left) Non-Format was invited to create a cover for the British design magazine *Creative Review*. Once again, a simple, elegant structure is overgrown with rich detail.

"WE QUICKLY REALIZED WE HAD A SIMILAR APPROACH TO DESIGN. WE ENJOYED THE SAME KINDS OF IDEA-BASED WORK."

WIRE SERVICE The rechristening coincided with the arrival of their most ambitious project yet. "The publisher of *The Wire,* Tony Herrington, wanted to move the magazine into a new design direction. Because he was very familiar with the music packaging work we were doing for Lo and Leaf, he offered us the chance to completely redesign the magazine, which seemed to us to be a great opportunity to explore a different medium for our design ideas.

"The first redesigned issue went on sale in 2001, and we have been pushing its design forward since then." Being in charge of *The Wire*'s look, Ekhorn and Forss got frisky. "Throughout 2002, we designed a feature type style, which we discarded and replaced each month with a new treatment. In 2003, we designed a typeface treatment that makes the feature headlines appear to be made of fraying cloth. At the moment we are working on a treatment with straw-blown ink. Next year, who knows?"

ROOTS AND BRANCHES Completing a circle, the advertising industry took note of their success and has reclaimed its prodigal sons, if only temporarily. "We have been working on illustrations for the advertising agency Mother. These illustrations are for a massive print campaign for the UK mobile phone company Orange." The resulting illustrations of

1825, mobile phone ad (above) The British mobile phone service provider Orange offers 1,825 free text messages a month with their service plan. Hired by ad agency Mother, Non-Format advertised the feature with lyrical illustrations of the number 1,825.

the number 1825 advertise a feature of the cell phone service—1,825 free text messages a month. Non-Format's exquisite graphics put to shame the bland stock-photo-driven ads of US cell phone service providers as well as the bulk of current advertising in general. Their work shows that clients outside of the editorial sector will accept graphically challenging work. Creating visuals for new music remains the duo's mainstay. They are unfazed by the industry's downturn. "It seems as the major labels are suffering at the hands of the Internet, they are actually starting to appreciate the added value that a piece of unique music packaging can have on sales. Not many people want to pay for a CD if it comes in a standard jewel case. There seems to be a lot less work in music packaging, but what there is seems more interesting to do."

Still, Non-Format is branching out, looking for new challenges and new creative playgrounds. "We're keen to be more involved in the fashion industry. Kjell has already art-directed a few photo stories for various magazines, and we've just shot another fashion story for the magazine *Tank*. It's an area in which we'd like to be more involved." Regardless of its ultimate method of distribution, Non-Format's work, with its unique mix of classic composition, joyful ornamentation, and airtight production values, remains a beacon in the ever-rising sea of mediocre graphics. "We just love doing what we do." ✄

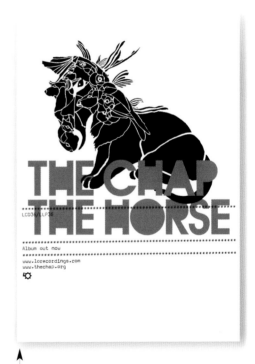

The Chap, *The Horse,* poster Look closely to find the various animals that make up the horse's head in this poster advertising the release of The Chap's album *The Horse*.

DEANNE CHEUK

23

Back in her native Australia, Deanne Cheuk tapped the creative energy of her friends and built *Mu*— a five-issue magazine empire. Then she came to New York to show the rest of us how it's done.

Deanne Cheuk was born and raised in the city of Perth, on the western tip of Australia. She stuck close to home and attended art school at local Curtin University. "I went to university to 'learn' graphic design, but I can honestly say that I learned more when I finished." Cheuk received her degree in 1994. Just 20 years old, she was hired to art-direct the Australian magazine *REVelation.* She stayed with *REVelation* for three years but felt a mounting urge to do better. In 1997, she struck out on her own and started a design practice under the name surfacepseudoart. Cheuk wanted independence and knew "that I knew more about what worked in design than the people I could work for."

MU Inspired by Robert M. Pirsig's 1974 novel *Zen and the Art of Motorcycle Maintenance* and armed with the know-how of having guided *REVelation* for the past three years, Cheuk started *MU,* a global subculture magazine. Turning to writers and photographers in her circle for content, she ultimately designed and self-published five issues, seeing them distributed throughout Australia, Britain, the United States, and Malaysia. "*MU* was my first magazine, and I started this after working at another magazine for a few years. I just decided I could do one better on my own—and I did! I asked all my friends to help me. We didn't make any money and no one ever got paid, but I learned so much and made so many great friends through the magazine. I still think it is one of the greatest things I ever made."

2003
***Big*, magazine covers** (left) While working at David Carson's studio in 2002, Cheuk was tapped to design the surf issue of *Big* magazine.

2002/2003
***TOKION* magazine, covers and spreads** (opposite) *Tokion* provides fertile ground for Cheuk's lyrical, intricate designs and typographic illustrations.

SEAN PAUL
Reggae's Future Light

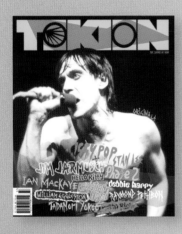

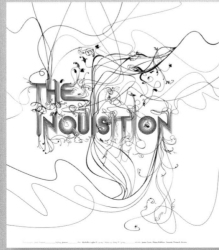

"My aim was to publish a magazine with stories that I wanted to read about—about music and art and fashion that I wanted to know about. It was quite a selfish thing because it was just about all of my favorite things! Luckily, other people also wanted to know about the same things, so it did OK. I also started *MU* so I could work on something independently and design it exactly as I wanted to. Actually, this was the beginning of the way I work now, in that respect."

In 1999, Cheuk traveled to New York and fell in love with the city. "I went to New York for a weekend vacation and didn't want to leave. Five months later I was living there!" In New York, she found work assisting David Carson and stayed with him for two years while simultaneously working as an art director for the ad agency Dirty Water. "Finally, I had so many clients and so much freelance work, I went out on my own." Going solo also proved a welcome opportunity to return to magazine design once again.

NEOMU "It didn't take me long to miss the publishing world; I still had all my contacts, and my friends were always sending me amazing illustrations and photos that they were working on. I also wished we all had an outlet to publish these things. Then at a bookshop one day, I thought about how most design books cost so much money and contain only two or three good pages. Wouldn't it be great to have a book that was amazing on every page and didn't cost anything? This is what I set out to do with *Neomu*— I called it *Neomu* because it was to be the New-*MU*. I called it a 'graphical progression' because it contained neither words nor advertising. I didn't want to make any money from it, so I decided to send it to stores for free, have them sell it for a dollar, and then donate the money to charity. It costs about four dollars to make each copy, and it looks quite good, so people have been very pleased to buy it. I wanted to pass on the inspiration from the people who are in the magazine to the people who buy it, to the shops that sell it, and to the charities that benefit from it. It has been an amazing success, because I think it doesn't try to present itself as more than what it is—it is a humble production"— at 4" x 4" (10 cm x 10 cm), it is, in fact, the world's smallest magazine— "but the work in it, I think, is better than in most design books out there."

DJ Shadow, flyer Cheuk created the promotional material for the Hong Kong stop of DJ Shadow's 2003 tour, twisting animal woodcuts into a strange yet undeniably modern circus poster. As Norman Rockwell said, "If in doubt, add a gorilla."

STU magazine, cover Each issue of *STU* magazine is shepherded by a different designer or design firm. Cheuk art-directed, designed, and illustrated issue #25.

Cheuk designs the magazine's covers and contributes several pages to each issue but functions primarily as its curator. Her own work ranges from intricate typographic illustrations to high school doodles elevated to the level of high design by her refined sense of style. In the context of *Neomu*, her design is part of an ongoing dialogue between her and her contributors. She is clearly influenced by the submitted pieces, which in turn were often inspired by her own earlier work.

Ü BERMU? Outside of *Neomu*, Cheuk has been the art director of *Tokion* since 2003 and has placed her mark on the magazine with her intricate, lyrical designs and typographic tableaus. She is also a sought-after illustrator, appearing regularly in the pages of *BlackBook*, *Cosmo Girl, Flaunt,* and *Nylon*. More important, she now counts Conan O'Brien among her clients.

With her 30th birthday almost upon her, she senses an urgency to move on once again. "I am working on a clothing line called *Liness* with two part-ners"— fashion designer Yasmin Majidi and Rinzen's Rilla Alexander [p. 200]. "I have a line of toys coming out through Sony Creative Products in Japan. I am working on a book of my own illustrations, which will launch with a show in Philadelphia. At the moment, I am working on a new issue of *Tokion* magazine and the new Urban Outfitters catalog. And I just released the latest issue of *Neomu*." This to-do list betrays an enthusiasm and sheer physical energy that makes it easy to understand Cheuk's wish for her future: "More of the same—all at once." ✌

"I STARTED *MU* SO I COULD WORK ON SOMETHING INDEPENDENTLY AND DESIGN IT EXACTLY AS I WANTED TO."

The Blow Up magazine, illustration In this illustration for *The Blow Up*, Cheuk wove snakes, earthworms, lizards, octopus tentacles, and neon lights through a porous leaf.

KIM ²⁴ HIORTHØY

Making the most of opportunities that present themselves,
Kim Hiorthøy has built an eclectic but always personal body
of work that includes not only graphic design and
illustrations but music videos, two documentaries,
and two albums of his own music.

300 Cheap Drawings "In 2000, I did a drawing
exhibition in Oslo of more than 300 drawings.
Each one was priced at 100 Kroner (about twelve
US dollars). Because they were so cheap I felt
free to also make sloppy or extremely simple ones.
That was a good and liberating experience."

2000

Kim Hiorthøy was born in Trondheim, the third-largest city in Norway, in 1973. "For as long as I can remember, I have always drawn. Both my parents were architects, I had no siblings, and whenever I complained of boredom, drawing utensils would be stuck in my hand. I grew up seeing a lot of buildings and art, and I spent a lot of time sitting alone, drawing or painting."

But despite immersing himself in the visual arts, his life ambition lay elsewhere. "A tremendous part of my spending so much time drawing and making things was because I didn't fit in so well socially. It wasn't something I chose. My real dream was that I would become an actor. I was intensely passionate about drama and theater and took drama classes. Drawing felt like a private thing." Then, at age sixteen, Hiorthøy felt a change within himself that shifted his interest back toward art. He can't explain what happened. All he knows is that he was ready to dedicate himself to art.

"When I began college, I choose art classes in addition to my regular subjects. The making of visual images became something more." College also provided Hiorthøy with his first chance to see his work published. "My drawing teacher was married to the editor of the biggest local newspaper. During my second year, she took my drawings to him, which lead to me getting my first jobs—illustrating crime novellas for the Saturday edition—when I was seventeen. I continued to do this for the next couple of years. By that time, I had begun to be seriously interested in what I understood as fine art."

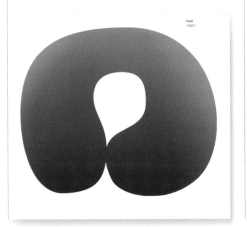

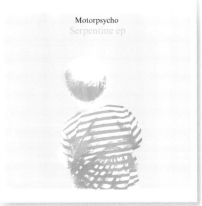

Food, *Veggie,* record sleeve "When I started working for Rune Grammofon, we wanted a distinct look for the entire label. For a long time the graphics were completely flat, but as time passed, the artwork began to change ever so slightly, this one being one of the first with a bit of shading of the form on it."

Oslo Cinematheque, program covers "I've had a long-standing working relationship with the Cinemateque, making posters and program covers for them for close to six years now. Sometimes the art is more linked to series or themes in the screenings, sometimes less."

Motorpsycho, *Serpentine* EP, record sleeve "I've done close to twenty sleeves for Motorpsycho since 1994, and in contrast to my work for Rune Grammofon, every Motorpsycho sleeve is completely different."

The Smalltown Supersampler, record sleeve Taking a break from the spare aesthetic of his Rune Grammofon designs, Hiorthøy indulges in vibrant 3-D typography for the this 2002 Smalltown record.

"GRAVE MISTAKES, DISASTER, AND COMPLETE INCOMPETENCE FOLLOWED MY WORK ON EVERY ISSUE, BUT EACH TIME I LEARNED MORE AND GOT ONE MORE THING A LITTLE BIT MORE RIGHT."

POP CULTURE JUNKIE During the early years of college, Hiorthøy's interests blossomed. He became a magazine and bookstore junkie. He was drawn to the art and the mystique of Andy Warhol's Factory, which led him to take an interest in the cinema. "I joined the Trondheim Film Society, where I discovered Hitchcock and Tarkovskji, Cassavetes and early Jarmuch. I began to walk with a slouch in a black coat." I remember being in a mild state of panic at the idea of finishing college. I was shit at doing my homework. I was unstructured and sloppy, and my grades were poor. When my mother asked me how I planned to ever make a living, I really had no answer to give."

TRONDHEIM A new possibility presented itself in short order. "One day our art teacher took us on a tour of the Trondheim Art Academy. Just the sense of the place made me intensely want to be there." Hiorthøy was hooked, and he enrolled at age eighteen. The school's liberal curriculum shows the genesis of his eclectic style and the disregard for disciplinary boundaries. "There was no formal teaching. There were lectures, one-on-one and group discussions, and technical courses. Graphic design was not a part of it. It was all fine art—painting, sculpture, experimental cinema. But they had Macintosh computers with Adobe Photoshop and QuarkXPress." Hiorthøy soon hijacked the machines to make art fanzines, which led to an early commission. "I had been accepted onto the board of the Film Society, where my responsibility was to do the layout of the semester screening program." This work would later find a parallel in his designs for the programs of the Oslo Cinematheque.

The Rip Off Artist,
Pet Sounds, **record sleeve**
Hiorthøy had designed
a similar cover that wasn't
accepted, so he added
more ink splatter and black
hair for the final piece.
"I thought perhaps they'd
like more power in it."

Seeing Hiothøy's Film Society program and newspaper illustrations, the makers
of a radical political monthly invited him and another student to work with
them. "It was unpaid work, but we would be given complete creative freedom,
and I would get to do the covers." This turned into a two-year crash course
in graphic design. "Grave mistakes, disaster, and complete incompetence
followed my work on every issue, but each time I learned more and got one
more thing a little bit more right.

"I was still in art school through this. After a couple of issues, the other guy
and I decided we should try and get outside jobs through the magazine."
They placed whole-page ads advertising their services. "Whoever picked up
the phone when an assignment came in would get that one. One day
I answered—it was the local rock band Motorpsycho asking if I would do
the sleeve for their next EP. Since that one sleeve, I have continued to do
all their artwork, and as their fame in Norway and abroad rose, so did my
reputation as a designer."

NEW YORK "In 1994, I took a one-year leave of absence from the art
academy to study film at the School of Visual Arts in New York. I didn't
find the school very good, and after one semester I quit, still having
six months left on my student visa." Luckily, he was refunded half of his tuition,
which allowed him to stay in town. Serendipity led him to a job assisting a cine-
matographer on music videos, commercials, "and one very-low-budget feature
film. Then the money ran out and I went back to Trondheim for my final year."

Various Artists
Gumball Variations

susanna and the magical orchestra
list of lights and buoys

Gumball Variations, record sleeve "It's a record of electronic music, and most of the sleeves of the records put out by the label Vertical Form have a look indicating this. I wanted to try to counter that a little bit."

Maja Ratkje, *Voice,* **record sleeve** "This was the first Rune sleeve with a photograph. It felt like a big change and ever so little like a sellout."

Money Will Ruin Everything, ad This ad promotes *Money Will Ruin Everything*, a book Rune Grammofon published in 2003, commemorating five years of the label's existence and thirty records released.

Money Will Ruin Everything

2 compact discs with 30 exclusive tracks by
Supersilent, Biosphere, Jaga Jazzist, Food, Deathprod,
Arve Henriksen, Alog, Phonophani, Nils Økland, Information and many more
In a 96 page book designed by Kim Hiorthøy
celebrating 5 years of records on Rune Grammofon.

Out now.

RCD 2032
Rune Grammofon
Money Will Ruin Everything

Before his trip to New York, Hiorthøy had illustrated several children's books written by another student. "While I was in the United States, two of the books were published in Norway." At the same time, one of his Motorpsycho pieces was crowned record sleeve of the year. "When I came back, I was already getting asked to do more record sleeves and other work while I was completing my final year at the academy." During that year, Hiorthøy also started experimenting in the school's sound studio. "I had a small book of freeform graphic design printed, as well as a CD with sound collages and little loop-based music pieces." Making music would return as a part of his life a few years down the line. For now, he graduated from the academy and left Trondheim once again.

FAME "I moved to Oslo, where I was able to support myself solely on freelance graphic design and illustration work, and that's what I've continued to do since." In 1998, he became the designer for the label Rune Grammofon and has done more than thirty records for them. He also got involved in a music collaborative and participated in several live performances. The label Smalltown Supersound heard a CD chronicling the events and asked Hiorthøy if he had more. "In the fall of 2000, my first record, *Hei*, was released, followed by *Melke* in 2002. These events changed my life. Suddenly I was asked to travel to play concerts. New connections and relationships have formed, and Smalltown has become a new outlet to do things—again without any money, but with complete freedom."

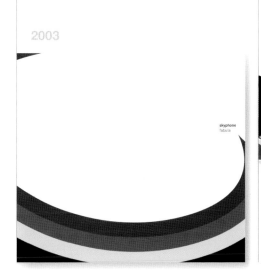

skyphone
fabula

Skyphone, *Fabula,* record sleeve (far left)
On another sleeve for the Rune Grammofon
label, Hiorthøy further explores the minimalist
visual identity he has established over
the past years.

Jaga Jazzist, *The Stix,* record sleeve
(left) The 3-D theme continues on this Ninja
Tune/Smalltown Supersound release, albeit
in a much more restrained color scheme.

Lars Horntveth, *Pooka,* record sleeve
(below) "I sometimes do sleeves for Smalltown Supersound, who also releases my
own records. Joakim, who runs it, is a good
friend, and all the work is done as a collaborative effort, with no one getting paid."

"IT WAS NEVER MY INTENTION TO BECOME A GRAPHIC DESIGNER.
EVERYTHING STARTED FROM WORKING WITH FRIENDS
AND FOR FREE, AND THEN MORE WORK CAME IN FROM THAT WORK.
WHENEVER WORK WAS SLOW, I JUST THOUGHT THAT MEANT THAT MY TIME
OF POSING AS SOMETHING I REALLY WASN'T WAS ABOUT TO END,
AND I COULD GET ON WITH WHAT I WAS REALLY SUPPOSED TO DO."

After submitting pieces for a design compilation, the German publisher
Die Gestalten Verlag offered to publish a book of his work; *Tree Weekend* was released in 2000. "It was never my intention to become
a graphic designer. Everything started from working with friends and for
free, and then more work came in from that work. Whenever work was
slow, I just thought that meant that my time of posing as something
I really wasn't was about to end, and I could get on with what I was
really supposed to do.

"For a long time, I really wanted to make films—I have done it a little bit,
doing music videos for bands." In recent years, Hiorthøy also filmed
two documentaries. He's had exhibitions of paintings and drawings.
He is getting more and more international work and has now re-located
to Berlin, but still keeps a second base in Oslo.

GOING FORWARD Considering everything he has achieved at age
thirty, it is surprising to hear him admit to common anxieties.
"I regret chances I've had that I haven't stepped up to, because
of hesitance and fear of not being able to cut it. Sometimes I just lapse
into some form of panic freeze." Still, he is eager to continue along his
path. "There's no divide anymore between work and what I do, because
I like to do it. To be in this situation is the best thing imaginable."
Hiorthøy doesn't see the need to search for the next opportunity.
He knows from experience that "it comes around anyway." ☙

Breakfast Identity, club flyers
"Breakfast is a new after-hours club that opened in London in the fall of 2003. The identity and flyers aim to capture the exhilaration of leaving a club or party as the sun is rising through the use of color and a surreal aspect to the photography."

Spitting London, book spreads
"Walking through London, I began noticing a landscape littered with spots that had become an all-too-familiar texture in the concrete. These pieces of gum have no time, no value, and no ownership, yet they seem to be a permanent fixture in the cityscape. I began to map or record the gum's patterns, recording its movement away from a tube station, charting its density, color, shape, and size. As I give these patterns new meanings, I am working on developing modes of tracking an invisible behavior, noting configurations of movement. It is a way of reading a chaotic and disorientating city. It's anthropological, and, in the same breath, it talks about space entangled with moments in time."

CAMILLIA 25
BenBASSAT

By traveling the world, seeking out the best schools, and working with the people she admires, Camillia BenBassat is working hard to shape herself into an extraordinary designer.

Camillia BenBassat was born into a life of art. "My father is an architect, my older brother is an immensely talented and well-known photojournalist, and my younger brother an aspiring designer with a natural gift for craft. Art and design have always been fostered in my family." Growing up in Los Angeles, she spent most of her time in art classes or working at studios and entered the design program at UCLA in 1996, just in time for her nineteenth birthday.

"To be honest, I did not really know what design was when I entered the major. It had just reopened at UCLA after a few years of restructuring. I had applied for the art major and was accepted to design. The counselor at the school pushed me to try it, because my work was already leaning in that direction. Within a week, I was hooked."

"At the school I met [teacher] Gail Swanlund, who showed me the potential of design as a method of communication. She was very influential in that she encouraged research and development teamed with a strong sense of style and craft as the basis for conceptual work." Beyond the conceptual underpinnings, BenBassat also picked up her mentor's aesthetic preference for line art combined with detailed decorative elements.

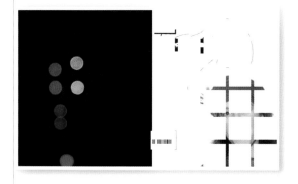

See magazine "*See* is a magazine that charts the loss and dissolution of love. A grid is used (ironically) to represent the foundation of a relationship, and as the woman watches her love fall apart, the grid itself also begins to disintegrate."

"I RETURNED TO THE ACADEMIC ENVIRONMENT TO CONTINUE TO QUESTION THE ROLE OF DESIGN IN SOCIETY, LOOKING AT QUESTIONS OF POLITICS, TECHNOLOGY, AND SUSTAINABILITY, FOR EXAMPLE."

AROUND THE WORLD During her junior year, BenBassat moved to Florence, Italy, for five months. She sensed an immediate influence on her design. "Florence was a scattered yet deeply moving city and my work became expressive, free-flowing, and full of texture. A lot of my work happened off the computer, and I had the opportunity to collaborate with other artists and photographers that I met in my travels there." From Florence she moved to Tel Aviv and, four months later, spent a month in Egypt to "live among the Bedouins in a bamboo hut on the beach."

REALITY CHECK After returning to Los Angeles, she began working for Red Channel Interactive, a husband-and-wife team that had designed the first Lollapalooza website. Following her graduation from UCLA, she took a job in the Maverick Records art department. There she was plunged into the deep end of the pool. Instead of having time to give scholarly consideration to the possibilities of a project, she had to produce instantly and constantly—CD packaging, promotional materials, merchandising tie-ins—while living up to her own standard of quality. "I began to learn how to maintain the essence of the work while engaged in a compromise with the client." Still, she relished the creative atmosphere of the label. "I can't believe how spoiled I was at Maverick. I was surrounded by great people."

WANDERLUST Yet within the year, she began to feel restless once more. "Traveling was still in my head, so to satisfy my wanderlust, I decided to move to London." Unfortunately, she hadn't secured the necessary permits for her move and was turned back at the border. Rebuffed, she traveled through Eastern Europe for the next six months before returning to San Francisco. "I began working at Macromedia. Within a month, most of the art department was laid off as a result of the dot-com crash. I was rehired to do some freelance work and ended up staying on full-time for over a year." Following her time in San Francisco, she decided to take a step back, "to take a year off and freely and consciously explore my process and work."

Amberlight, identity, logotype
"Amberlight is a usability company that works with leading corporations to provide a user-centered approach to the design and evaluation of digital interfaces. The mark plays off the traffic signal reference of the company name and reflects the company's position (between their client and the user) in the process of designing intuitive interfaces."

DOWN TO LONDON With proper legal documentation in hand, she returned to London and enrolled in the Communication Design graduate program at Central Saint Martins in London. "I returned to the academic environment to continue to question the role of design in society, looking at questions of politics, technology, and sustainability, for example. On a formal level, I was reintroduced to various modernist systems and design methods. Coming from a California school of thought, line art and decoration were a large part of my work, and I was constantly challenged about their purpose and intention. I realized I did not have a strong enough base on which to build this type of design and decided to step back to modernist simplicity to clearly assess my methods of working. Line work has returned as a part of my visual language, for example, but is now more carefully considered."

ONWARD AND UPWARD "Going back to school has given me a base to move forward in a more considered direction. The past year has given me the time to develop and consider the process of making my personal work—learning the process was key to continuing to work in this manner, outside of my degree. I began a series of self-initiated projects over the last year that I will carry with me as I re-enter the professional world." ✌

Butcher's Hook, exhibition flyer and poster Butcher's Hook, a reference to cockney rhyming slang "Take a Look," was a Central Saint Martins MA Communication Design work-in-progress show and fund-raiser at the club Cargo in London.

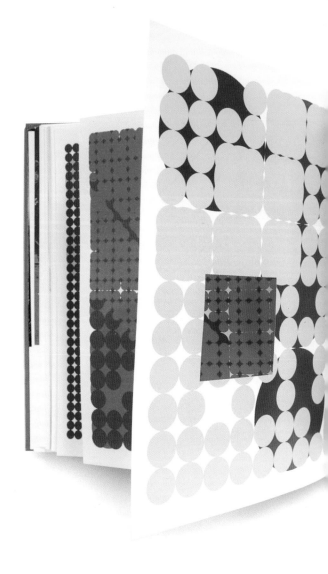

1999
spherize!, chair Valerie Kiock
and Kuno Nüssli originally designed
spherize! as a plywood lounge
chair containing a big rubber ball.
The production model is inflatable
rotary cast plastic.

1999
The Apartments, Clerkenwell, brochure
This brochure for a development in Clerkenwell,
London, where a '60s office building was
converted into apartments, gave Kiock her first
experience working on a project about architecture.

1999
N2, leaflet The name of the design group
is derived from the highway that connects
Basel and Luzern, the two cities where the
designers were living. Green was taken
from Swiss freeway signs.

VALERIE KIOCK

26

German designer Valerie Kiock
has integrated her love for graphics
with an ever-growing interest
in furniture design to forge
a unique body of work that benefits
from its exposure to both worlds.

Pretty much anything goes in graphic design. As in fashion, trends remain—currents and quirky little eddies that curl away and disappear— but the authoritative party-line style of earlier times is gone. At this point it takes desire and a tight focus to learn the craft of minimalist Swiss typography. It takes a young eye, guided by immaculate taste, to use its tools to create design that is relevant and holds its own amidst the flood of dazzling, more effects-laden work. Valerie Kiock describes her approach: "Stylistically, I tend towards the pragmatic approach: legible, clear, comprehensible, well-founded, rather straight ahead, strict, but certainly neither boring nor bland. I always like to play around, figuring out what works and how it works."

CANDY AND THE CLASSICS Growing up in Munich, Valerie Kiock started collecting candy wrappers as a child, attracted by the combination of colors and typography. She remembers small chewy squares wrapped in colored paper, ringed with printed tinfoil that identified the flavor of each piece with words and picture. It didn't take long for her to form a Pavlovian connection between sugar and graphic design.

The second push toward design occurred when Kiock went to see a Raymond Loewy exhibit. "I remember the progression of the Shell logo exactly. I was intrigued by the reworking, the mutations. I remember the Lucky Strike package, of course. Beautiful to begin with, it turns from green to white for nonaesthetic reasons. The brand, the application, following a need was what interested me. You might call it 'freedom within boundaries.'" Following the exhibit, she started leafing through magazines, clipping typestyles, pictures, ads—image/type combi-nations, colors, and patterns—and placing them in scrapbooks. "Also packages, postcards, and stamps— everything I thought was beautiful."

2002
Taylor Bloxham Diary 2002 The day planner advertising the client's new twelve-color press was a studio collaboration at Williams & Phoa. "My section is die-cut and shows dots and flowers that use eleven special inks, including day-glo and metallic inks and a varnish."

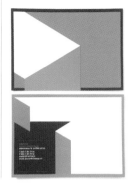

Jörg Boner, change of address card
This postcard was sent out to announce
the change of address of furniture designer
Jörg Boner. Recipients had the option
of keeping the entire mailer or tearing out
a perforated business card.

Werkbildnis, book "A book for a photographer who photographed
the studios of famous architects, as well as famous American and
German photographers to portray themselves by showing where they
work rather than what they themselves look like."

Konstantin Grcic, catalog The catalog for
Konstantin Grcic's work for the Nymphenburg
Porcelain manufacture features a white cardboard sleeve that contains individual cards and
accordion folds that vary in length according
to the size of each project. Working with Grcic
established a link that would soon allow Kiock
to design her own porcelain patterns.

THE JUMPING BIT After graduating from high school, Kiock took
on a series of internships. She moved from restoring paintings
to working for Rolf Müller, Otl Aicher's former second-in-command
and one of the lead designers of the 1972 Olympiad identity. From there
she went on to Studio Paco Bascuñan in Valencia, Spain, before moving
to Switzerland, where she enrolled in the undergraduate program at the
Schule für Gestaltung Basel. During her time there, the German company
KOKON gave her a freelance assignment designing and producing
a series of carpets, cushions, and tabletops, introducing her to the world
of furniture and interior design.

This interdisciplinary seed would later grow into a second career for Kiock
when, during her graduate studies at the Schule für Gestaltung Zurich,
she became a founding member of N2, a Swiss furniture design group
(named after the freeway connecting the two cities where the designers
were living at the time). "On my own, I am a graphic designer. I like and
look for flat things, strictly two-dimensional. Yet, I am interested in the
'jumping bit,' when something is slightly twisted from flat to maybe not so
flat. Putting things into an order or arranging things—flat or not—is the
connecting or interacting activity." Kiock describes the "jumping bit" not
as a digital term but as the sudden connection between separate
elements or objects, an idea coming into focus.

Being a part of N2 gave Kiock a chance to work on both aspects of
her creativity at once. She designed furniture and was also responsible
for the group's print graphics, including the identity that appropriated
the color of Swiss road signs.

Auer + Weber + Architekten, book
The monograph of architecture firm Auer +
Weber combines elements of prior Kiock
projects from the N2 leaflet to the Apartments
brochure and the *Werkbildnis* book,
but ultimately transcends them all in its
subtle use of typography and imagery.

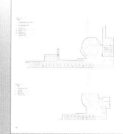

Valerie Kiock, change of address card This dog-racing scene, Kiock's own change of address card, shows her lighter side yet maintains her strict aesthetic standards.

Decor for a Konstantin Grcic china pattern Kiock developed the decor for this Konstantin Grcic china pattern to hit unique target terms such as young, contemporary, everyday, fresh, and different. An extraordinary eye transcends a mundane brief.

LONDON AND BACK After receiving her graduate degree, Kiock moved to London and spent four months working with Alex Rich. She then found a new home at the design studio Williams & Phoa. There she was given the opportunity to apply her skills to larger projects, including the lavishly produced day planner for the printing company Taylor Bloxham. Gone were the days of self-financed two-color mailers. This client had a new twelve-color press to promote, and Kiock began an orgy of metallic and day-glo inks, varnishes, and die cuts.

But independence called. While living in London, Kiock twice returned to Switzerland to teach at the Hochschule für Gestaltung und Kunst Lucerne, and, after a brief stint at the London offices of Imagebank, she moved back to her native Munich. She set up her own studio, and new clients appeared who allowed Kiock to once again expand her reach.

A catalog design for industrial designer Konstantin Grcic turned into a chance to create patterns for one of his porcelain lines. She recently finished work on the monograph of architecture firm Auer + Weber + Architekten, a thematic continuation of the piece she had done on an architectural brochure in her days at Williams & Phoa, and is now working on another project with Grcic. "Looking ahead, I'd like to see my work continue to be diverse, because I do find it interesting to learn about new things/situations/tasks/techniques/materials, ways to work, and make it work." To this day she collects the tinfoil wrappers of chocolate Easter eggs. ✄

"I LIKE AND LOOK FOR FLAT THINGS, STRICTLY TWO-DIMENSIONAL. YET, I AM INTERESTED IN THE 'JUMPING BIT,' WHEN SOMETHING IS SLIGHTLY TWISTED FROM FLAT TO MAYBE NOT SO FLAT."

27

ANGELA DETANICO

RAFAEL & LAIN

In the economic and cultural revival that followed the demise of Brazil's dictatorship, Angela Detanico and Rafael Lain were part of the first wave of young artists to bring about a renaissance of experimental design in their country. Today they are bridging the gap between graphics and fine art wherever they go.

2001

Santa Cecília, typeface "Santa Cecília is a typographic essay on the architectural lines of a São Paulo downtown district of the same name. São Paulo is a chaotic place where architectural elements are constantly colliding, thus creating complex networks of ever-changing lines. This liquid landscape is explored in a typeface featuring composable characters that draw new scenarios for this neighborhood."

Angela Detanico and Rafael Lain spent their childhood in Caxias do Sul in the south of Brazil. "It's the coldest state of Brazil, not as tropical and happy as the rest of the country, but it's still a good place to live," says Lain. Born in 1973 and 1974 respectively, both Lain and Detanico come from culturally aware families. Detanico remembers, "My mother worked as a teacher and used to bring me lots of books from the school library." Even though money was tight, Detanico's father took his family to Europe and North America in the late '80s. Says Detanico, "Thanks to that, I got to know people, museums, architecture, bookshops—and had the coolest CDs in my high school."

Rafael Lain grew up a boy's boy. "I had a lot of contact with nature, climbing up trees, eating fruits—a very healthy kid. My only problem was that I loved to draw, especially superheroes." This made him somewhat of an oddity in Caxias, an industrial town with no cultural scene to speak of, and a minor celebrity at his high school. He soon found ways to market his skills, illustrating event posters for a local club. It was around this time that he met Angela Detanico.

She remembers, "We met in 1991, and we became intellectually and romantically involved at the same time, so working together was a natural consequence. At the time, however, we were following personal paths." She pursued a degree in law at the Universidade de Caxias do Sul. He took a job as a sketch artist for an advertising agency, only to be replaced by the firm's new Macintosh computer six months later.

"By the time Rafael started working, things were changing a lot in Brazil due to the end of the military dictatorship that lasted from the '60s until the end of the '80s. In the early '90s, the media was no longer under the dictatorship's control, and the country became more open to the international market. In terms of design, that meant easier access to computers, magazines, and books."

DISCOVERING DESIGN Lain's drawing portfolio landed him a new job working on a Mac in the industrial design department of a footwear company. He recalls, "The manager was really interested in graphic design. Every time he traveled outside the country he brought back lots of books and magazines. That's how I discovered graphic design—in the pages of *The Graphic Language of Neville Brody, eye,* and *Émigré* magazines. I was allowed to borrow the magazines and books to read at home. Angela and I devoured each page. I immediately realized that this was the kind of work I wanted to do. But how? Where? There were no graphic design studios or clients in Caxias who would pay you to do that kind of work. The only place in Brazil that seemed to want this work was MTV in São Paulo." Lain managed to set up an interview and showed a portfolio of self-generated posters, CDs, and book covers. He was hired and moved to São Paulo in 1994. "That's how I got my first job as a graphic designer."

Detanico expands on MTV's importance in Brazil's nascent alternative design scene. "MTV Brazil was the only place to work if you wanted to do alternative design in Brazil. Most of the graphic designers who changed the face of Brazilian graphic design in the '90s worked there. At that time Brazilian universities offered no graphic design courses, so in the beginning of the '90s, MTV functioned as a kind of school."

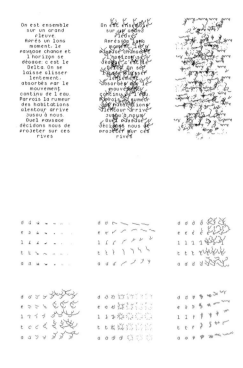

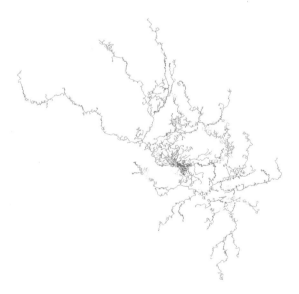

2002

Font Delta, typeface "Font Delta is an experimental typeface in which the design of the letters is gradually transformed. The project aims to represent, poetically, the processes trigged by language, using the geographic image of the delta as a metaphor. The river that divides itself into branches, redesigning its paths in its way to the sea, as the living language. The fertile terrain of the delta, fed by the water's flow, as the mental universe of the speaker irrigated by the use of language."

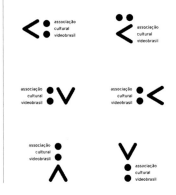

Associação Cultural Videobrasil, identity "This logo is a group of compositions using the elements V and a colon [:] for VideoBrasil, as the association is currently known. Every time the logo is shown, it is used in a different configuration, to refer to the mobility of the institution."

"WE CANNOT SEPARATE WORKING FROM LIVING.
THE SENSE OF LIVING IN A LIQUID REALITY,
THE CROSS-BORDER ATTITUDE,
THE DESIRE OF MULTIPLE POINTS OF VIEW,
AND THE AWARENESS OF THE IDEOLOGICAL WEIGHT
EMBEDDED IN EVERY CULTURAL PRODUCT
ARE ALWAYS THERE, IN OUR MINDS
AND IN OUR WORK."

BURRITOS DO BRASIL After a successful run, Lain left MTV in 1994 and joined his former colleague Jimmy Leroy at his new design firm, Burritos do Brasil. Detanico explains, "The idea was to do more experimental and contemporary work for the advertising and design market. In 1996, I moved to São Paulo and joined them. That's when Rafael and I started working together."

Their new venture flourished. As one of the first alternative design studios to appear in the wake of MTV Brazil, Burritos received a lot of attention. "We developed works for big companies such as Adidas, Pepsi, and Renault, and for big Brazilian advertising agencies." They developed the visual identity for Canal Brasil, the first cable TV channel for Brazilian cinema, and began to develop their own fonts for projects like *Tribo,* a skateboard magazine that became an artistic laboratory for Lain.

Gaining national exposure gave them the confidence and financial security to become more experimental. They soon started to feel hemmed in by the restrictions inherent to large corporate accounts. In need of inspiration, they took a trip to the Fuse conference in San Francisco in 1998. Here they came face to face with people like Malcolm Garrett, David Carson, and Lain's original design hero, Neville Brody. The trip proved to be a potent catalyst for change.

FÊMUR Upon their return home, they quit Burritos and founded their own two-person studio, Fêmur. "Our goal was to work with clients from the cultural and artistic environment, which gives us more freedom, more time, and a more interesting dialogue—and, of course, less money. As a small agency, we worked for art galleries and independent music labels, as well as big cultural institutions and exhibitions, such as Serviço Social do Comércio and the biennial art show Artecidade," which they handled in collaboration with Ronaldo Miranda "and Videobrasil." On top of all this activity, Detanico managed to return to school for a masters degree in linguistics and semiotics.

DISPLACEMENTS.
14 INTERNATIONAL ELECTRONIC ART FESTIVAL
VIDEOBRASIL

2003

14th IEAF Videobrasil, identity "The concept behind the fourteenth edition of the Videobrasil festival was 'Displacements,' conceived to stage some political questions raised by population flux, national identity, and territory disputes. The logo 'Displacements' has no fixed form but is composed of a series of frames. The Portuguese word *deslocamentos* gradually changes to the English *displacements*, and then to the Spanish *desplazamientos*, and back to Portuguese, in a loop. The concept of movement was extended to the whole visual identity by the use of images of border areas and stretched lines of pixels. Very often peaceful landscapes, the borders are in fact highly controlled places. We wanted to communicate that even though the population flux is restricted, and in some cases dangerous, it stands as a possible way to cultural exchange and mutual understanding in a world transformed by the globalization process, for the best and the worst."

FROM NEW YORK TO PARIS In the summer of 2001, the pair went to New York to attend the Tomato School, an intensive one-week workshop hosted by the experimental British collective, Tomato. They found themselves surrounded by other young artists from around the world who were united by their desire to evolve. "These days were very important to the path we followed afterward. It was the first time we worked on space—outside the computer." The influence of Tomato's process-centered approach is now clearly visible in the couple's output. Stripped of all ornamentation, their work is a sinewy manifestation of the thought behind it. Luckily, the couple has kept their design from becoming a purely academic exercise. Their keen aesthetic instincts and visual sense of humor inform all they do and are readily apparent in the final result.

In 2002, they were selected for an eight-month art residency at Le Palais de Tokyo in Paris. Says Detanico, "It gave us the opportunity to research, work, and exhibit in a big art center. We developed and showed installations and video, as well as typefaces and graphic design. They welcomed the challenge presented by different media and exhibition spaces. "It opens up new possibilities for our work."

LIQUID REALITY Following their time in Paris, the couple returned to Brazil and put to work the new ideas they had gathered abroad, dividing their time between design work and fine arts projects. Preparations are underway for their first solo exhibition in São Paulo at Galeria Vermelho, and they are working as curators on a Brazilian graphic design show at La Ferme du Buisson in Paris.

Detanico and Lain see work as a space for reflection and as a means to discuss issues they consider relevant. "We cannot separate working from living. The sense of living in a liquid reality, the cross-border attitude, the desire of multiple points of view, and the awareness of the ideological weight embedded in every cultural product are always there, in our minds and in our work." ✌

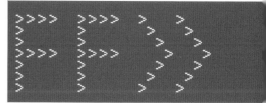

Fast Forward, logo *Fast Forward* is the electronic magazine of Associação Cultural Videobrasil and, thus, utilizes multiples of the Videobrazil V in its logo.

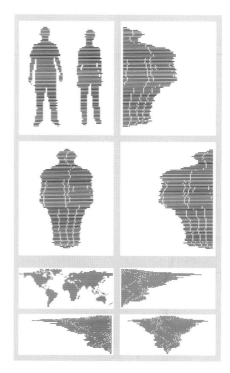

2003
Align, experimental piece "We align shapes as texts. World Align shows the map of the world in four alignments. The other series shows our silhouettes, which we use as a kind of logotype."

2003
Possible Narratives, logo (above) "Possible Narratives," an art show on artistic practices in Lebanon, was part of Videobrasil 14. "We had to design the font in Arabic. One of the curators of the show wrote it by hand and sent it to us by fax. We designed the logo, not knowing if it was readable, then sent it back to him for a legibility test."

Utopia, typeface (left) Brasilia, the new capital of Brazil, was inaugurated in 1960 as a symbol for a new era of industrial development. Putting the modernist lines of the city with chaotic elements that have appeared over the years, the Utopia font "re-creates the unplanned situations found in Brazilian big cities, where these elements coexist and modify each other in ever-changing landscapes."

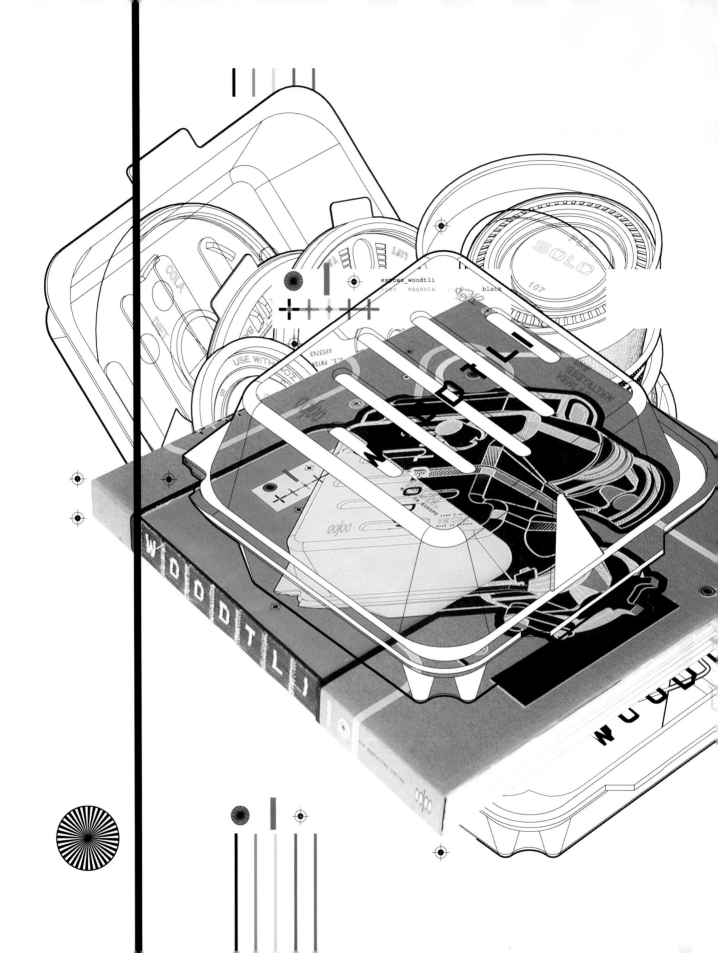

MARTIN
WOODTLI

Born, raised, and educated in Switzerland
and inspired by working in New York,
Martin Woodtli set out to become an author-designer
and established himself with his signature style
of subversive technical illustration.

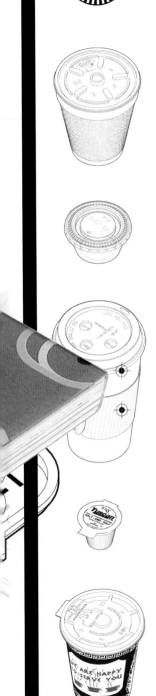

"A basic idea is still the most important thing to be able to do work. But if all you do is start with an idea and execute it, you'll end up with something you—or others—have done before. I want all the insecurities and doubts of the production process to be part of the finished piece."

Martin Woodtli began his formal art education at the Schule für Gestaltung Bern und Biel (School of Design in Bern). He spent two years majoring in ceramics, then decided to switch to graphic design instead, only to learn that his school is no different from most others: The administration balked at the transfer. They insisted that to switch his major, Woodtli would have to reapply to the school. Woodtli relented, reapplied, and was—remarkably—rejected.

Instead of seeking a place at another college, he took an apprentice position at a local graphic design studio where he designed projects for research institutes and clients in the cultural policy sector. "Working as an apprentice, you have less room to experiment than you would at school, because you have to wrestle with the reality of clients, but you quickly learn to take responsibility managing projects." By the end of his apprenticeship Woodtli had a few clients of his own, mainly emerging artists on the local scene. One of them was Kiosk, a gallery that would later become the Stadtgallerie Bern, for which he still designs today. Working for clients such as Kiosk allowed him to start developing a strong, highly idiosyncratic visual language. Using exactingly detailed technical renderings, he created a constant flow of machine characters and Dadaist objects, such as rotary picture phones and memory-chip-enhanced remote controls.

Schooled in production techniques and printing, Woodtli loves to push the boundaries of his tools. One of his techniques involves saving files and opening them in other versions of a program to generate errors and artifacts. "I don't take for granted the functions of the computer. I combine them in new ways to discover new possibilities.

"The idea used to be that it's only good design if it's anonymous design, without a detectable signature style identifying the designer. Today we see an established school of graphic authors, well-known names such as Neville Brody or David Carson, for example. I enjoyed a lot of freedom with these assignments. I didn't want to practice anonymous design, so I accepted only jobs that would benefit from authored graphics."

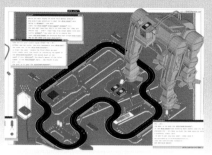

***Skim.city,* magazine spread** For the magazine *Skim.city,* Woodtli envisioned spreads that allowed him to discover and expand his vision over a number of frames. Beyond a series of toys and mazes, we find robots of the industrial variety as well as a big mechanical gorilla.

ZURICH TO NEW YORK Woodtli left the studio in 1996, and moved to Zurich to continue his education at the Zurich Academy of Art and Design. Life at the academy, however, proved less than satisfying. "I found it to be a place too tightly focused on concepts without developing those concepts to a truly high level." Luckily, other opportunities presented themselves. "I had two separate tracks going at the same time." On one end he had the academy; on the other, more and more offers came in to design for clients in the cultural arena.

Woodtli graduated from the academy in 1998, and took his portfolio to New York. He left at home everything he did in school and took only samples of his professional work. Woodtli showed his book to David Carson and was surprised to find himself freelancing for the man the next day. "Obviously, it was great to get an inside look at a place like that, but in retrospect it wasn't all that interesting." He left Carson and started interning for Stefan Sagmeister [p. 44]. Life was different there, and Woodtli immediately felt at home. "My time working for Stefan Sagmeister was the complete opposite [of working for Carson]. I experienced Stefan and Hjalti [Karlsson, p. 160] as very communicative personalities. I still remember the team discussions fondly." When Sagmeister created his infamous AIGA Detroit poster and needed copy carved into his body, he let Woodtli wield the blade. "I would have never done that with David!"

2003

door to door, die Berner Ateliertage, poster
In Woodtli's language, even a simple typographic poster becomes a machine object, each letter a small piece of technology.

digital brainstorming, invitation cards To invite people to the traveling digital brainstorming exhibit, Woodtli had these machines silk-screened on coarse cardboard with a precision that would make most offset printers weep. Shown here are Jodi, a remote control with memory card, and Alan Turing, a rotary phone dial with monitor.

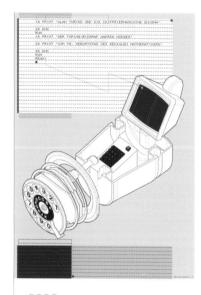
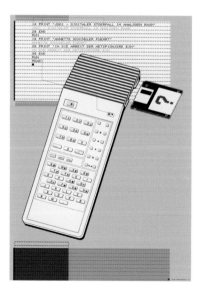

2003

2003

***soDA* #21 aktion, poster**
Woodtli turns to clock radios
to alert the masses to the
new issue of *soDA* magazine,
which dealt with subjects
such as action at the super-
market, lowered prices,
special promotions, rebates,
and so forth. "The alarm
clocks display twenty-five
hours instead of twenty-four.
That's another special
promotion—this day has
twenty-five hours, which is
an ironic statement on
the theme."

"I DIDN'T WANT TO PRACTICE ANONYMOUS DESIGN, SO I ACCEPTED ONLY JOBS THAT WOULD BENEFIT FROM AUTHORED GRAPHICS."

2003

expo2002, poster For
the Expo 2002 World's Fair,
Woodtli allowed himself
a pun, playing the word
Expo off floating Xbox
game consoles.

ZURICH TO NEW YORK—AGAIN A year later, Woodtli returned to Zurich to open his own studio and promptly won the
Swiss Federal Design Prize based on the strong body of work
created in his own machine idiom. The prize came with a 20,000-
franc check. He was off to a good start, but he did find that he missed
New York. He returned to the city for another six months to work
on his first monograph, *woodtli,* and to help on occasional design
experiments during Sagmeister's Year Without Clients. Sagmeister
asked him to stick around and work for him full-time when he reopened his studio. It was a tough decision, but by this time Woodtli
wanted to go his own way and returned to Zurich, where his studio
and a number of teaching engagements were waiting for him.

Woodtli is, by his own definition, a full-fledged graphic author. His
style is too highly developed, too immediately recognizable to make
him a viable ghostwriter to others. To ensure his work won't be com-
promised by financial necessity, he, like Sagmeister, keeps his overhead expenses low and lives a humble life. This way he can afford to
take only the jobs he wants. He continues to work for cultural
institutions, but commercial clients knock on his door more and more,
knowing that they don't want a random designer to fulfill their brief—
they want Woodtli. ✍

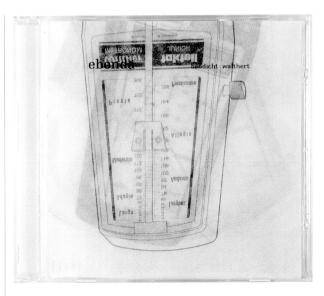

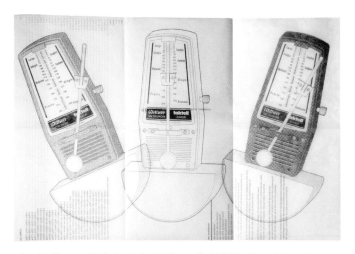

ebenda, CD cover For the band ebenda (German for ibid), Woodtli created a metronome
on a round base that effectively kept the pendulum standing still and moving only the
machine around it—a mechanical tail wagging the dog.

2003

29 RINZEN

VIVA LA VECTOR proclaims one of Rinzen's promotional stickers, and it is clear that the Australian design collective has internalized the motto. Following the success of RMX, the project that brought them together, the five partners are spreading their optimistically stylish line art far beyond their Australian base.

Rinzen is an obscure Japanese word meaning "sudden awakening, commanding, or awe-inspiring." As such it serves both as mission statement for this group of Australian artists and as a friendly jab at the occasional self-importance of the design scene. The group comprises five members: Steve Alexander and his wife Rilla, Adrian Clifford, Karl Maier, and Craig Redman. Born between 1973 and 1978, they all entered the profession at different times and worked for different employers, but during the early to mid-'90s, all of them attended the Queensland College of Art in Brisbane.

EVOLVING DESIGNS The five partners first collaborated as an escape from the drudgery of their day jobs. Inspired by music remixing and the Surrealists' "Exquisite Corpse" concept, they adapted the technique for graphic design, reworking each

other's pieces, then handing them to another member of the group to be augmented again. They collected the results and dubbed the project RMX. Adrian Clifford remembers: "At the time of the first RMX project, we were all deep in corporate design projects for various clients and employers and felt the need to do a collaborative project outside these restrictions—something spontaneous, free, fun, and tax-deductible. Each of us produced an initial piece for one of eight themes. The files were then passed progressively to each designer, being remixed each step of the way—modified, augmented, and erased—and no one saw the work before it was his or her turn to remix it."

2001
RMX Extended Mix, book *RMX Extended Mix* documents Rinzen's second foray into graphic remixing.

"Remixes were handed over at the drunken weekly project meetings, and at the end of the eight-week process the resulting 64 pieces were compiled," recalls Clifford. "The collection is a chaotic merging of vector, pixel, and hand-drawn work filled with colorful and repetitive design elements—some themes evolve gracefully while others chop and change awkwardly."

The pieces formed the basis of shows in Brisbane and Berlin and were later published as a book. "It didn't take long to see that what we had created together outside of the world of monolithic corporate design was the direction we should pursue. People responded to the genuine spontaneity and energy in the project and were happy to see us apply that to more projects—both commercial and personal," says Clifford.

Rinzen's decidedly contemporary ideas, as well as their refined use of color and vector art, unites their body of work and gives it its modern presence. "Our work is a response to design and culture," says Clifford, "We see an opportunity to build

The New Conservatism, illustration Invited by *THE FACE* magazine to illustrate their article "The New Conservatism," Rinzen captured the dreams of a sullen boy with an über-happy rainbow-colored cloudscape of teenage love.

Underbifrost, mural The studio was commissioned to create a mural for the "Other Worlds" show by the Queensland Art Gallery. The piece depicts cyclical themes. "Norse mythology is the basis for the figurative content—Bifrost being the rainbow bridge linking the mortal plane to the abode of the immortals. Death and rebirth, good and evil," explains Rilla Alexander.

The Valley, promotional materials To promote "The Valley," Brisbane's entertainment district, the team created a series of illustrations representing the history of The Valley—from the settlers' voyage from London to a scene of today's shopping and entertainment district.

a collection of works that are expressive but not kitschy or pandering to nostalgia—something that reflects a joy of life without forfeiting craftsmanship and design skill. It should be possible to be serious but not sober, playful without being apologetic. Unfortunately, in the current cultural climate, a lot of artists' approaches to these themes tend to be mired in irony and redundant referentiality, which reduces them to mere sound-bite status or fashionability."

The RMX project proved to be such a success that it spawned two sequels. The resulting pieces, featuring the visual remixing talents of more than 30 designers from Australia, the United States, the United Kingdom, Switzerland, Japan, and Germany, were collected in the follow-up books *RMX EXTENDED PLAY* and *FRESHRMX*.

INDEPENDENCE Working on the initial RMX project, the five designers relished the freedom that their regular jobs could never match. "A mind that is stretched by a new experience can never go back to its old dimensions," says the poet Oliver Wendell Holmes; thus, Rinzen was formed in 2000. "We saw a brighter future in the combination of our energies, both creatively and organizationally," declares Craig Redman. Clifford elaborates: "In the first couple of months we were in various locations—Berlin, Switzerland, Tokyo, Brisbane—so pulling the group together was more an exercise in communications than anything. The plans had been on the table for some time; we just had to take the step of saying 'now' and flying the flag."

Finally sharing one office space helped the principals grow closer. "Whereas most of us had worked together in studios in various combinations, having everyone working side by side and back to back in the new office accelerated the group development and the flow of ideas. It helped to form the creative common ground."

Rinzen is clearly a labor of love and is structured to allow the maximum amount of personal and creative freedom for all involved. Having started as a virtual office that connected its members by electronic means, it comes as no surprise that

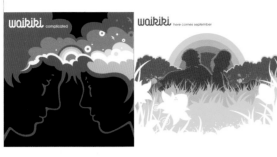

Nouveau :
Cosmopolitan,
CD artwork
Inspired by the title, Rinzen appropriately reference Czech artist Alphonse Mucha for this piece of album artwork.

Waikiki, graphic identity Rinzen developed a graphic identity for the Australian band Waikiki, which references the optimistic illustration style of the 1970s—including the studio's trademark rainbows—while staying very much in the moment, thanks to the way color and typography are handled on the various record sleeves.

"THE 'RINZEN OFFICE' IS A CONTINUOUSLY EVOLVING THING—CHANGING TO ACCOMMODATE THE WORK WE ARE DOING AND OUR NEED TO ABSORB LIFE IN DIFFERENT PLACES."

Rinzen is not tied entirely to its Brisbane headquarters. Clifford explains: "The 'Rinzen Office' is a continuously evolving thing—changing to accommodate the work we are doing and our need to absorb life in different places to keep our approach fresh. At present, Rinzen are again working from several locations in Australia and overseas. We have a strong structure—underlined by a long friendship—which allows us to continue to work collaboratively, even when not in the same space."

Today the partners handle an ever-larger roster of international clients, while continuing to generate their own projects and self-produced works, which they sell through the online Rinzen shop. Still, their prime focus remains artistic. Says Redman: "Every project contains a moment of alchemical miracle—the point where the possibilities solidify into something complete and meaningful. Hitting that point each time is the perpetual challenge. We're always conscious of having more things to create and more places to go." ✌

2003
Planet Earth, flyer
To promote a Sunday club night at the Lychee Lounge, the group created a flyer that carries the DNA of '70s band logos and period illustration.

The Brasil Series, book spreads Working in collaboration with photographers Lyn Balzer and Anthony Perkins, Rinzen give their simian interpretation of Brazil for a book contribution.

FIEL
VALDEZ

Fiel Valdez isn't interested in labels or boundaries. She is interested in things like art and integrity. Using her uncanny eye for the cool and quirky, she has created a thriving one woman design boutique that allows her to do the work that challenges her and her clients.

2003

Tree Hair, illustration (left) Valdez uses her personal illustrations as playground and laboratory, expanding her artistic vocabulary beyond the more mundane solutions often made necessary by more mundane projects.

2001

Tomodachi, illustration (opposite) Over the years Valdez has created a growing collection of characters that have found their way into a number of her self-promotion items. She calls them her Tomodachi—the Japanese word for friends.

"I believe that when you create, you can create in any medium. Each medium has its own language, and I believe one simply needs to be sensitive to the language of a particular medium in order to create in it." Fiel Valdez uses graphic design as the base that allows her to reach freely into the worlds of illustration, fashion, fine art, and product design. She doesn't trumpet breaking through these boundaries, because she doesn't perceive them in the first place. "I'm passionately interested in many things… and I try to connect as much of them with my work as I can."

Growing up in Daly City, California, she was influenced early by embarking on various craft projects with her mother and being mentored by her piano teacher, Betty McNeil. She took her first visual arts class the summer before enrolling at UCLA as an aerospace engineering student. This led to a class schedule that started with chemistry and calculus and ended with photography and tool shop. Two years into her studies, she switched to Art Center College of Design in Pasadena, California, where she received her degree in photography in 1996 and was awarded an honors term in typography.

CREATING NEW LANGUAGES In her last year at Art Center, she was offered an internship at Hotwired.com, the new online division of Wired magazine. "The company was small at the time, and there were some amazing, creative people there who I worked with directly, specifically Barbara Plunkett and Erik Adigard. I'll always remember preparing images for Erik and missing the boat on the importance of aliased edges to create the illusion of transparency in Director. At first, he was disappointed that I had made such a big mistake, but then he decided he liked the images better with the sloppy edges. It was a happy mistake, so to speak, and sort of the beginnings of my ideas about letting one's tools speak in the work one makes with them.

"It was also a wild, rather ungrounded experience where the paradigms of the Internet (visual design, information architecture, interactivity, etc.) were being invented as we were all going along." Her work for Hotwired.com soon led to an assignment creating the web graphics for NASA's Jet Propulsion Laboratory, an unexpected chance for Valdez to tap into her early aerospace engineering education.

Following this, Valdez returned to the Bay Area to become one of the first employees of Circumstance, a burgeoning interactive studio. "That was a complex experience. I came in as a very junior graphic designer, and by the time I left, I was a senior designer/art director. I was only there for about a year and saw the company grow from about eight people to about 40 then back to about 20. It was slightly insane."

Circumstance brought awards and national exposure to Valdez's work on James Cameron's *Titanic Explorer* CD-ROM, Neimanmarcus.com, and Artmuseum.net.

"The most valuable lessons I took away from Circumstance were about the business of design and the politics of business, all the things they don't teach you in school. I started freelancing right after that and haven't been on staff anywhere since."

Urban Nature CDs With a partner, Valdez launched Color Crush's line of recordable "Urban Nature CDs" that were sold at high-end boutiques and bookstores in Los Angeles.

Since then, Valdez has created apparel graphics for Nice Collective, Reebok, Puma, and Disney, identity design for various entertainment clients, as well as costume and set design for musician Blevin Blectum. She has written and designed for *Macromedia Flash: Art, Design + Function,* a book on the construction of the Mighty Assembly website she helped birth. She now presents all her work under the Gesamtkunstwerk umbrella *lovelybrand.*

ON LIVING WITH ANOTHER DESIGNER Valdez lives with her husband, Peter Vattanatham [p. 150]. They met at UCLA while Valdez was still studying aerospace engineering and they later attended Art Center together. She reflects on the benefits and difficulties of sharing life with another designer: "We don't always agree on things regarding our work and creativity. It took us a while to be comfortable with disagreement.

"One of my favorite things about it all is that we constantly learn from one another. It's like having another 'me' who goes off and has different experiences (though still applicable to what I do) then returns to share the best and worst parts."

Their bond also provides support and perspective in the struggle to translate her fine arts sensibility into work that keeps the lights on: "I do my share of attorney stationery for money and always keep an eye out for opportunities to do more interesting work. I'm always in the position to work on something engaging even if it doesn't pay (well). Peter taught me that if a project winds up being fun, interesting, and good enough to stick in my portfolio, then that might be pay enough." ✄

Chigai, illustration Valdez. frequently contributes. to *Neomu,* the illustration. magazine created and. curated by Deanne Cheuk. [p. 174]. This piece shows. Valdez's love of vector art. and.unexpectedly elegant. color combinations.

Nice Collective, poster (right) Valdez. created this poster advertising Nice. Collective, a San Francisco group of. fashion designers, based on a photo-graph by Ian Hannula of Nice Collective.

Horses, illustration (far right) For her. latest piece for *Neomu,* Valdez drew a. group of horses by hand, then transferred. them onto cloth with a sewing machine.

Puma, t-shirt designs (opposite, far left) Valdez's t-shirt designs for Puma subtly absorb the company's logo, instead of blatantly putting it front and center, to appeal to fashion-conscious consumers loath to become corporate billboards.

Heels, sculpture (opposite, left) Valdez created this object as part of her personal collection to explore the fetishistic pain caused by high-heeled shoes.

Mighty Assembly, identity (above) An exploration for the Mighty Assembly identity, based on the animation that launches their website and serves as its main website interface.

Mighty Assembly
The book *Macromedia Flash: Art, Design + Function* by Mighty Assembly demonstrates the high-end capabilities of the Flash software suite, using as an example the Mighty Assembly site Valdez helped create.

"WE CONSTANTLY LEARN FROM ONE ANOTHER. IT'S LIKE HAVING ANOTHER 'ME' WHO GOES OFF AND HAS DIFFERENT EXPERIENCES THEN RETURNS TO SHARE THE BEST AND WORST PARTS."

Macromedia Flash: Art, Design + Function

THANK YOU

Thank you to the designers
who allowed me to tell their stories.
It's been a privilege.

Neal Ashby
Alexandria, Virginia

Anne Burdick
Los Angeles, California

Margo Chase
Los Angeles, California

Ed Fella
Valencia, California

Tom Hingston
London

Allen Hori
New York, New York

Mirko Ilić
New York, New York
Thanks to Simona Barta

Eike König
Frankfurt

Hideki Nakajima
Tokyo
Thanks to Kiyoshi Takami

Stefan Sagmeister
New York, New York

Paul Sahre
New York, New York

Paula Scher
New York, New York
Thanks to Kurt Koepfle

Rick Valicenti
Chicago, Illinois

James Victore
New York, New York

Paul White
London

*Hey, wait a second.
That's more than thirty designers!
Ah hell — it's too late now.*

Camillia BenBassat
London

Gerard Saint
and all at Big Active
London

Deanne Cheuk
New York, New York

Evan Gaffney
New York, New York

Denise Gonzales Crisp
Raleigh, North Carolina

Kim Hiorthøy
Oslo / Berlin

Angela Detanico
Rafael Lain
Sao Paolo

Harmine Louwé
Amsterdam

Hjalti Karlsson
Jan Wilker
New York, New York

Valerie Kiock
Munich

Kjell Ekhorn
Jon Forss
London

Steve + Rilla Alexander
Adrian Clifford
Karl Maier
Craig Redman
Sydney/Brisbane

Fiel Valdez
Los Angeles, California

Peter Vattanatham
Los Angeles, California

Martin Woodtli
Zürich

Mom + Dad
made it all happen for me.
This book is for them. Alles Liebe!
Special thanks to my dad for giving me the book
Friedrich Stowasser 1943–1949 many years ago.
It was one of the early seeds of this book.

These are two of the people
who made me want to make books:

Ingrid Haberland
produced some exceptionally beautiful catalogs
for the Wilhelm Busch Museum in Hannover, Germany.
Those were the first cool books in my life.

Elke Imberger
and I have been pen pals since 1985.
Her letters first taught me how to write like a mensch.

These are the people
who made me want to make this book:

Hjalti Karlsson + Jan Wilker
asked me to write a page for their great book *tellmewhy*.

Ronnie Lipton
read the piece I wrote for Jan and Hjalti and told me
that it would make a good book proposal.

Petrula Vrontikis
convinced me that Ronnie was right and egged me on
to tilt at this particular windmill. She then had to listen
to me natter on and on about The Book for a solid year.
I wouldn't have made it without her support.

Thank you to my friends and
colleagues for your inspiration,
support, and patience:

Sean Adams
Hans Akrok
Linda Aldredge
Jed Alger
Michael Apponi
Neal Ashby
Troy Boane
Melanie Bruns
Joni Caldwell-Couch
Josh Chen
Bill Eckenrod
Mary Fagot
Ann Fox
Stefanie Freiberg
Saam Gabbay
Daniel Goldscheider
Teresa Hale
Mark Heflin
Jim Heimann
Toni Hollander-Morse
Clark Hook
Gary Koepke
Keith Knueven
Michael Langone
Rudy Manheim
David Mayes
Joerg Metzner
Noreen Morioka
Jennifer Morita
Nancy Nimoy
David Norland
Lauren Nukes
Kavi Ohri
Chris Pekoe
Vesna Petrovic

Maggie Powers
Alan Proctor
Tobias O. Rink
Heather Robbins
Norm Schureman
Theresa Seelye
Cathy Solarana
Jennifer Stone
Terry Stone
Gregory Sylvester
Peleg Top
Charles Trotter
Alice Twemlow
Kai Ulbricht
Bettina Ulrich
Fiel Valdez
Peter Vattanatham
Allen Voskanian
Aidan Walker
Helen Walters
John Waters
Nina Weiner
Brian Welsh
Scott Williams
Tamsin Wilson
Kathi Wogrolly
Amanda Wray
Doyald Young

Thank you to Kristin Ellison
and the team at Rockport Publishers.

Read profiles by John Lahr
and listen to Bill Hicks records.
It's good for you.

A special thank you to Karla,
Charles, and Janet Field for being
good friends to me and my family
for ten years and counting.

Tony Arefin and Jim Ludtke:
You are missed.

Have a lovely day!

*And there you have it. That's all I got for you today.
I hope you had fun. Now put that tootle away
and go get some fresh air. I bet it's nice outside.*